FRAMEWORK FOR A POLITICAL SOCIOLOGY

This ambitious work offers a new and systematic conceptualization of the factors necessarily involved in the conduct of social and political enquiry. Professor Bélanger analyses and criticizes the concepts employed by the past masters in the fields of communications, anthropology, sociology, and political science, and then creates his own original synthesis or framework for understanding political dynamics. He proposes sets of relationships that take into account the interplay of interests and their intermediates that socialize and mobilize people through culture, ideology, and ultimately regulation in order to legitimize control. Control, conditioning, and conflict emerge as the basic social relations involved in the political arena, into which are fitted social classes whose interests permeate most organized actions. The last chapter uses the framework to consider the feminist movement, from the diffused nature of male controls over women to the diversity of the modes of mobilization adopted by women to combat these controls.

The author dissolves the concept of society into those social relations; the framework is not a theory but more of a map of the essential features in the whole social landscape, where technology, ecology, and demography are the basic motors of change. His description of these features illuminates them all and should serve to sharpen the sociological perception; political sociologists especially should be interested in this all but Herculean attempt to redefine their ground.

ANDRÉ J. BÉLANGER is a professor of political science at the University of Montreal.

ANDRÉ J. BÉLANGER

Framework for a Political Sociology

UNIVERSITY OF TORONTO PRESS
Toronto Buffalo London

© University of Toronto Press 1985
Toronto   Buffalo   London
Printed in Canada

ISBN 0-8020-5666-0 (cloth)
ISBN 0-8020-6571-6 (paper)

Canadian Cataloguing in Publication Data

Bélanger, André-J., 1935–
Framework for a political sociology

Bibliography: p.
Includes index.
ISBN 0-8020-5666-0 (bound). – ISBN 0-8020-6571-6 (pbk.)

1. Political sociology. I. Title.

HM33.B45 1985   306'.2   C85-099365-2

It is not the 'actual' interconnections of 'things' but the *conceptual* interconnections of *problems* which define the scope of the various sciences.
Max Weber

All the world's a stage,
And all the men and women merely players;
They have their exits and their entrances;
And one man in his time plays many parts,
His acts being seven ages.
William Shakespeare, *As You Like It*

Contents

ix Contents

A structural view of feminism; or, What can the framework tell us about feminism? 175

Preface

Any theoretical endeavour is in itself pretentious; in this respect, this book is no exception. Any attempt on my part to put myself in the clear would be of little avail. Indulging in the elaboration of a theoretical device bespeaks a degree of discomfort with former developments in the field, whether theoretical or empirical. Hence, an explanation of my epistemological *parti pris* offers more than an attempt at modesty.

The discussion that follows is based upon an exclusively sociological approach coupled with a determinist and relativist apprehension of reality. Without discarding all other perspectives out of hand, the disquisition uses social determinants, as far as possible, to account for human behaviour. Besides, the discourse does not flow directly from any recognized school or any specific mode of thinking in the social sciences – functionalist, systemic, behaviouralist, individualist, or Marxist. Although I borrow at times from different schools of thought, I try to avoid any form of syncretism while hoping that the discussion does not take too eclectic a tack either. I build a framework out of a set of elements and their interactions, and in so doing pay critical attention to current usage and significance, within the discipline, of these elements and interactions.

The table of contents and the sequence of figures in the text show quite well how the argument unfolds: from the centre to the periphery, like a spider's web spun in reverse, becoming ever more complex. This procedure is but a strategy of demonstration; it is no more than an artefact of presentation. No hierarchy of importance of the different elements involved is implied. It would have been possible to set out the argument the other way around: to present the whole structure of concepts in the first chapter and then develop segments. Nonetheless, the sequence chosen for the argumentation follows quite closely my own original logic of functioning, a logic which provides for a sociological perspective at a micro level and then expands it to a macro level while keeping the micro level constantly in relationship with the macro.

The first three chapters develop a number of notions into two series: a/control, interest, and resources (chapter 1), b / conditioning, socialization / culture, mobilization/ideology (chapter 2), leading to a structure of conditioning (chapter 3). The notion of collectivity (chapter 4) is considered before we cope with the phenomenon of regulation (chapter 5), which has to do with a combination of both the control and the conditioning series: collectivity stands as the referent for any form of regulation – one rules or regulates in the name of a given collectivity, whatever its nature. Classes (chapter 6) are dealt with last since they involve the whole social dynamic from which they emerge both as products and as active elements; they constitute the diffuse reality of the whole set. Owing to their universal character, they are likely to permeate all the relationships discussed.

As for its use, the present framework lends itself to comparative studies but does not preclude stricter methods of application, whether experimental or statistical. Methods, though, are not discussed; in this respect, readers are left on their own. As a sort of guide, an illustration on feminism is furnished at the end to show how the framework can be applied.

I wish to acknowledge with gratitude the stimulating comments given to me at the initial stage, when parts of this work were submitted to a number of scholarly groups, the Departments of Political Science at York University and Laval University and my own at the University of Montreal.

My thanks go to David V.J. Bell for his encouragement to put the work into writing and to André Blais, Guy Bourassa, James I. Gow, and Vincent Lemieux who made extensive comments after reading it in its earlier version.

This book has been published with the help of a grant from the Social Science Federation of Canada, using funds provided by the Social Sciences and Humanities Research Council of Canada, and a grant to the University of Toronto Press from the Andrew W. Mellon Foundation.

FRAMEWORK FOR A POLITICAL SOCIOLOGY

Introduction:
a sociological framework

Political studies address a wide variety of phenomena, some amenable to scientific treatment, others better adapted to descriptive approaches. Debates on the status of these studies have been going on for long enough; there is no necessity to recapitulate the highs and lows. It is in any case not the intention of this book to try to define what should be considered political and what should not. Politics can hardly claim to be, in its entirety, an object of scientific endeavour (Bélanger 1984). It is a concept drawn from common-sense experience and, for this reason, seems an imposition on social scientists; it is a concept waiting to be finally recognized and attributed a scientific status. Whereas the sciences usually determine for themselves what objects they will observe, and acknowledgment by the general public comes later, such is not the case for politics. An Aristotelean propensity to assign specific goals to different disciplines may have had some impact in the past. But nowadays, whether we are considering chemistry and physics or sociology and economics, none of the sciences takes particular care to furnish a clear-cut definition of itself. They leave the definitions to philosophers of science. For a chemist, chemistry will often amount to what chemists usually do. Economics has exhibited a little more vulnerability to this type of questioning, opinions agreeing with or diverging from the definition proposed by Lionel Robbins (1952, 16). On the whole, few scientists pay much attention to such an exercise, except some belonging to possibly the oldest discipline among the social sciences: politics. It may be the oldest, but it is still in a fledgling stage, and is still at the mercy of common usage.

In order to avoid any misunderstanding or ambiguity, I shall avoid the term 'politics' as much as possible. The reference in the title of the book is meant only to indicate an approximation of the field under investigation. In the final analysis, the discussion probably covers somewhat more and somewhat less of what is commonly understood by politics. Instead of coping with a rather fixed web of activities, I shall concentrate on relationships and more specifically on patterns of relationships, with particular emphasis on the recurrent character of certain patterns, granted that science is responsive to repeated observations but blind to events considered in their singularity.

Furthermore, it is a framework and not a theory that is being offered. The latter generally refers to sets of propositions tied together by logical links, either of a deductive nature or otherwise, whereas a framework contents itself with delimiting a field of theoretical propositions to come; it sets frontiers and determines the types of factors to be reckoned with. In other words, it identifies the sorts of objects susceptible to scientific investigation. At the same time, a framework disqualifies a series of possible aspects and approaches; these have to be identified as well, establishing beyond any doubt the precise limits of observation. So, before broaching the major concepts governing the framework, let me describe the nature of the approach itself and leave the development of specific elements for later.

This framework is sociological. For the sake of illustration, I shall adopt that distinction dear to J.S. Duesenberry, which established economics as 'all about how people make choices' and sociology as 'all about why they don't have any choices to make' (1960, 233). Whether the first proposition on economics is well-founded or not, is not absolutely essential to my purpose, except in so far as, in its contrast with the second, it elicits the full sense I want to attribute to sociology. Of course, the ways leading to sociology are many, and many are the schools. The approach puts the emphasis on the intervention of social determinants in human actions. There is no question of denying freedom a role in people's choices. But in the present discussion attention is focused entirely upon the socially determined aspects of such choices. A psychologist might adopt an analogous approach in extracting the emotional content of an individual's decision. Such undertakings can never claim to exhaust the meaning of any action; in any event, no science would make such a claim.

Any action is amenable to numerous scientific considerations. In this vein, one may speak of the necessity of pluralism in the handling of analytical instruments. An event may be envisaged as totally determined by a series of factors which intervene in its definition. Some may resent the idea of confining human expressions to such limiting parameters. I do not wish to become embroiled in such a discussion. In order to remain aloof from this discussion, one may simply state one's intention to either maximize the possibility of finding determining factors (of any sort, be they biological, psychological, or sociological) or proceed as if human beings were entirely preconditioned. Considering all possible determining factors opens the way to a pluralistic rather than a reductionist outlook. Human beings, for instance, are not solely biological entities, nor are they solely psychological or social. At this stage in the development of the sciences, there is little likelihood of a synthesis of them all coming about in the near future. Almost all indications lead us to put our faith in the multiplication of models in all directions.

Some authors have submitted typologies without depriving human beings of their freedom. Talcott Parsons broke down human action into four levels of components: culture, society, personality, and behavioural organism. More than a mere typology, this division presents a structured view by introducing the notion of interrelationship between the parts. The observer becomes aware of a system, but also of components propelled by their own sets of activities. However, there is nothing to prevent the exclusive treatment of one component provided, as I have said, no reductionist view is imposed upon the whole. Parsons's systemic disposition serves here as an illustration, although I do not intend to resort to it for further developments.

WHERE I BEG TO DIFFER

Basing the argument upon social determinants entails the dismissal of factors that might be relevant in other types of exposition, such as sociobiological factors, psycho-individualistic factors, and human needs.

Sociobiology
Sociobiology explains social life by genetic programming. Some of its most extreme pronouncements propose no less than to sound the knell of sociology and anthropology. Its most prominent exponent, Edward O. Wilson, has managed to suggest that the discipline is alternately on the attack and in retreat, displaying great ambition at times and a great deal more modesty at others. Coming after the well-trumpeted *Sociobiology: The New Synthesis* (1975), his *On Human Nature* (1978a) is more elaborate in matters directly connected with the social sciences. The conclusion of the first book led to a heated debate that the second has tried to clarify and cool off somewhat.

In his moderate moods, Wilson agrees that at least 'the evidence is strong that almost all differences between human societies are based on learning and social conditioning rather than heredity' (1978a, 48). He agrees, therefore, to limit the scope of investigation of his discipline: *some* behaviour is genetically imposed. The message remains intact but is less sweeping than in its first versions, which provided for 'programmed predispositions' that supposedly lead human beings to be altruistic, aggressive, homosexual, religious, and so forth, the whole process evolving along the lines of evolutionary requisites of adaptation. This too obviously imperialist and reductionist approach is toned down in his second book, where he writes: 'The form and intensity of altruistic acts are to a large extent culturally determined. Human social evolution is obviously more cultural than genetic' (1978a, 153).

From then on, it is the 'underlying emotion' (altruism) which, he assumes, is derived from genes. One may dispute the actual aims of the discipline as working *de facto* towards getting rid, sooner or later, of the encumbrances of social science. Some adepts, like Van den Berghe, have been quite outspoken in this respect, or disrespect: '[Social scientists] manipulate great masses of dubious data but make few findings; they use a lot of jargon but their so-called concepts and theories are largely reiterations of old ideas, pretentious platitudes, or worse yet, pompous nonsense' (1978, 35).

Wilson's clarification of sociobiology's relationship with the social sciences, while more diplomatic, is nonetheless intended to give the social sciences a good jolt. In his mind, sociobiology is an 'antidiscipline' (1978a, 7) of the social sciences just as physics is of chemistry, chemistry of molecular biology, molecular biology of physiology, and so on upward. The antidiscipline stands as the unit of the lower level of organization and for this reason is often understood to subordinate the other disciplines layered upon it. Wilson's motives are not to denigrate the social sciences but to situate them within a scientific continuum in which disciplines lie in levels of complexity in terms of their objects of study. One might wonder, first, where psychology stands among these tiers; second, whether the social sciences occupy the highest tier; third, how and whether the social sciences should be broken down into a similar spectrum (anthropology, sociology, economics, political science); and, fourth, whether sciences fit one into the other like Chinese boxes or Russian dolls. In short, from Wilson's point of view there is room for sociological discourse, but only when the postulates and approach harmonize with the more basic evidences of biology.[1]

The spontaneous reaction from some quarters has been to adopt a moral stance and put the conservative bias of the approach on trial. Sociobiology is discredited because it reproduces, *à la* Darwin, the structure of capitalist dynamics (Sahlins 1977). The argument is levelled at the consequences of the approach which are bound to agree with the requisites of the capitalist conception of society. However, this objection does not reach the core of the argument. A more persuasive stance is that adopted from the standpoint of culture as distinct from any biological inference. In *The Use and Abuse of Biology* (1977), Sahlins puts forward the integrity and autonomy of culture as a thing in itself. He argues, like many others, that symbolic production is proper and exclusive to human beings. Animals, he notes, may resort at times to some form or another of language but do not confer on

1 Along the same lines, but in a less systematic fashion, P.A. Corning (1976) submits an approach based upon the biological paradigm of survival and natural selection.

it a symbolic content. The response of the anthropologist to sociobiology rests upon the basic distinction to be drawn between humanity and animality, just as animals probably distinguish themselves from plants. The intention is to grant to human collectivities a status that puts them in a distinct category. It is still debatable whether such a neat distinction is indispensable.

Sociobiology's projections and analogies from animals to human beings do not always make for the most convincing arguments. Is aggressiveness the main cause, or even a significant cause, of warfare? Is altruism the real origin of nation-building? To cap it all, explanations based on both 'group selection' and 'individual selection' shed little light on the discussion. But whatever its present treatment, sociobiology can hardly be brushed aside as invalid. On the contrary, systematic research should be encouraged, even if the conclusions present difficulties of interpretation.

In 1981 Wilson published a more sophisticated but also more ambitious work entitled *Genes, Mind and Culture*, written with Charles J. Lumsden. This time, the authors aim at no less than putting culture in direct continuity with biology by considering cultural behaviour 'as an ultimate product of biology' (Lumsden and Wilson 1981, 350). They argue that culture is the product of a multitude of 'personal cognitive acts' which follow a genetically determined process of natural selection based on genetic fitness (176, 16). Their search is for 'biologically grounded rules in human cultural evolution' (58). Social sciences are therefore called upon to become subordinate to biology, even though Lumsden and Wilson propose a coevolutionary process of genes and culture, as the subtitle of their book suggests.

I do not mean to deny that there is a degree of determinism in biology. But, as Wilson implicitly grants a degree of autonomy to biology in regard to chemistry, I claim that the same rationale should apply to the autonomy of social relations in regard to biology and also any other physical determinants. The claim stands as a postulate for the rest of the discussion. Any sociological discourse rests, in the last analysis, on a form of autonomy analytically granted to a dynamic proper to social relations.

Psycho-individualism

While the biological school has gained prominence recently, psycho-individualism is also alive and well. It hails from a deep tradition embedded chiefly in the Protestant canons. It is more or less in such terms that, especially in his work in the fifties, George C. Homans has defined his position, arguing that it conforms to the western intellectual stream, which claims that the nature of individuals ultimately defines the nature of society (1962, 8). He argues that institutions derive their existence from drives or needs found in individuals who, from self-interest, proceed to satisfy these drives or needs by interacting with other people. From his point of view, therefore, any rigourous observation of reality ought to merge two already existing approaches: behavioural psychology (which does research by means of experiments on animals; Homans claims he took his inspiration from B.F. Skinner's works) and elementary economics (1955, 15; 1961, 12). In a nutshell, Homans contends that sociology has to stand as a corollary to psychology; sociability is construed as a by-product of psychological urges.

There is no point in searching for historical precedents for this view; they are legion. It is of greater interest to mention in passing those who have remained in Homan's wake. Peter Blau, while recognizing some sort of dynamics which emerges from association itself, conforms to the view that 'primitive psychological processes,' feelings of attraction, and desires for rewards preside over the formation of associations. Individuals precede group formation, which is the effect of 'motivating forces' (1964, 19). An immediate follower of the same trend may be found in Sidney R. Waldman (1972), who bases his theory of politics on individual action and choice.

Critical of the 'oversocialized conception' of man found among many sociologists, Dennis Wrong called, some two decades ago, for a 'more complex [and] dialectical conception of human nature' as a remedy for the unidimensional approach that he felt prevailed in the discipline (1961, 183). Oriented towards what he labels 'problems' for human societies, he proposed a more sophisticated approach which would cope with questions such as 'How are men capable of uniting to form enduring societies in the first place?' or 'How is man's animal nature domesticated by society?' (ibid. 184). This sort of questioning is classic, even traditional, and the author is conscious of the fact. Apart from being sweeping, such psychological reasoning is quite surprising on the part of a sociologist. It spontaneously evokes Rousseau's *Discourse on the Origins of Inequality Among Men*, where humanity is first conceived as a nature in itself which later acquires another nature quite distinct from the first. Rousseau's intention was to illustrate that human beings, before becoming social, were entirely different. But even before engaging in this demonstration, Rousseau was quite aware, as he mentions, that this state of nature might not have existed at all.

One may question the utility of trying to track down events that probably did not even take place, along the line of our rationalistic mode of imagining the making of societies. Why imagine that human beings developed first as human entities before aggregating into collectivities? Why not imagine instead, until proved wrong by convincing ethnological proofs to the contrary, that humankind developed as a social kind at the same time. Until there is proof to the contrary, the hypothesis of people joining together at a certain stage looks less plausible than the counter-hypothesis of human beings evolving in their formative period as social beings, acting one upon the other.

Whether one reduces social activities to emergent individualistic interests at work or tries one's hand at expressing the complexity of human collective endeavours in terms of hybrid combinations of psychological and social components, the intention is to exclude the reductionism of a strictly sociological frame of reference. There is no point, at the present, in trying to determine the value of Homan's, Blau's, or Wrong's propositions. Suffice it to say that they exemplify the resistance to any attempt to explain social behaviour as exclusively social events. The individualistic approach is still very strong, even pervasive, today.

Used as a heuristic tool, Emile Durkheim's hypothesis that humankind's alleged instinct for sociability may simply be an effect, instead of a cause, of human beings living in society, puts us, I think, on more secure grounds ([1938] 1966, 107). It has the advantage of reversing the old psychological perspective into a sociological one. Pushing a sociological perspective to extremes would be as detrimental as the extreme psychological perspective was. Reducing human behaviour to a sole logic of action, whatever its nature, is sure to lead to simplistic and mechanical generalizations. As a matter of fact political philosophers of former centuries had a propensity to attribute to society, as it evolved into more complex relationships, the same basic impulses that propelled it in its earlier stages. Marx, for one, held to an economic explanation in the last resort. Interestingly enough, such conceptions of humankind serve best as reflections of how society defined the nature of human beings at different times.

Human needs

By discarding individualistic explanations, I exclude all presumed needs so easily attributed to human beings. Bronislaw Malinowski's assignment of needs to humans in society, or more precisely, his designation of society as a creation ordered to the satisfaction of basic human needs, exemplifies the perspective I want to avoid. As already implied, I automatically discard teleologies of any sort. The same argument applies to reasonings educed from some nature which one might confer on a human being, be it moral, rational, sexual, economic, or aesthetic.

More often the 'human essence' (Macpherson 1977) is seen as taking the form of 'human needs,' which are understood to be fundamental and universal. These needs, proposed these days by progressives, follow an order of priorities elaborated by Abraham Maslow: physical, security or safety, social-affectional or love, self-esteem or dignity, and self-actualization. Established as a hierarchy, they are supposed to be reached by stages which follow one after the other (Davies

1977b, 161). Human beings are called upon to progress along a psychological path that society is expected to facilitate.

Some, like C.B. Macpherson, though cool to Maslow and more open to Marx, especially the *Manuscript of 1844*, distinguish between false and true needs: the former are those 'imposed by relations of production [requiring] domination'; the latter are those which 'could be met by a rational, non-class-dominated organization of production' (1979, 49). In the same vein, wants as opposed to needs are identified as the result of 'manipulation' (Fitzgerald 1977). The Frankfurt School has adopted a more sociological stance in calling for a distinction between true and false cultural needs (Mennell 1979). Interestingly enough, a good number of these proponents recognize the problems raised by the conceptualization of needs.

While it has all the trappings of a conception inspired by a psychological outlook, the human needs approach is in fact directed at the transformation of society from a moralistic point of view: needs are meant to provide a criterion for the evaluation of societies. Some societies can be considered as better suited to meeting basic human needs than others, some as more responsive or more 'alienating' than others (Etzioni 1968a, 624; 1968b, 873ff.). The 'is' as recognized in needs provides a basis to proceed to the 'ought.' This way of thinking harks back to an old ethical preoccupation which assumes that society is conceived for the benefit of human beings.

Whether societies are fit for human beings or not is of little concern if one is solely interested in the functioning of societies. The intention is not to judge or evaluate the degree to which societies conform to basic needs or generous ideals. The so-called human needs can be considered as secured only in some societies and not in others; the needs vary as to the importance socially ascribed to persons as individuals. The Maslow scheme corresponds to a liberal conception supported by the western legacy. But what really counts is what is happening, not what should happen. 'What should happen' becomes an interesting ideological framework which has to be submitted to sociological scrutiny.[2]

The general purpose is to put an end, at least momentarily, to individualistic concepts such as attitudes, volitions, desires, and other psychological phenomena which can be summed up as 'soul stuff,' to use a Bentleyan expression.

Without being Durkheimian to the hilt, it seems quite sound to accept that social facts should not be submitted to psychological or ethical explanations. In this way, the existence of determinants that are exclusive to social relations can be presumed without denying the effects of other factors at other levels of observation. Some behaviour or, to be more specific, some aspects of behaviour can only

---

2 The present framework does not claim immunity to any values; such is not and cannot be the case.

be accounted for as patterning after ready-made models that life in society provides.

The adoption of this guideline avoids the lure of an incipient form of functionalism, and sometimes teleologism, that grew up with Radcliffe-Brown. It should never be forgotten that Durkheim's sociology relies first on the efficient causes of social events, resorting to functional explanations only as a second step ([1938] 1966, 95). We need not have recourse to either of these modes. The negation of individualistic concepts belongs to an approach shared by numerous sociologists, although it does not imply our being enthralled by these sociologists' conclusions. Such a direction contradicts the Protestant ethic; human conscience and responsibility are reduced in importance.[3]

FRAMEWORK FOR A FRAMEWORK

Durkheim's seminal work provides a perspective, a way of looking at social reality. For one thing, his emphasis on the exclusion of consciousness as a relevant or reliable indicator of people's behaviour should be of some use. In other words, one should never count on the reasons put forward by the actors as necessarily explicative or satisfactory. Durkheim himself admitted that in this respect he was in agreement with Karl Marx, who contended that social relations stand outside people's wills and should not be explained from the actors' conceptions of their actions (1897, 648).

Leaning towards Durkheim's sociology should result almost automatically in a departure from Max Weber's sociology, which is grounded in the 'subjective meaning of action.' But this does not necessarily have to be so. Of course, the notion of personal motive is at this juncture of little avail. We are not interested in knowing what people think of their own actions or how they interpret them. On the other hand, values remain of great concern so long as they are construed as products of social determinants instead of as the effects of personal preferences. There is certainly a departure here from Weber's goal of comprehending events from the actors' presumed intentions, although there remains an adhesion to some of his intruments of sociological analysis – the ideal type, for instance – to the extent that these instruments can be deprived of their motivational aspects. Indeed, it is possible to question the practicability of such a divorce.

For the purpose of the present framework, all individualistic facets of people's

---

3 Parsons's conciliation of Durkheim with Weber, Marshall, and Pareto is illustrative. One may question, as some have done, whether Durkheim would have recognized himself in this convergence oriented towards a voluntaristic theory of action, but Parsons's approach reflects a deep concern for respect of man's free will.

behaviour are dispensed with, and whether actions are conscious or not does not make any difference. Rationality is of no concern either, unless it shows up as a value in itself: the systematic application of efficient rules for the achievement of specific purposes. Calls for rationality have, by necessity, to make appeals to goals of some sort. The end may be, for instance, production at the lowest possible cost, an entire life devoted to work, or the total reinvestment of earnings for the sake of increasing capital. Such objectives are values in themselves, and thus social products, no more and no less rational than other values. They can just as easily be labelled *arational*, that is, lying outside the realm of rationality.

Works of undeniable value have revolved around rationality as explicative of human behaviour. Largely inspired by the economists' perspective of efficiency maximization, some studies have reached interesting conclusions regarding, for instance, the propensity of individuals to participate in collective endeavours and in the expression of social choices (Downs 1957; Olson 1965; Riker and Ordershook 1973). Efficiency is bound to be estimated by comparing costs and goals. But in fact both costs and goals are matters of preference, and for these authors are considered as givens. Therefore the usefulness of their models should always be gauged in terms of the assistance they provide in examining particular social sets.

I do not mean to devaluate or even question the disciplines that make extensive use of concepts that are momentarily put aside for the sake of the present discussion. The aim is to extract from the complexity of reality a specific area of interrelationships affected strictly by social conditions.

This area cannot be isolated by considering individual cases in themselves; a sequence of recurrences must be explored, a series of singular events grouped together because they have certain determining characteristics in common. It is commonly accepted that there is no room for a science of the singular. Nonetheless, it has been the lot of political studies – purportedly called science – to be constantly solicited to explain particular events per se: the last election campaign in the United States, the last dispute in the Middle East, or, more pretentiously, the evolution of a given society. Behaviouralism at least offers the advantage, depending upon its use, of selecting sets of recurrences. Whether these sets and these recurrences are generally of any significance is another matter.

Besides, the discipline has frequently pursued its course in conformity with classical canons that see society as in need of therapy. The new dimensions of development and modernization, which are part and parcel of post-war decoloni-zation, confirm a trend connected with political studies, as well as sociology, from time immemorial. The intention of acting upon society is collateral with ethical preoccupations understood in the broadest sense: what is desirable, ideal, or advisable for society or societies. The 'good life' introduced by the Ancients still permeates present-day research. We are still very much influenced by the moral weight of political theory. Democracy remains a term of common usage, whether defined or not. Robert Dahl's book on the *Pluralist Democracy in the United States* is ostensibly an attempt to vindicate the happy juxtaposition of pluralist practices and a political ethics of the same nature: the democratic rules of 'polyarchy'[4] happen to find their full expression in the American Eden.

Under the guise of strict scientific prescriptions, Karl Popper's 'social engineering' is also entirely absorbed by an activist stance which gauges knowledge, and especially social knowledge, from its utilitarian impact.[5]

Fundamentally, it should not make any difference to the analyst whether the behaviour observed is of a supposedly democratic, authoritarian, or totalitarian nature. The same observation applies to the notion of exploitation which is appreciated differently depending upon time and place; Marx's sociology may be said to have limited its own breakthrough by basing its disquisition upon moral appreciations of economic relations.

Philosophical concepts designed to depict the state of people's minds – such as alienation and false or true consciousness – belong to a different set of analytical instruments, but do refer, at least implicitly, to realities closely associated with values which are to be shared or forsaken. False consciousness refers to a state of mind alien to its true interests, that is, those interests identified as true by the observer.

To sum up, all humanist considerations, whatever their pretentions or origins, are being set aside, not because they are judged to be unreal or even unscientific – although in some instances such may be the case – but because, by and large, the present framework plans to extract all that can be drawn out by examining social determinants – not more, but no less either.

A call for an unqualified study of social determinants may easily let loose holistic approaches which verge on a reification of society. All such approaches must at all costs be avoided. This point will be clarified as the discussion proceeds. Suffice it to say, for the time being, that questions about the supposed essence of

---

4 The term used in later works by the same author.
5 'As Professor Hayek says, "economic analysis has never been the product of detached intellectual curiosity about the *why* of social phenomena, but of an intense urge to reconstruct a world which gives rise to profound dissatisfaction"; and some of the social sciences, other than economics, that have not yet adopted this outlook, show by the barrenness of their results how urgently their speculations are in need of practical checks' (Popper 1961, 56). David Easton comes close to the same point of view: 'Like all social knowledge, political science has its origins and continuing support in the obvious fact that human beings find it useful ... Men want to understand the political system so that they can use this knowledge for their own purposes' (1953, 223).

society, its nature, and its ends are therefore excluded. Furthermore, any attempts to reduce society to the parameters of the individual will be thwarted from the start.

If society is dismissed as an unamenable concept, it is only in order to focus on a more specific set of phenomena to be derived from the social reality. *Relationship* is the seminal concept here. Scientific endeavours look for phenomena couched in terms of relations of properties of things, not for things in themselves. Social relations are multifarious; however, they are all forms of communications that may be construed as networks of production, consumption, conflict, and the like. Social relations need not be circumscribed within the conventional boundaries of what is usually understood as society. Direct reference to social relations, rather than society, will make my objective clear: the managing of sets of analytical units without trying to explain the working of a single collective whole. The intention is to examine not aspects of society, but rather aspects of social encounters. A dynamics of their own emerges when we examine relations, not when we consider society as a single entity.

The inquiry is deliberately sociological and focuses on a specific social relation: control. The whole framework is geared at delimiting a field of investigation from that social relation of reference, just as economics deals with relations of exchange. In other words, the proposal is to bring out a tentative network of social conditions, intertwined social relations, that make possible the emergence and maintenance of controls and sets of controls. Though it may shed light on certain current issues, the framework stands outside the realm of solutions to what are considered social problems. The purpose is explanatory but not prescriptive. Being sociological, the approach is not meant to have a say on strictly individual behaviour; it therefore excludes considerations, for instance, on the personal fate of politicians.

This book elicits sets of social relations identified as control and conditioning, and also as regulation, which is a combination of control and conditioning. These phenomena are discussed as analytical devices which account for recurrent behaviour. To this end, the definitions are intended to remain nominalist throughout the discussion. They may at times appear somewhat declaratory, but the purpose is solely to outline the contours of certain social realities without any claim to being definitive, exhaustive, or even explicative. No definition stands by itself but only in conjunction with others; the explanation lies in the relationship of concepts and not in the concepts themselves.

1

Control and its immediate components: interests and resources

A good many terms in the power family have suffered from over-exposure. A whole book could probably be devoted to trying to exhaust their different connotations and usages much in the way Kroeber and Kluckhohn have dealt with the concept of culture.[1] It would be redundant to tackle the semantic discussion once again. Social scientists are already familiar with the transfers and swaps of meanings imposed upon the various terms for power. The social reality identified as power by one author is called coercion by another, and vice versa. Academic tradition calls for trite reminders of either Shakespeare's 'What's in a name?' or Humpty Dumpty's familiar pronouncements. Scholarly tradition aside, there is little advantage in getting entangled here in a quarrel over words and meanings, for I have no intention of situating the notion of control along a spectrum of influence and power terms. Another word could have been chosen or, better, coined, to suit my goals: the identification and delineation, for analytical purposes, of a series of recurrent social phenomena.

CONTROL

By control I mean a social relationship based upon a recognized social pattern, in which a person or a group of persons avail themselves of a right over another person or group of persons.

First, control is considered as given; it is present in most social activities. The primordial origin of control in human behaviour is not my concern. I do try to explain the reasons for the existence of specific controls within specific conjunctures of events, but do not consider it my business to elucidate the purportedly profound underlying principles of control in general. Whether control

1 For recent coverage and new developments see Nagel (1975), Martin (1977), and Wrong (1979).

is found among animals or not does not in any way affect the discussion. Nor is the question of morality of any relevance: whether controls are good or bad, desirable or undesirable.

To posit control as a social relationship based upon a social pattern is already to dispose of a familiar form of dyad, a theoretical formulation that assigns relationships strictly atomistic or individualistic settings. Game theory, which has achieved high levels of formalization, and Robert Dahl's approach in *Modern Political Analysis* are good instances of this type of perspective. Studies of the interaction between two actors, either pitting one against the other or putting one in a situation of influence, power, or authority over the other, certainly have some value if the analyst contemplates the study in terms of optimized rationality, psychological response, or concrete events and proposes to check if A's intervention affected B's decision (Dahl 1976, ch. 4). The question is not primarily 'Who governs?' although I do provide information which should help to cope with this question in the future. The question I am dealing with is closer to a Laswellian formulation: 'Who controls whom or what, and how?' In a less lapidary fashion, I attempt to assess the extent to which certain social patterns facilitate or, conversely, interfere with some people's actions towards others. Consequently, I see control as a reproducable phenomena; it is precisely its recurrent aspect that makes it interesting and not its uniqueness or singularity.[2]

Controls are not models of behaviour as such, but are based upon models of behaviour. There are controls in so far as there are people who follow the same pattern in exercising rights over others, and often in deriving advantage from the exercise. The patterns are abstract, while the controls refer to real actions. Control is recognized in a variety of actions that have in common the submission of one actor to another, or one group of actors to another, with respect to specific values or sets of values. Let us look at a few examples. Controls are the actions that lead in certain societies to the subordination of women to their spouses, the latter exercising the right to, for instance, decide on the place of residence, the budget, the children's education, and so forth. The same may be said of the control of teachers over their pupils, employers over their employees, police over offenders. I am not concerned, of course, whether such control is opportune or not, rational or irrational. For instance, in some societies control over children's education is almost entirely left in the parents' hands; in others, this control is monopolized by the state or other similar agencies.

These illustrations bear in common a relationship based upon a mode of conduct shared by a number of actors. The actors' acceptance of the mode of conduct, however, does not mean adherence or consent, especially on the controllee's part;

2 See Harry Eckstein's reliance on the recurrence of his authority patterns (1973, 1150).

he or she may consent, but does not have to. So long as an actor submits to the pattern imposed upon him or her, control is understood.

Force

Many sociologists are departing with reason from the consensual, if not 'consentual,' approach that relies almost exclusively on adhesion to common values (Goode 1972; Wrong 1976). As a matter of fact, the use of force as the 'final persuader' is implicit in most controls. Control takes place under threats of varied impact. Some controls imply the loss of symbolic or material goods, which in some instances is felt as more severe than death itself; exclusion from the collective sharing of basic values – such as excommunication from the Catholic Church – can be an experience of extreme deprivation. Other controls provide for loss of physical freedom, or even life. Eventually, it is not imprisonment which serves as the instrument of submission, but the threat of imprisonment (Lively 1976, 8). To be respected, a pattern of control must impose some form of deprivation as a consequence for non-compliance. If, on the other hand, the pattern offers an opportunity for an advantage or inducement of some sort (be it financial or symbolic), exchange, which will be discussed later, not control, is involved. Thus, controls are necessarily an alternative to a worse condition, even when they are greeted as desirable or acceptable by those who submit to them.

Resorting to force marks a failure in achieving control. By force I mean the use of physical violence, not what is commonly known as coercion, that is, the threat of the use of violence or a show of force to impress potential controllees. True, apart from the deliberate elimination of people who stand in one's way, force is usually employed to affirm the controller's ability to follow up in case of resistance: it serves to illustrate the capacity to make good a threat, the aim being compliance in the future. Those subjected to alternatives under duress may feel they have a very limited choice indeed.[3] The point, though, is not the margin of manoeuvre open to controllees, but compliance as opposed to non-compliance; the goal is respect of a pattern of behaviour on the part of designated controllees. The use of force proves most efficient when negative controls are pursued, controls which forbid access to certain goods. It soon shows its limits when it is designed to have people do things, rather than prevent them from doing things.

Since coercion is generally costly as well as unreliable, controllers contrive to

3 'Even in the most oppressive and cruel cases of subordination, there is still a considerable measure of personal freedom ... Actually, the "absolute" coercion which even the most cruel tyrant imposes upon us is always distinctly relative ... The super-subordination relationship destroys the subordinate's freedom only in the case of direct physical violation. In every other case, this relationship only demands a price for the realization of freedom' (Simmel 1930, 182).

establish their authority through internalized recognition of patterns: automaticity in acceptance is the goal.

If conscience has any part to play in this framework, it is precisely at the level of common recognition of specific patterns - the diffusion of a collective state of conscience about the appropriateness of certain actions, the word 'appropriateness' being used here without limiting it to moral judgments. In many instances recognition remains at almost instinctual levels, no precise justifications being given for submission. Traditional behaviour frequently embraces actions that are taken for granted, finding their supposed *raison d'être* in the beginnings of time. In such circumstances the dictates of conscience do not have to be explicit, so long as people conform to the behaviour expected from them. Patterns upon which controls are based range from automaticity to emphatically legitimized modes of behaviour.

The dyadic character

Controls are part of a more complex structure of conditioning which I will develop later. For expository purposes I will treat controls first *per se,* and integrate them as the discussion proceeds into a more complex whole. For the moment, let us examine the control relationship itself as an enforced pattern involving two parties. Whatever their degrees of explicitness and extensiveness controls always display a bilateral mode. They deal with protagonists designated in dyadic terms: the controller and the controllee. Though there may be innumerable controllers and controllees, the basic relationship remains bilateral. The employer, whether a single individual or a group of people constituting an administration, entertains a dyadic relationship with his or her employees. The same reasoning applies to all sets of controls, from the family network to the more complex structures of governmental action.

Parties frequently have within a control-set counterparts to controls originally exercised by only one agent, so much so that one may wonder at times which controls really came first. Formerly, an employer's controls over his or her workers were considerable; they have since been progressively whittled down and contained by other controls. Controls by men over their families usually imply financial obligations, a form of control wielded by family members. Rights and duties as they operated in the Middle Ages under the vassal system epitomize a condition of great bilaterality in the distribution of controls. It is hard to imagine controls that are absolutely unilateral, offering no counterparts to the controllee although some instances of slavery may be cases in point. Besides, the notion of justice or equilibrium among roles within a given network is bound to vary and call for frequent reappraisals by the controllees, opening the way to conflicts.

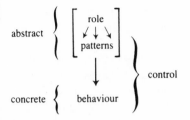

FIGURE I Immediate components of control

Roles

Roles are made out of patterns; they may be defined for our purposes as the sets of behaviour patterns one is entitled, from a given status, to make one's own, as well as those one is expected to conform to. Controls, which follow patterns, usually designate only parts of roles, hardly ever entire ones. The parent role, for example, incorporates a good many controls but also implies actions that are alien to control. The same consideration applies to roles defining other extended face-to-face encounters: the boss's role as well cannot be summed up strictly as a set of controls. Management is familiar with the necessity of rendering working life sufficiently attractive. If controls conform to a dyadic pattern, such is not the case for the roles which sustain the pattern. Being a professor, for instance, means not only exerting forms of control over students, but also having exchanges with them and with colleagues, conforming to decisions from the administration, and keeping contacts with the scientific world. By and large, patterns may be construed as dyadic by nature, but a role, seen as a whole, does not have to be.

Controls are actualized patterns of behaviour (Figure I); they may be confirmed in the actors' minds as acquired rights, or may be normalized by tolerance or imposed by the sheer threat of force. However, the most essential element of control is its social character: it must be a collective practice, a model of conduct that is reproduced a number of times. The element of generalization is crucial. From a purely logical point of view, three occurrences should be satisfactory: the first occurrence is a singular event, the second a copy of the first, and the third the adoption of a social pattern based on the previous two occurrences. This minimum of three may seem a caricature, if not blithely ludicrous. Some events, however, do not have to repeat themselves very frequently to show a pattern of considerable interest: government actions need few precedents, in some cases, to confirm their validity. All controls are not of equal impact; some need a high degree of frequency to deserve even slight attention, while others need a lower degree, although they are nonetheless controls whatever the amount of concern they get.

Frequently, controls are thrown into the limelight when they are considered too frequent or qualitatively too exorbitant. For analysts, controls are coped with differently. Since they are numerous, the analysts' job is either to put them into analytical sets and subsets or to single out some they find more representative or more relevant. Subjectivity certainly affects the observer's scientific choices, whatever they are. In the final analysis, no criterion seems absolutely satisfactory as a basis for selection. One tentative hypothesis might be to propose the study of controls deemed decisive in the fates of societies, those whose suppression would be most shattering.

Although controls submit to abstract pattern formulations, they are also embodied in concrete actions, identifiable even when performed in secret; they are always open to discovery. Whether overt or covert, controls exist whenever social patterning and acquisition of rights or advantages coexist. Controls are elements of an action and seldom the whole of it: men may exercise their fatherly rights over education in a wide variety of manners, including psychological twists that vary greatly from one individual to another. Since controls are specific, total control over anyone is next to impossible. The ideas of domination, subordination, and the like are conducive to inferences too vague to render any rigourous observation satisfactory. Such terms, however, suit polemic designs and, as a result, are frequently employed. One might break down domination into a series of controls – in other words, specific identifiable actions – and in so doing probably dilute the impact of the term. The specificity of control, as a notion, also implies varying degrees of control achievement, the possible spectrum ranging from more than zero to a hundred per cent.

Controls are multifarious. They can be found in almost all our daily activities, at home, at work, at social gatherings, or on the street. For an observer to cope with them, levels of analysis have to be introduced; a sole matrix which lumps them together into one whole seems hardly realizable. The recourse to levels being an analytical artefact, one may imagine a great variety of possible levels, unless one entertains an essentialist approach to things and deeds. A strategy of observation therefore becomes necessary, a strategy which automatically involves grouping sets of actions. Controls, while real, are based upon patterns which may easily be broken down into sub-patterns or conversely clustered into more comprehensive patterns. It is up to the analyst to determine the most desirable extensions: one which covers all the control patterns included within a dyadic relation – man and wife, employer and employee – or one more limited in scope, covering only part of the ensemble of control patterns in a dyadic relation.

On a macroscopic level of observation the phenomenon of the division of labour proceeds from the assignment of controls within a production network. The production of goods, services, and ideas involves the allocation of rights over these matters, rights that entitle some agents to determine where energy will be spent and for what purposes. So emerge industrial enterprises, military ventures, and symbolic expressions – the arts, sciences, and religions. Controls also intervene in the way the fruits of production are distributed. These illustrations are discussed in greater detail as we proceed.

Up to now control has been considered mainly as an action. At the source of action, however, lie values and agents. Enter interests.

INTERESTS

Control, as has been posited, subsumes two other concepts: interests and resources. As a corollary to an earlier definition, control may be said to be the social actualization of specific interests over specific resources. Interests must be reckoned with first. For purposes of analysis, control is construed as an action directed by interests which are the necessary condition of the control's existence. There are no controls without interests. But what are interests?

A whole tradition links interest with aspiration. Lasswell and Kaplan envisage interest as a 'pattern of demands and its supporting expectations,' putting the emphasis upon the actors' calculated involvements which may be conducive to the formation of organized groups (1965, 23, 40–1). Robert A Dahl prefers to steer clear of the term and to stick to less contentious concepts such as motivation and aims (1976, 37–8, 59). Distinguishing interest from demands, David Easton endows interest with an instrumental value; for him interest is a means for a person or a group to arrive at the implementation of fundamental goals which serve as the ultimate aspirational reference.[4] Most of these authors provide ample room for atomistic and psychological interpretations of social relations which amount in consequence, on the whole, to a sum of individuals interacting without their interactions involving the emergence of a new reality.

Value

I view interest in this study from a sociological perspective, as part of another whole, part of a structure of value. Values and interests are abstract entities that lend themselves to circular relationships: values arousing interests and interests promoting values. A closer circumscription of what values are is in order. A value is a form assigning a standard which is attributed to an identified order of entities. Values rank the significance of either concrete or abstract entities – things, persons, actions, ideas, representations, roles. The weight accorded any particular

---

4 Interestingly enough 'interest' is not defined in Almond and Powell's classic *Comparative Politics* (1966) even though the concept is extensively used (interest articulation, aggregation).

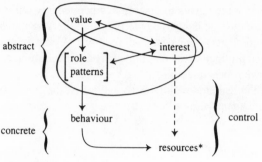

note to figure,

* From their tangible aspect

FIGURE 2 Value components of control

entity varies with time, place, and common experiences, but it is always relative. Nothing is of value in itself; an entity is ascribed a value in so far as other entities are similarly ranked. Hence values are social products. What is fundamental in one society may be of little or no importance in another. Even life and death are ascribed meanings that differ from one set of values to another. The kamikazes, the suicide squads sent by Japan against their enemies during the second world war, are almost unthinkable in western tradition. Suicide is honourable in some places and despicable in others. The right to life, which is basic in the Hobbesian perspective, nevertheless remains at the mercy of social diktats. Traditions vary in determining when non-productive elements in a society become a burden and must be disposed of. Arch-sociologism is inclined to state that all needs found among human beings derive from society, and that what is called human nature amounts to social values that are mistaken for individual ones; the arch-psychologist, on the other hand, sums up social values as extensions of individual drives; while the arch-rationalist describes them as extensions of personal choices, and so on. Where do we draw the line, if there is any to be drawn? At this juncture, it does not seem desirable, as mentioned earlier, to get bogged down in distinctions that would satisfy very few people. The problem seems insoluble anyway in the foreseeable future. Our best bet is to try to maximize the sociological approach without lapsing into an undue reductionism.

Although I have selected values as units of reference, I do not mean to suggest that they owe their existence to themselves; I have already alluded to their existence in connection with interests (Figure 2). Furthermore, the existence of values can never be verified. Clearly, values are embodied in physical expressions, be they signs or symbols like letters, numbers, or sounds of the voice or more concrete expressions like pictures or buildings. But letters, numbers, syllables, and paintings are not values in themselves. The world of values is completely abstract and unfolds in people's minds. For this reason, one becomes easily entangled if one counts on values as the cornerstone of one's theoretical constructions, unless one believes in their essential reality or autonomy. Values, understood as fundamentally social in this disquisition, are only amenable to discretionary identification; whichever way they are singled out, identified, and arranged, they are no more than intuitions or personal deductions on the part of the observer. Values, as well as the value systems that serve as integrative supports, are then bound to be constructs, imagined particles that move and evolve within a hypothetical field of reference, interrelated from the outset either antithetically, conflictingly, complementarily, interdependently, or otherwise. This hypothetical field remains the observer's construct and therefore can hardly be imagined to be found reproduced in the actor's mind. Should such a coincidence ever occur, it can have no particular significance, except to show that both observer and observed share the same code of behaviour.

Any professional of social science will already have confronted the above development with Max Weber's ideal type. Both developments, Weber's and mine, obviously share the construct principle upon which they are based. Neither intends to transcribe faithfully the composition of sign and symbol circulation within social relation circuits. They diverge with respect to the premises of Weberian sociology, a theory developed through an understanding of people's inner motives. Otherwise, both models respect the same analytic rules.

In my view, interest is an activated value, activated in the sense that a value or a set of values is taken over by agents who proceed to its promotion and implementation. Indeed, the properties ascribed to value become entirely applicable to interest. In the final analysis, interest can be said to be a value saddled with a value of activation. For instance, private property is a value; it becomes an interest when it is actually promoted as a desirable end by some agent or when its principle is implemented in reality. As was said about values, interests are also constructs which, as will be discussed later, cannot provide other than tentative interpretations of the motivation for actual controls.

Founded upon values, interest is necessarily a collective concept which applies to situations that are shared by a number of actors. Within the present framework, an individual acting on his own behalf is not regarded as representing interests. (In common usage one may be said to hold interests of one's own, but this is a different matter.) Interests are social products which are promoted collectively. Actors may work for their common cause separately, on an individual basis, and still serve their interests. Bentley establishes as a quasi axiom the coincidence of groups with interests, one owing its existence to the other and vice versa. In his mind, a group is more than a mere collection of people with a concordance of views and actions; its members must strive for a formal organization of involvement. My definition of a group is more extensive; it covers a wide spectrum of collective actions ranging from individual actions parallelled by a series of identical endeavours to the most organized of activities.

The terms 'group,' 'organization,' and 'actor' pertain to more intellectually accessible realities than interests; they seem, so to speak, more concrete. But in fact actors and their behaviour are the only concrete reality. Groups and organizations are mere abstractions of the mind (as will be elaborated more extensively later on). How then can we relate the notion of interest, which is inherently abstract, with that of agents or actors? People are not interests, but they may be considered as agents of interests; in other words, they are vehicles of interests without being the interests themselves. Interests, as an analytical abstraction, are served, or perhaps fulfilled, by agents. Actors are situated in a network of relationships that match socially assumed roles: age, sex, occupation. To speak, for instance, of a 'prosperous industrialist' is to describe a status achieved from an accomplished role which puts into play controls that are essential to the accomplishment of the role; in a nutshell, this manner of speaking underlines the set of interests for which the person is an agent.

Interests are as intimately connected to roles as they are to values. Whereas roles account for static expressions of accepted patterns, interests point to a dynamics of promotion for the maintenance of current patterns and, at times, the introduction of new ones. Since roles are static, they are dependent upon the way they are defended by interests. From a lack of interest, a role will have its control-patterns fall into disuse. Interests represent values served by controls, objectives to be attained through control. Interests correspond to a valorization not by the role itself (which is passive) but by the agents filling the role (or the role to be) who come to share values specific to that end. The move may be in favour of the introduction, maintenance, or extension of controls; it may also be geared to the defence of a status by removing barriers of access to other agents, or geared to the reduction of controls wielded by others. Even the exercise of a controlling pattern is done in the name of interests. All these properties of interest bespeak the autonomy of the values specific to the holders of a role, as a whole. This autonomy marks an area of particularistic, segmentary, often contending claim.

To sum up, interests are values proper to a role without being parts of the role. They are, from an analytical point of view, the starting point of controls, the controls being the fulfilment of roles and operating on behalf of interests which are conveyed by agents.

Epistemological status

To what extent, then, are interests subjective or objective? Political science is quite familiar with the problem raised by the analytical consequences of the objective/ subjective dichotomy. Making reference to interests may be to unlock the Pandora's box of the discipline, but nobody can seriously elude the question. Debates have been raging between the objective school and the subjective. The former goes back at least as far as Karl Marx. It affirms the existence of interests that can be objectively identified by the observer. Whatever the actors' moves, it is deemed possible to determine their real interests (Balbus 1971; Connolly 1972; Lukes 1974); for if the actors actually understood their real interests, they would follow the right course of action. The supporters of the subjective school consider the observer's supposedly objective interests as pure projections of his subjective preferences. Subjective interests are defined as those interests openly expressed in the arena, for or against an action or a policy. The observer is then supposed to consider, for purposes of analysis, only those interests that are openly associated with a movement or an event. Those that do not show up are not to be imputed any reality (Polsby 1963, 116–17; Dahl 1961 – though the term 'interest' as such is never used). A less rigid approach will content itself with the agents' conscious desire to intervene, or more simply their desire to obtain a change of policy.[5]

Both the objective and the subjective perspectives rely one way or another on the participants' consciousness as their main axis of explanation. My point of departure is entirely different and does not stand on this link with reality. The notion of interest does not constitute a checking point in the present framework but is rather an analytical device, so much so that the opposition between the two schools over consciousness remains of incidental importance.

The notion of interests certainly has all the appearances of a powerful abstraction subduing mankind to its irresistible attraction. Human beings thus divested of their 'natural' capacity to choose, seem merely irresponsible entities. This would certainly be the case if the claim of the model were to explain the whole reality of human beings in society. However, viewed as a construct, interest can be used as an analytical tool. In itself it does not have any other value; it does not purport to reveal inner motives or bring to light sublimations or deceptions, on the part of either individuals or collectivities. For the sake of this discussion, interests do not exist except in the mind of the observer, who uses this device as if human beings were so managed.

For me, interests, like the values from which they are logically derived, cannot

---

5 Interest is referred to by La Palombara (1964, 16) as 'the conscious desire to have public policy, or the authoritative allocation of values, move in a particular, general or specific direction.'

claim any existence of their own; they owe their existence, whenever mentioned, to the author who decides when and how to make use of them. More often than not, we integrate them into a value structure, which is also a construct. One might venture to situate sets of interests in relation to each other, using the notion of culture as a serviceable background. Culture then stands for a sort of canopy of values legitimating these interests. Ideology, on the other hand, is another way of integrating values and reflecting interests in a more wittingly systematic and, sometimes, studied fashion. I see both culture and ideology as intellectual constructions built up for analytical, polemical, or interventional purposes. Culture and ideology usually aim at different analytical goals, culture being more inclusive than ideology. Nothing forbids the introduction of intermediate levels or the entire reshuffling of the approach towards the observation of value and interest structures. Besides these macromodels which encompass rather large systems, it may be opportune to build up more sectorial or segmentary frames of references, selecting a limited number of value-units put into relationships. Depending upon the extent of the analysis, the model can take more or fewer units into consideration.

Interests stand at the origin of controls. They are analytically conceived of as social products entitled to what is collectively considered an advantage, or exercising rights over people. Controls remain, as has already been stated, the sole concrete element of the whole framework. Interests nonetheless stand as the theoretical fulcrum; depending upon their arrangements they may or may not offer rewarding results. Controls are meaningless if they are not tied to interests as their *points d' appui*. Controls serve to achieve mastery over objects valued by interests; we call such objects resources.

RESOURCES

Resources are identified as any objects, abstract or concrete, which are designated as desirable by interests. Resources may be human beings, material things, or symbolic representations, but they must be tangible to some extent; they cannot be completely abstract. Agents may exercise control over other agents. Slavery, as institutionalized in former times, is an obvious example, as is conscription. Agents may hold control over material things; in this case they exercise a right of property. Control via property – whether private or public makes no difference – is a way of limiting or determining access to resources for some people. It implies at least indirect control over others by forbidding them tenure, use, or abuse. There is no way of checking the exercise of such control except in the negative. So long as nobody intervenes to thwart its application, control over property may be assumed to exist. It must be remembered in passing that since control is held only in conformity with a social pattern, it cannot be said to occur on Robinson Crusoe's island, if one presumes that Robinson and Friday have the island all to themselves.

Control over symbolic representations is exerted over the spectrum of abstract signs, from pure symbols such as flags and anthems to the most recondite expressions such as complicated mathematical equations. But controls stop short of affecting minds – at least it is impossible to verify such effects. Hitler, for instance, could control to a large extent the symbolic manifestations diffused in Nazi Germany, though no one knows the depth of their impacts on people's minds. In day-to-day dealings we are accustomed to exchanging symbolic tangibles – money, cheques, receipts, contracts – which express abstract capacities of different sorts. The state's generally recognized exclusive control over money printing is a good illustration of control over symbolic items. Copyrights indicate a monopoly held over the diffusion of other types of symbolic tangibles: books, records, and drawings.[6] Censorship stands as the final recourse for stemming the flow of sign and symbol transmission. Although the diffusion of signs and symbols may be so canalized, ideas, as abstractions, cannot be said to abide by controls. We shall see later that conditioning should not be confused with control. Finally, status positions recognized by symbols, written endowments couched in terms of money or title-deeds, and other like forms, constitute, in their own right, a control over symbolic expressions.

Reckoned as significant by interests, resources become valuable in themselves; or they may become valuable as means to the attainment of other resources, that is as a way of gaining control of further resources.[7] One can imagine an almost infinite chain leading to the management of more and more resources. But, whatever they are, resources remain valuable because social conditions keep them so.

In other words, interests emerge when scarcity appears. Where there is plenty, there is no room for interests. Rarefaction is largely a social process. Human beings come to believe in some sort of scarcity after having been sensitized to it. They either have been accustomed to a level of consumption and have to satisfy

6 The following statement often found in books strongly limits the owners' ability to dispose of them physically as they wish, even for lending purposes (libraries are particularly concerned here): 'This edition is sold subject to the condition that it shall not, by way of trade or otherwise, be lent, resold, hired out or otherwise circulated without the publisher's prior consent in any form of binding or cover than that in which it is published, this condition being imposed on the subsequent purchaser.'
7 Evoking Marx's model of the class society Ralf Dahrendorf comments in a sense quite suited to our purpose: 'Property,' he writes, 'must not be understood in terms of purely passive wealth, but as an effective force of production, as "ownership of means of production" and its denial to others' (1968, 21).

themselves with less – because of famine, war, depression, or other factors – or have been submitted to new expectations which themselves create a sense of scarcity. I postulate that the notion of scarcity is meaningless except as an offshoot of social conditions. Of course, interests are readily at work stimulating some needs and not others, campaigning for certain controls and for the suppression of others. But interests are in fact active because the resources they already hold give them a vantage-ground. These resources are amenable to a variety of typologies; for my purposes they have to be collectively distributed and cannot rest upon individual skills.[8] The gamut of resources is widespread indeed. It ranges from the panoply of advantages over the use and production of goods and services, including organizational know-how and brains trusts, to more abstract entities such as symbols and status. Depending upon time and place, resources which were once assets may become liabilities; although titles of nobility opened doors in France before 1789, at that time they were more likely to open those to a tumbrel. On a still more abstract level, information, defined as efficient signs in the organization of action, remains one of the most coveted objects of control, since it serves as a basic instrument in the procuring of resources. On the other hand, control over resources is no guarantee of control over further resources. Wealth, for instance, is no obvious indicator of significant control over production or public policies.[9]

CONCLUSION

Controls put in action interests which are abstract entities. These interests are taken charge of by individuals, identifiable as such, who get in contact with other individuals upon whom the control is exercised. The examples given, of men's controls over their wives, illustrate the management of male interests – which are constructs – as actualized by concrete people in concrete situations within the confines of a precise social network. The notion of interest enables the observer to extract a single aspect and ignore others, while remaining in a position to make the necessary verifications of his hypotheses. In other words, controls are identifiable events which may be defined as the realized social capacity of getting some action done, or of getting hold of resources which in turn may be directed at the acquisition of new resources in an unending process. In order to achieve their goals, controls frequently call for the threat of recourse to force, force as such being only instrumental, though quite efficient on many occasions.

8 Here I strongly depart from Dahl's aperture which focuses on resources as held by individuals (1976, 37).
9 In this case, Dahl's caveat seems quite à propos (1976, 27).

Among its many acceptations the term 'power' is at times used to describe a potentiality,[10] a situation where actors are in a position to intervene without necessarily taking advantage of the situation. Parsons put forward the idea of power as a circulating medium. In my discussion, however, control refers to an actual state of determination over others and on specific grounds. I do not purport to use the notion of control as an instrument for the analysis of future courses of events or as an indicator of potential capacities.

Since they are based upon patterns which are enmeshed in roles, controls exist to the extent that they are socially institutionalized. That is not to say that they have to be legitimized by authorities, but rather that they have to be recognized by some – at least those who exercise them – as a social mode of behaviour. Controls are thus parts of institutions just like any other behaviour deriving from roles. Their objects or goals, then, also have to be social in conformity with the logic that binds all the components.

Resources are galvanized under controls set up to satisfy social needs of either direct consumption or use for the production of further resources. Any control is aimed at people, for control is intrinsically a social relation. Private property, for instance, would be meaningless in the case of two people lost on a forgotten island. In other respects, control is not effected upon persons as such, but upon some of their actions which can at times be systematized into processes. So, control may apply to production capacities within a given division of labour.

All controls are not of equal importance for any particular analyst; consequently a choice must first be made of the controls which are to be emphasized. In some instances, the analyst may be concerned with the controls he or she finds most prominent in a given social network. Since a consensus on what is prominent is highly unlikely, I will leave the question open for the time being, until other elements shed light on possible arrangements.

Since they are founded upon patterns of action, controls must be transmitted from actor to actor. A medium is necessary to get people to conform to the patterns. The intricate system of diffusion operates under an embracing social phenomenon called conditioning.

10 Sociologists and political scientists are familiar with Weber's use of the term 'power' as the 'chance' to exercise one's will over another (1969, 180).

2

Conditioning: the management of interests through culture and ideology

Controls are, by definition, sustained by patterns of behaviour whose maintenance relies on the mediation of signs which, depending upon their style and the observer's impressions, are usually labelled as information, advertising, propaganda, manipulation, or otherwise; the purpose here, however, is not to make value judgments about the agents' motives.[1] The term 'conditioning' suggests, perhaps, a cynical outlook on sign transmission but such is not my purpose. I intend no pejorative connotation by my choice, which is aimed at a neutral description of reality. I posit that conditioning exists whenever agents are exposed to patterns of thinking or behaving which are directly or indirectly conducive to the performance of some action. Patterns of thinking or behaving are abstract entities we devise in order to account for repeated actions. Patterns are clearly legion, and for this reason only limited numbers can be examined at a time. But, more important, they remain abstract models devised to allow a systematic observation of facts. Most patterns, as stated earlier, may be broken down into sub-patterns or, conversely, integrated into more global patterns; they are analytical artefacts.

From conditioning resurges the vast domain of values, but this time viewed in the process of transmission. Conditioning points out which values are to be adopted and which to be repudiated. It proposes, through strong inducements to mildly inciting illustrations, types of actions to do or not to do, to allow others to do or to prevent them from doing. Hence, conditioning is not only limited to the performance of acts; it also provides for cases of abstention where tolerance or submission is the model of behaviour.

---

1 A literature exists on manipulation and other means of concealment of one's interests (Wrong 1979, 28ff.; Goodin 1980; Dahl 1976, 46).

The emotional aspect

Conditioning is of a rather psychological nature whenever it relies on emotional devices to ensure its impact. Symbols are one of its richest instruments, since they can easily mean different things to different people. They are signs which, for the purpose of the present discussion, are directed at irrational feelings – of belonging, strength, love. Flags, regalia, national anthems, and parades are obvious instances. Nonetheless, there exist more subtle symbols which lend themselves to contradictory interpretations: for example, the code of traditional etiquette can be superficially deciphered as illustrating the influence of women in society, or, more cynically, as underlining women's social weakness. Nobody is ever in a position to reveal the exact meaning of such a set of signs, if it ever has a meaning other than what people assign to it, according to their interests. Intentionality has no place here. The motive invoked by a symbol producer is no guarantee of the meaning imparted to other people. Whenever a symbol is expressed, there is no semantic proprietor to endow it with meaning. It is let loose for others to grasp and give it a sense. For example, for some people Cadillacs are the symbol of the *parvenus,* not the well-to-do. Spending-symbols are interesting because they express what the actors, taken collectively, want observers to see. Everyday life is fraught with symbols for others to notice. One might say that life is so rife with symbols that its meaning is hardly decipherable. There is the rub. Provided with an extensive halo of ambiguity, which is its strength as well as its weakness, the symbol cannot always be tracked down to a specific meaning. The multiplicity of meanings for individual symbols is one aspect of ambiguity; the symbol contributes to a polysemic world, a world of convertible referents. What a hunting-ground for the humanist intellectual in search of meanings!

The intractability of the subject does not spare one from examining its bearing. Whatever the difficulty in rigorously circumscribing this protean reality, it is imperative both to cope with the symbol and to avoid any claim to reveal a supposedly concealed sense. In spite of their multidirectionalities, symbols are part and parcel of the control entity. Omitting them from the discussion, for whatever reason, would mean depriving the analysis of a fundamental component. All symbols, to start with, are not that enigmatic. The semantic aura of a good number of them may be closely approximated. Or, to put it differently, some aspects of them may be readily decrypted. It should not be forgotten that we are only considering collectively produced symbols. Individual expressions are automatically excluded from the discussion, in so far as they do not conform to any transmitted pattern. Variations and discrepancies in appreciation have to be of a collective nature as well. Groups or classes of people disagree at times about resorting to one symbol rather than another. Different evaluations of a status symbol, such as the Cadillac mentioned earlier, must be understood as a collective difference of appreciation over what value is evoked by the use of a Cadillac as a social indication of achievement or unachievement. Personal approbation or disapprobation still remains of no particular interest.

Although a good number of symbols are known to be appraised quite differently by generally opposed groups of people, it is nonetheless possible to imagine a situation where the analyst, as a scientific observer, perceives a symbol conditioning no one has grasped before. Since urban ecology is to a large extent the effect of social relations, it is well adapted for semiotic analyses. Building architecture may convey good taste, prettiness, or functionality, as well as awe and respect. The Grecian facades of banking premises, which in the nineteenth century wore the guise of antique temples, were probably erected to impress both patrons and employees: banks were perhaps called upon to become the new sacrosanct places. On the other hand, a strictly functional building arouses quite different feelings. Here the decoding is no easy job and many different interpretations are possible. But whether we like it or not, diffuse conditioning can hardly be discarded because of its plasticity, although it cannot be assigned determinant importance. It certainly complements more explicit conditionings and controls and should be considered as an adjacent factor. For instance, the impact of American capitalism or Soviet socialism cannot be summed up in their buildings, although these buildings may be deemed useful instruments for impressing people. They serve at least as incidental expressions of might, being a sort of 'signature of power on environment' (Lasswell 1979, 44).

Finally, threat and intimidation are also part of the psychological apparatus used for conditioning. The militia, whether the army or the police, personifies the capacity to repress, for whatever reason. Intervention strictly through armed forces belongs to the military. But whenever armed force is used to impress an aggregation of persons, it must also be ranged as a conditioning device. The German occupation of France during the second world war serves as a good illustration of control acquired through intimidation and seconded by force.

The rational aspect

Seldom is conditioning uniquely the product of emotional appeals. Ideas are called upon to buttress the desirability of using designated controls. They act as rational legitimizers, putting emphasis on the logical organization of concepts and propositions. Any discourse, be it of the most dispassionate nature, is, for our purposes, a sort of conditioning, in as much as it is conducive to desired controls. In other words, ideas take part in a conditioning undertaking when they are geared to the transmission of control patterns directed at controllers, controllees, or both – whether potential or actual. Ideologies are an illustration of one of the most structured forms of conditioning. At the other extreme, advertising is more circumscribed, though quite pervasive in its cumulative effects: spot after spot, advertisements add up to a mosaic which is, however, of little interest as a rational whole.

Rational conditioning tries to defend logically the creation of new controls or the maintenance or abolition of existing ones. While the discourse, like an ideology, may look very logical and well articulated, it necessarily carries values which, in the last resort, cannot claim total rationality. No pronouncement can be entirely equated with rational conditioning.[2] Almost any conditioning is a mixture of rational and psychological appeals. Returning to the example of Germany's occupation of France, one might note the great emphasis put on 'la collaboration,' in which both rational and psychological registers are strongly implied.

The arena of value production
Whole societies are subjected to the extolling of collective goals, couched in terms of desirable levels of output. Goal-attainment is familiar to the Parsonian ear, but goal determination is a lot less so (even though Parsons made reference to both). Likewise, the allocation of values has been a concept in common usage since the work of David Easton. But what if the whole game takes place before wants are submitted to a conversion into demands, that is, at the threshold of the political system? Easton certainly has a few words to say on the subject, but only a few; he puts aside the whole process as an externality pertaining to the outside world of the environment. Expectations, opinions, motivations, ideology, preferences, and interests are somewhat left in the lurch.[3] The arena of value production, which has a direct effect on the emergence of demands, is kept in abeyance.[4]

The world of goal- and value-determination, as a social process, is wholly embraced by the phenomenon of conditioning which openly or covertly induces people to conform collectively to standards of behaviour. The acceptance of the standards is determinative in the overall production and organization of collectivities: thus are defined roles that constitute a social whole. Capacities are socially evaluated and roles allotted in consequence. At this point interests intervene, trying to draw in their favour whatever they can. Division of labour in practice is

2 The distinction between rational and psychological conditioning has only indicative use; otherwise we are faced with the moot question of what rationality is. The issue of such a discussion, whatever it is, would probably be of limited use.
3 Easton (1965, 71–2). He agrees that wants are affected by social determinants but adds that they are, for his analytical purposes, taken as givens. He does not presume that wants are static either, although he says 'the conditions of the wants, whether they are static or changing, will be accepted as parameters of the system' (72).
4 Easton's propositions about socialization will be dealt with in due course.

indeed a reality of controls, while the patterns sustaining it are products of conditioning.

In order to strengthen the patterns and to reinforce their legitimacy, recourse to the rule of authority is frequently contemplated. Rules indicate controls that are either imposed, permitted, or prohibited officially. The absence of rules in specific cases of control are as indicative of the authority's intentions or abilities as is a code of rules in other circumstances. No rule is a rule too. Legitimization by the authority is in itself a sort of conditioning. Rule-making is no more than uttering propositions in a formal context, the application of which may necessitate controls only if rule-application propositions are not followed. Conditioning through rules carries weight and legitimates stringent means of application in cases of non-compliance. *Per se*, conditioning remains strictly speaking an inducement to do something or to abstain from doing something; by nature, conditioning is associated with threats in the form of sanctions for non-observance.

Conditioning is most efficient when patterns have become so internalized that they are automatic, a sort of second nature; it has reached a stage of irresistibility when the norms have been completely assimilated.

To sum up, conditioning is the *sine qua non,* the indispensable condition for control, for otherwise control would loose its social character; conditioning provides for the emergence of controls.

Controls over conditioning

Conversely, conditioning processes are submitted to controls that are institutionalized at different levels of social relationships. In some cases, conditioning unfolds on a face-to-face – though horizontally universalized – basis, as for example, in the family or at school. In other instances, it is more generalized, as through the mass media. And finally, on a vertical plane, it takes the form of government rulings. But whatever the channel of expression, since it is organized in one way or another conditioning is amenable to controls that try to have a hold over its content, direction, and style. But conditioning is indispensable for controls, and therefore controls have a direct stake in channelling conditioning to their advantage. Apart from interests obviously having an axe to grind, I assume at this stage of the exposé that there are some interests more intimately linked than others with conditioning itself – the interests of all people engaged in the production of signs and symbols, for instance, such as intellectuals, journalists, or politicians.

Hence, conditioning is generally controlled, and controlled in different fashions. Some types of conditioning necessitate substantial investments of a financial nature in order to reach vast audiences – education and the mass media, for example.

While conditioning is quite amenable to controls whose intention is to determine its direction, there are no guarantees as to whether or how the conditioning works on people's minds, for there is no sure way of ascertaining its real impact. Conditioning works at unconscious as well as at conscious levels. Nobody is even qualified to evaluate the effects on his or her own mind. Interviews are unlikely to reveal more than what the interviewees believe to be the effects of the conditioning action on themselves, though it is always conceivable that deeper soundings might give more conclusive results in the future. Under questioning, people may be able to give sufficiently accurate accounts of former deeds, or even reveal the nature of their motives while they were performing specific acts. But regarding events to come, the interviewer obviously cannot rely on the interviewee's intentions in the future. Any attempt to gauge the effects of conditioning strictly from the conditionee's perceptions is bound to give limited results. Reasons evoked by the conditionees for behaving in a specific manner are not necessarily good indicators.

The conditioners' intentions are no more reliable than the conditionees' statements. Again, it is results that count, not the motivation behind any conditioning undertaking; and results must be translatable into controls, for otherwise they must be considered non-effective, whatever the cause: the messages may have been directed at the wrong people, or they may have been couched in unattractive terms. Conditioning can be geared towards short- or long-term effects, but whatever the lapse of time envisaged, conditioning must be examined in terms of its fruition – control relationships.

As must be obvious by now, conditioning refers to a very diffuse reality. Ignoring conditioning for this reason would be, as stated earlier, to deny oneself the instrument indispensable for analysing controls. The vector leading from conditioning to control is bound to be imprecise. No direct link can be readily established in most cases, owing to the diversity of conditioners. It becomes the observer's duty to extract sets of conditionings whose object is to legitimize, strengthen, or introduce controls within social relations. This operation is strictly analytical, the selection being based solely upon the observer's criteria. No further considerations are indicated until the means of conditioning, socialization, mobilization, and regulation have been explored.

Human nature
So far, I have dealt with relationships among people as determined by their social setting. Control and conditioning have been analytically coined so as to make exclusive reference to the action of the collectivity on its members. The analysis has remained within a strictly sociological frame of reference. No consideration has been given to the nature of human beings, and any attempt to do so would have been cast aside on the grounds that dealing with human nature introduces parameters which I feel are incompatible with a framework dedicated to the study

of social determinants. Without denying the pertinence of more humanistic endeavours, I prefer to concentrate on a more limited area of observation, on the assumption that, at this stage of our knowledge, the results are likely to be more rewarding.

Notwithstanding the limitation thus imposed, it is impracticable for us to ignore completely the instrument used in the operation of the phenomena here examined: control and conditioning are performed by individuals who are part and parcel of these realities. Being considered now agent, now resource, where does the human being stand? Any theoretical development of social matters automatically involves a conception of the human being. This conception may be explicitly elaborated or, as quite often is the case, simply assumed. But the more transparent are the faculties vested in the human being, the less are the risks of misunderstandings.

In introducing a notion of human beings I am not attempting to cope with the totality of possible meanings. Rather I propose to select, following an a priori approach, the aspects I feel are relevant to the discussion. The selection may be questionable; it may be too reductionist to be serviceable, but the risk must be taken anyway. Without leading to the construction of an abstract human being, this procedure, like any scientific endeavour, simplifies in order to understand a singularized system of relationships.

Whether acting as agent or as resource, whether submitting others to controls and conditioning or being submitted to them, human beings are assigned roles they are expected to perform. They are put in a situation of fulfilling collective expectations. But in order to do so, they must be vested beforehand with capacities that qualify them to assume these roles. Nobody expects from a child the same behaviour expected from a mature adult. It is primarily from the standpoint of abilities that the subject will first be circumscribed.

Human resources are converted into productions, processes requiring a consumption of energy for the transformation of things or for a performance of some sort. Physical, psychological, and intellectual abilities combine to produce a diversity of possible actions. Some abilities are more readily recognizable than others: age and sex categories, for instance, already imply capacities as well as incapacities; weight, height, and health give an idea of possible performance. Education, though a more fluid factor, also serves as an indicator: education cultivates intellectual resources, an activity which is the function of socialization.

Human nature remains somewhat at the outskirts of our inquiry. Attention is drawn instead to certain capacities that have been collectively developed. Some societies impress by their appeals to will, to rationality, to order and discipline, to cool-headedness, and to diligence, while others do not. The question that comes to mind does not pertain to humankind but rather to an investigation of the social factors which contribute to form humankind as we know it. The primary question focuses on the effects of sociability on humankind and not the other way around, which would mean proceeding from a psychological approach. The aim is not at all to disparage psychology, but rather to envisage one aspect of a reality which derives from determinants outside the inner impulses of humans.

It may seem paradoxical that behaviourism comes to our rescue in delimiting the frontiers applied to our inquiry into human beings either as controllers or controllees. The idea of the black box is of some use since it is directed at the observation of effects or responses from specific stimuli, without any consideration of the medium, which happens to be the human mind. In somewhat the same fashion, the human being reacts to incentives which are of a different nature: physical, intellectual, or moral. These incentives are also negative or positive, that is, either punitive or rewarding. Of course, the notion of incentive reintroduces surreptitiously by the back door an idea rejected earlier. Inducements, by themselves, must appeal to some inner disposition of the recipient, otherwise there would be no reaction. Granted, most of our preferences are products of conditioning, but in the last analysis they have to find their beginnings somewhere. However, the concern is not to find primordial explanations for human behaviour. Whatever the intricate operations at work in people's acting in conformity with formal and informal rules, it is nonetheless possible to extract facts at both ends of the process; at the input stage, a state of collective conditioning, and at the output stage, a state of compliance – or non-compliance or partial compliance – with the original stimulus. Depending upon eras and areas, social inducements vary; rewards, for instance, take the shape of financial or monetary compensations, symbolic considerations, even physical pleasures. The purpose is not to exhaust the spectrum of possible gratifications (or deprivations) that are effective incentives for people. On the other hand, it is interesting to shed light on the values that are dominant within given systems of social relationships. Monetary incentives may work within one system and be ineffective within another. So, instead of trying to emerge with a picture of humankind, my framework focuses on the dynamics of interests at work in the acceptance and rejection of social values and norms. Whether these values and norms conform to 'basic' needs is irrelevant. It is the social reality that counts. The fact that such a reality exists is sufficient reason to examine its functioning. These dynamics bring into play the conditioning processes of socialization and mobilization, which are usually backed by regulation.

SOCIALIZATION: PATTERN-MAINTENANCE/CULTURE

Conditioning may effect the transmission of already existing patterns to new members of a social network. It may strengthen or reinforce patterns threatened with extinction or weakened by the introduction of competing patterns. Conditioning may also serve to introduce entirely new patterns or yet unrecognized ones. In the first instance we are confronted with a case of pattern-maintenance which is commonly associated with socialization. In the two other instances, 'pattern-preservation' and 'pattern-formation,' the action has more in common with the dynamics of mobilization.

As an expression, pattern-maintenance conveys more specificity than socialization, which embraces a much wider scope of interventions. Even the term 'political socialization,' while restricted to more circumscribed frontiers, lends itself to a variety of semantic contortions. David Easton and Jack Dennis (1969) are among the few to have put forward the necessity of endowing the expression with a theoretical content if we want it to have any analytical bearing. Their understanding that a political theory of political socialization had to underlie any theory of political socialization amounts at first glance to an elementary pronouncement, but it constitutes in itself a stricture on the plethora of studies that paid little attention to their own analytical foundations. Even though studies in socialization have at times gone astray, or at least drifted in directions that would lead us too far from our subject, they have produced a sufficient amount of propositions for us to choose from.

Students of political socialization recognized early on the joint character of a process that straddles two fields of study: psychology and sociology or anthropology. Depending upon the school, emphasis has been put on either one discipline or the other. There is no use renewing the debate about where the emphasis belongs. Suffice it to say that the reference to two levels of analysis, the individual and the collective, is prone to introduce theoretical confusion if the frontiers of observation are not well defined. The same problem is raised with the evolvement of any consideration of culture. Both socialization and culture studies belong, at one and the same time, to two levels of observation: the macro and the micro. Socialization and culture also exist one for the other, socialization being the process of transmission of culture – when culture is considered solely from its sociological aspect.

Pattern-maintenance is concerned exclusively with the transmission of values which, in turn, are conducive to the explication of existing patterns within a given social network. Pattern-maintenance pays no regard to how the acquisition of values takes place, whether in terms of deep or shallow internalization of values which, for all practical purposes, we dismiss as no guarantee of future behaviour. Attitudes reveal only what one thinks at a given time one is supposed to think or do; they do not preclude the possibility of doing the contrary in real situations to come.

Parsons and Shils (1962, 58ff.), following an attitudinal approach, put forward a triptych which describes orientations of action in terms of cognition, cathection, and evaluation. The typology has been welcomed by students of political culture and political socialization. It has been transcribed as cognitive, affective, and evaluative orientations by Almond and Verba (1963), and in about the same terms by Easton and Hess (1961), as well as Froman (1962). Openly influenced by the 'understanding' approach expounded by Max Weber, the Parsonian sociology purports to evaluate individual voluntaristic actions while keeping in mind the stream of influences flowing from the individuals belonging to a social whole. Motivation and the way goals are construed are considered of interest to these analysts.

Almond and Verba's *Civic Culture* is probably the most thorough exemplification of attitude gauging as applied to political matters. The approach makes no secret of its ideological preoccupation with the achievement of 'democratic' ideals through attitudes that conform to rules governing the internalization of dispositions leading to the existence of 'stable and democratic polities.'[5] Societies are compared with this measuring rod which, refined into a series of appropriate questions, should lead to the expression of propositions (from answers to questionaires) that one could evaluate as to their congruency with democratic principles. The Parsonian schema, too, could probably be proved to be ethically loaded from the start.

Accompanying the question about democratic orientation is the question of trust in general, which, partaking of psychology too, implies at least a judgment on people's dispositions. In Latin societies like Italy and France, mistrust has been regarded by scholars as an impediment to a participatory sense of politics (Crozier 1964; Pitts 1963). Here again, the intention behind this type of reasoning is amply normative. Participatory and trustful intentions are deemed desirable, though it seldom crossed anyone's mind whether these lauded dispositions might not in some instances be mere expressions of naïvety and unrealism. Almond and Verba at least take into consideration the gap existing between their respondents' actual behaviour and their statements about potential actions. Norms here do not always match with actual behaviour. Nor are these authors deceived by their respondents' sanguineness about their ability to affect policies through personal involvement (1963, 344ff.) The world of attitudes is prone to mislead both the actor and the observer and to be finally of little use in ascertaining the real impact of value diffusion in general. While studies in socialization are more often than not directed at the receptivity of individuals, one can, without depreciating work done in the field, ascribe more reliability to less fluid variables.

Pattern-maintenance operates through the assignment of roles that are trans-

5 The authors have more recently confirmed the 'rationalist-activist' intentions of their 'democratic' aspirations (Almond and Verba 1980, 16).

mitted from generation to generation. For patterns, as we have seen, are ways of expressing roles, and thus it is through role reproduction that patterns of control are passed on. But roles too do not stand on their own. As social entities they gain meaning by being coupled with other entities of identical, complementary, or opposite nature: roles legitimize the recourse to controls, and they also belong to an abstract whole that we call culture.

Culture

It is very easy to become embroiled in an unending discussion over the definition and status to be assigned to the notion of culture. Kroeber and Kluckhohn's effort to arrive at a synthetic definition after having established an impressive repertoire, while not fruitless, has not, for all that, prevented the debate from continuing. The solutions proposed within the confines of anthropology have often tried to make do with a definition in the abstract, one which would stand by itself, as if culture, like a statue, had to be unveiled. At the same time, most authors would probably agree that the notion is generally used as an analytical device to explain behaviour or its effects. But any such contrivance must be appreciated in terms of its analytical capacity with respect to other components with which it is associated. The following definition only fulfils the purpose of satisfying a need with respect to our whole framework; its validity will have to be determined from its heuristic cogency.

In general terms, culture consists of a structure of accepted forms which give shape to abstract as well as concrete endeavours.

The structure may be of two sorts. It can be construed as real, in which case it would amount more or less to existing forms which have to be discovered. More subtly it may be conceived of in the fashion proposed by Claude Lévi-Strauss, whereby universal structures of apprehension could be reached through examining the unconscious activity of the human mind. Here again the structures are thought of as being pre-existent to any investigation. The other way of coping with the notion of culture is to confer on it the status of a logical construct, as do a good number of authors (Kroeber and Kluckhohn 1952, 375, and others), and as I plan to do.

I conceive of culture first as a non-verifiable abstraction, and second as a holder of some sort of coherence. Culture is an abstract device designed to give some consistency to modes of behaviour which otherwise would have nothing in common. It does not purport to exhaust the meaning or the causes behind modes of behaviour, but does purport to extract a social aspect that the different modes may have in common. The structural aspect draws on a presumption of congruence among parts (Hoyt 1961). It does not follow that no contradiction will show up, but at least some degree of cohesion or complementarity is indispensable; otherwise, it is useless to imagine any culture at all.

Cultural forms

Culture is equivalent to accept forms. It rests on recognition, by the agents involved, of the desirability of such forms. The term emphasizes the social dimension of the construct without allowing for any humanistic provision. But why refer to forms in the first instance? To start with, culture is not to be equated with material phenomena, like people, things, or behaviour; these are manifestations or expressions. They act as signs – Leslie A. White (1959a) would call them *symbolates* – which refer to forms or models, in their material representations (Goodenough 1964, 36). The forms are strict abstractions which are rendered real by the signs which account for their communicability. In other words, there is on the observers' part the presumption of forms that are transmitted by signs, signs which are visual, auditive, or sensitive as they derive from images, noise, manners, or gestures (Vermeersch 1977). This mode of communication allows a process of identification and discrimination, whereas habit may easily make the process unconscious.

Cultural forms affect the whole gamut of expressions that human beings are capable of. They range from perceptions to conceptions of all sorts, from the most abstract productions to the most concrete. A few examples will be sufficient to illustrate the pervasiveness of the phenomenon. Forms model the perception of the environment, which is the first step for human beings in grasping and expressing the reality surrounding them. Forms shape our way of looking at things, our way of circumscribing them. Eskimos, for instance, use a variety of terms to designate what we indiscriminately call 'snow.' Language alone imposes modes of perception. English is suited to expression through concrete terms, according to the third rule established by Fowler and Fowler's *King's English*, while French is better suited to the use, and sometimes to the abuse, of the abstract. Language provides a code for further cultural forms (Goodenough 1971, 23ff.). In his classic *Tristes Tropiques*, Claude Lévi-Strauss dismantles the mechanics of demonstration in use at the Sorbonne when he was a student, in order to show a pattern of response to the demands of an academic culture.[6]

6 'I first began to learn that every problem, whether serious or trifling, may be solved by the application of an always identical method, which consists in contrasting two traditional views of the question; the first is introduced by means of a justification on common-sense grounds, then the justification is destroyed with the help of the second view; finally, both are dismissed as being equally inadequate, thanks to a third view which reveals the incomplete character of the first two; these are now reduced by verbal artifice to complementary aspects of one and the same reality: form and subject-matter, container and content, being and appearance, continuity and discontinuity, essence and existence, etc. Such an exercise soon becomes purely verbal, depending, as it does, on a certain skill in punning, which replaces thought: assonance, similarity in sound and ambiguity gradually come to form the basis of those brilliantly ingenious intellectual shifts which are thought to be the sign of sound philosophizing' (Lévi-Strauss 1974, 51).

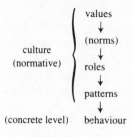

FIGURE 3 The components of culture

Artefacts stand as manifestations of cultural interventions on nature. We are accustomed to thinking of artefacts as physical entities, but they can also be abstract; languages are artefacts too. All artefacts derive from frames of reference which – to cover the whole range of human production – we characterize as follows: informative,[7] contemplative, or normative. Informative frames cover forms whose signs have a utilitarian purpose, contemplative frames cover roughly forms of scientific and aesthetic character, and normative frames prescribe which forms of behaviour are desirable. Although the description is for the moment rather succinct, the triad will be explained in detail much later in the discussion. At this stage it serves to distinguish the normative dimension of culture from the other two dimensions. Most references made henceforth will deal with the normative aspect, which, after all, is the determinant when dealing with control.

From a normative perspective, culture can be coped with in terms of four levels of abstraction which ultimately find their manifestations in concrete behaviour (Figure 3).

Values
Values appear at the upper level of generality. They are defined as forms which assign standards to people, things, and actions. Values, in other words, impose an order of desirability or quality on entities or behaviour. In themselves, the entities or behaviour are indifferent, devoid of normative sense: values endow them with normative sense. Values may be said to be 'directions of actions' (Parsons 1960,

7 'I shall assume that *all* the various non-verbal dimensions of culture, such as styles in clothing, village lay-out, architecture, furniture, food, cooking, music, physical gestures, postural attitudes and so on are organised in patterned sets so as to incorporate coded information in a manner analogous to the sounds and words and sentences of a natural language. I assume therefore it is just as meaningful to talk about the grammatical rules which govern the wearing of clothes as it is to talk about the grammatical rules which govern speech utterances' (Leach 1976, 10).

172). But contrary to Kluckhohn (1962 [1951] 395ff.) and others, I do not feel that values have to be justified; they can just as well be implicit. It should not be forgotten, after all, that values are meant to be constructs of the investigator, who may easily note a structure of forms never explained by the actors themselves. Consciousness on the part of agents is not necessary to the detection of values; the consciousness may well be, in some cases, an impediment, for it can distract the analyst from basic forms.

Signs express values through sets of artefacts which can be words, sounds, images, or gestures. Certain signs are symbols aimed at evoking values, inducing people to rally around a common cause.

Situated at a high degree of generality, values have to be pulled together somehow, for otherwise they are dispersed as atomistic entities. They need, so to speak, a common denominator, a common referent. This referent is the collectivity. Culture is bound to rely on collectivity in order to set orientations or goals that act as factors of consistency. Culture is not society. The two concepts are utilized here in two distinct perspectives that preclude any confusion.[8] 'Culture' refers to the analyst's construct whereas 'collectivity' (the term preferred to society) refers to the actors' conceptions of their group or community of reference.

We are accustomed to immediatley recognizing societies, or more precisely nation-states, as the group to be reckoned with. Such does not always have to be the case. Religious, racial, or ethnic groups share values of a cultural nature which do not belòng to other groups. Identifying these groups as sub-cultures amounts to subordinating them to a more all-encompassing whole, society; as an analytical device such as identification is quite deceptive, for it takes for granted that the cleavages are all within the boundaries of a common denominator. The advent of sociology as a field of study is concomitant with the advent of the nation-state it has frequently served to promote. The propensity is still strong to imprison all social values within the frontiers of recognized countries. At least in some cases, it will be worth while to ignore these borderlines for more meaningful ones. The European proletariat in the nineteenth century may have had a culture of its own, exactly as the aristocrats and bourgeoisie have developed a culture at different times in the past. It was easier for Marx to attribute class consciousness to the labouring class than it is today, even for the most convinced Marxist, since labourers then lived in a confined world of their own, not through deliberate choice, but in the sociological sense that they had a way of life that was peculiar to them and which could be thought of as the incipient stage of the ascendency of a new class on the way

---

8 Without adopting Kroeber and Parsons's classic distinction (1958) between culture and society (or better, social system) I nonetheless keep the two distinct.

to destroying the bourgeois confines of nation-states. Extranational collectivities like churches also account for group referents that bespeak realities of their own.

Whereas values may be unconscious or implicit, collectivities are conscious and explicit. Values can be transmitted from one collectivity to another through diffusion, the members of the adopting collectivities being unaware of the shift. But in order to crystallize in one way or another, values need a referent which serves to bind a given number of people to them.

Roles

If values are at times diffuse, norms come out at a level of greater specificity. Norms exemplify values (Blake and Davis 1964, 460); they serve to make values explicit, conferring on them a degree of operationality. Norms set ways of putting values into practice. This distinction, while orthodox in American sociology – Parsons 1961, 42ff. is a good example – is seldom retained as such in the present discussion. We could also say that norms provide criteria for legitimating roles and determining their allocation.

If values are at times diffuse, such is less often the case for roles, which set values within a network of interrelationships among people. Roles define how values are to be fulfilled by individuals or groups; roles determine who is entitled to do what. Status traditionally determines who is entitled to a function, whereas role determines what the function amounts to. Both status and role, two sides of the same coin, proceed from values that legitimate them. Roles make possible the actualization of values in terms of agents that are called upon to operate within a given set of values. They often contribute to the assignment and consolidation of what some would call 'identities': man, woman; boss, worker, etc. From a cultural perspective, roles derive from values which determine, finally, how roles are to be expressed by patterns.[9]

The analytical level of patterns comes closest to the concrete level of behaviour. Still, behaviour remains the reality which takes place before our very eyes, while patterns remain abstract. (Patterns respond to norms which exemplify values [Blake and Davis 1964, 460]; they are ways of putting values into practice. Norms dictate how roles are to be accommodated, how patterns are to be governed.)

The level of patterns is the most propitious for contemplating an analysis based upon the notions of reciprocity or symmetry in social relations. Anthropology is the discipline most advanced in making extensive use of these concepts. The pitfall to avoid is claiming to reach, through examining given situations, a form of objectivity which would entitle one to claim the existence or absence of reciprocity

---

9 While differing from Linton's personality approach, I accept his way of designating a role as 'the sum total of the culture patterns associated with a particular status' (1945, 77).

in the abstract. To be serviceable the notion must keep away from any ethical inference in the absolute. Of course, reciprocity or symmetry involves values which should be derived from the actors' culture and not from the analyst's own cultural frame of reference. To assert that there is symmmetry or asymmetry in a social relationship is to affirm a value judgment unless such a judgment is inferred from the standards of the culture under observation.[10] This analytical imperative departs from resorting to asymmetry as a useful notion for identifing relations of authority (Eckstein 1973; Eckstein and Gurr 1975, 9) or using the absence of reciprocity as a litmus test for the recognition of politics (Clastres 1974, 168ff.). It purports to suggest that, contrary to expectations, patterns in their ruling over behaviour are to be considered as providing for a global reciprocity within given collectivities. Relations look asymmetric when they are examined by themselves. For instance, children have to obey their parents, but if one looks more closely one has to add that the parents in return have to take care of their children. On a larger scale, it is possible to construe status as allocated within collectivities in such a way that resources are meant to be distributed along with reciprocal sets of rights and obligations, the rights and obligations being weighed according to values that determine how they can be compared. Reciprocity is merely proposed here as a hypothesis. For the time being, I must emphasize that patterns must ultimately be gauged not through compartmentalization but by examining the totality of patterns. A relationship between A and B may appear to be non-reciprocal, but the situation may possibly be better understood by considering the import of a third party, C. The whole set of norms (as ascribed to roles and expressed through patterns) is to be judged in turn from the values which are attributed to the series of rights and obligations.

The four layers just analysed – values, norms, roles, and patterns – make up sets of forms that belong to culture. The layers are considered as static. Once introduced by some interests they become accepted, after a while, as natural or normal.

Culture, an analytical concept
The choice of a widely embracing delimination for the cultural field is deliberate: it allows conditioning its full extent. Taken collectively, people are influenced by a wide variety of artefacts to which control patterns are susceptible. Since the latter are part of everyday life, it should not be surprising that the value framework that tops them all should be extensive. There is no question, indeed, of trying to explain at one fell swoop the entire structure of values, roles, and patterns, just as it is irrelevant to single out, all at once, the totality of controls existing in a given collectivity. Control patterns find their legitimation in roles which are in turn

10 A value judgment is formulated from one's own cultural stock.

integrated with more general values. The rationale for this process comes only after values have been well set, though in reality the chronology may be reversed, imposed patterns being legitimized later by appropriate values.

Cultures can hardly be dismantled into pieces readily amenable to analytical treatment. The notion of value itself being a construct, its adequacy can never, in practice, be proved beyond all doubt. A hypothetical *découpage* becomes necessary: the analyst is called upon to make a selection among values, sorting out from the cultural material those values, or more likely sets of values, which he or she sees as logically fitting the corresponding roles which always top patterns.

The type of group to which a culture is expected to fit varies depending upon the sort of control network to which the analyst is applying himself or herself. A preordained structure of values is of no avail. Any analysis of culture must proceed from the observer first looking at controls, then explaining or articulating the controls as they function in relation to roles and ultimately to values. The sort of controls looked at will determine a network, or if one prefers a structure, of social relationships to which may be imputed a set of common values which serve to define roles.

The articulation of values among themselves, roles within a network of roles and patterns within sets of roles, depends upon the observer's ability to produce the most efficient, that is, the most heuristic structure. Two main avenues are open. The first envisions the emergence from the observed values, roles, and patterns of main features that dominate the dynamics of the whole. The second, instead of expecting the object itself to furnish any explanation, entrusts the observer with the task of producing, on his or her own, a grid that will expose revealing traits. To be of any interest, dominant features or revealing traits must be able to provide clues about their possible conjunction with other factors. Within the present framework features have to be linked with controls from a conditioning perspective. The chances are, under these conditions, that the use of a grid will be more suitable than a search, in the abstract, for some integration of features from within a given culture.

Conclusion

Pattern-maintenance is part and parcel of culture, although it does not embrace it all. Values transmitted through different channels maintain a state of control patterns. As a rule, there is no way of delineating precisely the part of any behaviour or utterance which is to be labelled as strict pattern-maintenance. First, no objective judge can establish a definite causal relationship between the generalized and diffused conditioning we have been looking at and any precise situations of control. Second, the area of observation varies according to the analyst's own selection of control patterns. Values that appear at first glance to be quite innocent in themselves may in fact serve to prop up patterns that first looked quite distinct from, if not adverse to, such effects. The link is to be found in the role which serves as an analytical bridge between values and patterns. For instance, a culture largely centred upon consumption as an important value will provide for roles that bring sophistication to the exercise of buying and selling. One can imagine a cultural arrangement which is more advantageous to sellers (as a role) than buyers: in such a case the contractual advantages would be on the sellers' side, with, say, the only obligation on their part being to deliver, at some indeterminate date, goods in whatever condition. Such values are conducive even to complete acceptance by consumers (collectively speaking) of rules laid down by the sellers. Conversely, controls could be vested in the hands of the buyers (as a role), who might then be entitled to full information on the goods offered to them, together with, say, conditions of payment and delivery suitable to their whims.

Pattern-maintenance draws from culture as it gives recognition to the transmission of values and roles to specific modes of behaviour. But as such, pattern-maintenance can only be assessed by its outcome. It certainly remains as diffuse as culture; it permeates everyday life and becomes explicit only occasionally. Most values one is exposed to during the course of a daily routine have a direct, or at least an indirect, bearing on roles and their breakdown into recognized patterns. But this process can only be evaluated by its outcome. Here, my approach departs markedly from the general tendency of students of socialization who tend to favour the processes (Schwartz and Schwartz 1975, vi) at the expense of the outcome. My divergence from this general tendency can easily be explained by a difference in analytical perspective. The processual approach derives from a psychological questioning about how values are passed on, on a one-to-one basis either from generation to generation or from one set of people to another. Within such an approach, the stages of acquisition – from childhood onward or otherwise – become relevant, and degrees of awareness of and commitment to values stand out as explicative; the pattern-maintenance approach, however, remains unconcerned about the consciousness or unconsciousness of actors.

MOBILIZATION: PATTERN-FORMATION/IDEOLOGY

While pattern-maintenance proceeds from consensus, if not unanimity, pattern-formation usually evolves in a climate of conflict. Pattern-formation is oriented towards the legitimization of a new order of things, whereas pattern-maintenance does not unfold primarily in terms of justification but rather progresses through imitation from a diffuse replication of values.

Pattern-formation can be summed up as a process by which changes in values or roles lead to the introduction of new patterns.

In some instances, pattern-formation is surreptitiously introduced through a diffusion process that becomes apparent only when the pattern in formation already enjoys a certain stature. For example, the actions of combines and monopolies in the nineteenth century often had time to consolidate before arousing significant opposition. The same can be said of many commercial practices that have to be quite cumulative in their effect before becoming an issue. It is common these days, for instance, to see queues in front of bank tellers and supermarket cashiers: this is a way of controlling the customers' time in order to reduce the number of employees, and amounts to a sort of conditioning by a progressive adaptation on the part of the controllees. Conversely, some patterns will wither away from a progressive extinction.

Mobilization
Most of the time, however, pattern-formation involves resorting to mobilization. The word in itself spontaneously evokes a military usage. Political scientists and sociologists have applied the term 'mobilization' especially in the field of 'modernization.' Amitai Etzioni's *Active Society* relies heavily on the term, in an acceptation of his own which aims at characterizing increases of control, by overall 'units,' over assets formerly in the hands of sub-units (1968a, 388); J.P. Nettl (1967, 32ff.), on the other hand, sees mobilization in an élite's ability to impose upon a population a commitment to new referents (goals), and new actions in consequence. Well aware of Etzioni's conception, Charles Tilly (1978, 69) identifies mobilization with a process of collective commitment to public life activities, in which case there is no primary insistence on any élitist core of action, even though mobilization is meant to connote (from the discussion that follows) a commitment to 'deliver resources' (70).

Most connotations of mobilization refer to actual control over resources. The usage I propose is entirely different. It aims at designating a process whereby, through an emission of signs and symbols, people come to defend, oppose, accept, or simply tolerate changes in values or roles. On the one hand, mobilization serves to galvanize and crystallize new controllers' interests, to trigger off or simply strengthen a sense of solidarity; on the other hand, it serves to induce actual or potential controllees to be submissive. In such a case it draws on justificatory discourse (ideology) or, more openly, on threats of coercion – or both. Mobilization points ultimately towards both controllers and controllees. It serves two purposes, as ideology does.

Ideology, a concept of mean extraction
The word 'ideology' usually bears a pejorative connotation. It is either equated with 'false consciousness' or with simplifications devised to cope with too complex

realities. A long tradition in the wake of the young Marx's works has considered ideology as an alienating perception of social praxis. Relying on the works of the older Marx, Louis Althusser (1970 [1965] and Nicos Poulantzas (1973) apply themselves to repudiating a philosophy of the subject – an individual or a class – based upon self-consciousness, but they nonetheless come to the conclusion that, being imaginary, ideology, as opposed to science, is by its nature partially false. Both schools agree upon the discrepancy between ideological propositions and real knowledge even though they are at odds about the practical consequences of the discrepancy.[11]

Non-Marxists too usually confer a negative sense on ideology, which they regard as a form of intellectual simplification in an attempt to cope with too complex realities. Almond and Powell (1966, 61) consider ideology as an outmoded form of thinking which entertains a rigidity alien to the 'bargaining' realism of a modern secularized world. Before them, others had announced the imminent doom or at least exhaustion of ideology. In the early sixties Daniel Bell (1960) proclaimed the end of ideology, which as a faith structure would be taken over by another type of utopia of an incremental nature,[12] a sort of Popperian (1961, 58ff.) victory, in fact, of piecemeal perception over global constructions of the mind. Following the same path S.M. Lipset could claim that, while continuing to exist, the 'democratic' class struggle would no longer be animated by ideology.[13] Whether these pronouncements are well founded or not and whether they are of some limited application in a number of western societies is not immediately relevant here. All these points of view concur with Marxist points of view, whatever the school, in illustrating the negative character attributed to their respective notions of ideology. The use of the term usually arouses an idea of irreality and undesirability: the word 'ideology' serves to describe how poorly others collectively structure their own thoughts.[14]

As used in the present discussion, the concept of ideology remains outside any ethical reference to goodness or badness, rightness or wrongness. Nor does it purport to convey an idea of distortion, falsification, false consciousness, or even simplification. I do not intend to pronounce judgments on the cognitive status of

11 It might be appropriate to recall Karl Mannheim's conception of ideology as the ruling groups' rationalization about their interests, a position quite close to the standard Marxist interpretation but with an added psychological twist (1936, 55ff.).

12 The author later claimed to have been misinterpreted (Bell 1976, 34).

13 'The democratic class struggle will continue, but it will be a fight without ideologies, without red flags, without May Day parades' (1963, 445).

14 Ideology is also, at times, opposed to 'scientific objectivity' (Parsons 1967, 153) or to theory (Althusser 1970 [1965]) – the 'pratique idéologique' belonging to prescientific knowledge, as a follow up of Bachelard's 'rupture épistémologique.' Althusser has backed out of this rigid distinction (1976 [1974]).

ideology. Ideology is considered a social product arising out of a necessity for some agents to explain or to illustrate in order to avoid, or at least to limit, the imposition of naked threat and coercion in the introduction of new patterns of control or in the removal of existing ones. Ideological discourses may indulge in threatening propositions, but when they do so, the discourse is embodied in a more encompassing whole which is directed at adhesion via logical propositions or emotional rallying cries. The fact that an ideology is emotional in content does not necessarily reduce its status in comparison with a more rationally organized ideology.

Ideology, a positive concept

Ideology is a construed structure of forms which through signs and symbols collectively legitimate an order of values, norms, or roles, and which has a bearing on patterns of control. I conceive of ideology as I have conceived of culture – as a construct. Ideology can be construed by an analyst as well as by the proponents themselves; but in both instances the system of propositions remains the analyst's or the proponents'. Nobody is in a position to reveal the one and only structure of, say, liberalism, fascism, or any other ideology. Ideologies may seem at first glance well articulated and organized in themselves, but whatever their degree of consistency they remain, as social products, a mixture of explanations and illustrations that cannot be embodied in one, and only one, abstract construction. Ideologies are many, and detractors of any ideology will take great care in showing how differently they can be reconstituted.

Basic authors make significant contributions elaborating the frame of a doctrine. Their works make up a corpus on their own but cannot claim to constitute an ideology. Individuals, as individuals, remain outside the reach of ideologization. Such a process is triggered off only when a number of people come to share common views about the organization of social relationships, views which purport to legitimize a given state of controls. A thinker's school may be accounted for as a group of people who share common views about changes in the structure of values or roles – Marx's writings for instance. By themselves they cannot be reckoned as being of an ideological nature, whereas the same writings, or part of them, when well integrated into a tradition of intellectuals, considered as a whole, constitute part of a collective endeavour and therefore part of an ideology. The same applies to the connection linking, say, Adam Smith to Milton Friedman through the classics and neo-classics in the defence of free enterprise.

Some ideologies look more diffuse than others. Liberalism, for example, has spread into multifarious developments that nowadays make it look like a rather motley whole, assuming that any whole exists except in one's mind. Communism, if it describes anything specific, has also produced a wide diversity of projects that only have in common the proposal of some form of collectivist goal. The same logic is applicable to fascism.

At this stage the question of delimitation becomes problematic. All-embracing concepts like liberalism, communism, and the like rapidly reveal their lack of specificity. It then becomes the analyst's responsibility to carve out an ensemble that has some meaning. In so doing he builds up a system with his own hands, articulating propositions in a fashion that does not have to respect the order of values as they are usually expressed. Being a construct, ideology can never be tested as such. Illustrations may be put forward as examples, but the pulling together of propositions and values as representative of a group's thinking can only be tentative, even if it is undertaken by the group itself. (At any one time, ideology indicates at best what the proponents think the collective values are, and, more often than not, what they think these values should be if the group were better informed. We shall see later on how mediators often act as precipitators of events.) The analyst may pretend to extract exact propositions of values as they have been expressed by the group. But even on this basis one may question whether it is feasible to arrive at a high degree of precision, for the notion of value is open to objections: is it not in the last analysis a construct itself, a way of encapsulating collective aspirations in abstract nuclear entities? Whatever our opinion on the validity of value as an operational concept designating 'atoms' of the discourse, the problem still persists unsolved when the time comes to aggregate or integrate the values into a single system. Ideology remains a composition, just as much as culture.

Ideology is thus an abstract structure of representations which, whether through symbols or signs, exists as a structure and as a whole in people's minds. It is not a finite or a definite discourse that we can recognize on sight as always revealing the same arrangement of propositions. Ideology can be identified from some of what we believe to be its parts. For this reason, it is most amenable to the Weberian approach of the ideal type.

In principle one expects proponents of an ideology to stress the strong coherence of their pronouncements, since their purpose is to provide grounds for legitimating new patterns: consistency in determining new collective goals is seen as a condition of success. But this does not have to be the case in all instances. Symbolic displays of strength, prestige, feelings of togetherness, through the appropriate channels of parades, rallies, or exhibitions of all sorts, may contribute to the same impact. It is probably more realistic to presume a combination of both consistency and symbolic actions. Adhesion to new sets of values and roles can never be said to derive strictly from cogitation. Analysts are not expected to pass judgment on the rationality or logic of the structure of propositions as offered by a given ideology; their interest lies rather in the impact on changes within sets of existing controls. What is being gauged is not the profoundity or the articulation or even the soundness of ideologies as such, but rather their mobilizing effect: the sharing and diffusion of values among a large number of people, as well as the casting (or not) of the values into actual roles and patterns. Indeed, my concern is whether some arguments or symbols or illustrations have more impact than others when compared with other collectivities. In such cases, the comparative factor serves as a major criterion.

Up to now I have treated ideologies, if only for the sake of illustration, along the lines of the common 'isms' repertoire. Let us depart somewhat from these familiar grounds in order to cope with less ready-made syntheses. Problems of identification and delimitation are abundant in any operationalization of the concept. The analyst may, for one thing, sort out only a part of a discourse, which is then assigned an ideological nature. Religion, for example, may be considered in some of its aspects as belonging to ideology. The *Rerum Novarum* and *Quadragesimo Anno* encyclicals would lend themselves to this treatment as shared views of the Catholic Church, which can be considered within the limited scope of the church or in a wider perspective of conservative proclivities. Philosophers' views, as well as the views of thinkers of all stripes, are susceptible to the same type of approach. Parts and only parts of their works may in some cases be considered ideological.

Artistic works, whether literary, pictorial, cinematographic, or even musical, may expose, illustrate, or reflect ideological values. A sociological school in the line of Lukacs's interpretations of fiction have led followers like Lucien Goldmann (1955) into deciphering the implicit ideological structure of classics, such as the seventeenth-century works of Pascal and Racine. Whether all readers are sold on this type of interpretation is a different matter. I would like to call attention, nevertheless, to the possibility of looking more closely at roles and patterns suggested as desirable, or undesirable, through the mediation of fictitious events.

Ideology vs culture/mobilization vs socialization
As we progress it becomes increasingly apparent that ideological discourses do not unfold in a linear fashion. They express themselves at a multiplicity of levels and in numerous ways. Ideology comes to be as protean as culture is, and for this reason, like culture, it may become a source of confusion for the observer.

In the present framework culture and ideology are basically differentiated by their functions, which happen to affect their content. Culture is an abstract construct devised to account for the reproduction of values, roles, norms, and patterns, whereas ideology, which is also a construct, is designed to reckon with the introduction of change in the values, roles, norms, and patterns conveyed by culture. Culture seldom has to furnish extensive explanations, whereas ideology calls for more explicitness since it has to legitimize change; it carries the burden of proof. Cultures hold their momentum, so to speak, until challenged by ideologies.

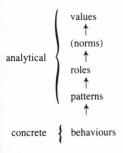

FIGURE 4 Degrees of acuteness of change

Culture acts as a rule, and ideology as a challenge. Ideologies are by their nature combative. Still, they unfold within cultural frames which sustain, to some extent, these moves for change. No ideology evolves *in vitro*.

The acuteness of the urge for change can be gauged from the level of forms which are affected. The degree of severity can be evaluated by its remoteness, analytically speaking, from actual behaviour along the spectrum already familiar (Figure 4). So, a change in roles will be considered more acute than a change in patterns, a change in norms more acute than a change in roles, and a change in values most acute of all. Changes at upper layers are bound to bring modifications at lower ones. It is in the logic of the hierarchy itself.

Ideology may convert into culture and vice versa. Content, in terms of values or roles, does not determine in advance whether we are discussing culture or ideology. It is the necessity to legitimate, in a context of a possible conflict over values, that makes all the difference. The 'organization man,' as exemplified in W.H. Whyte's book of the same title, derives from a cultural arrangement that obviously did not exist before the accession of the company to the stature of an overwhelming goal in itself. A new way of life is described in which private life conforms to the values of the organization. This totalitarian approach to everyday life may seem ideological, but in our vocabulary it is basically cultural. Louis Hartz's (1964) thesis on the fragment illustrates quite well the conversion of the liberal ideology that was brought from England into a cultural reality once it took root in America. Conversely, culture is transformed into an ideology when its values are threatened and must be more systematically described (a case of pattern-preservation to be discussed in the following pages).

This distinction which differentiates ideology from culture and mobilization from socialization derives from my perspective. Another outlook might have made away with this distinction and reduced the two to a sole field of diffusion. The purpose in bringing up the difference is to underline the particular dynamics that I believe characterize each of the two processes, one relying on the momentum of tradition and habits, the other having to struggle, in some way, for or against the former.

Of course, mobilization takes a variety of forms. As an indication, let us suggest two levels of intervention: one for the defence of a cause, the other for the defence of an issue. Ideology lends itself to expounding a cause. A cause evokes the idea of sets of roles to be rearranged; it evolves at a certain level of generality which calls for the achievement of collective goals in favour of a community of some sort, a group, a social class, or a nation. The justificatory function of ideology is obvious. Issues, on the other hand, give rise to more precise references in the mobilization they elicit. Issues aim at the definition of already determined roles, norms, and patterns; they get down to the specific demands causes imply. Mobilization surrounding, say, the adoption of measures setting working hours revolves around an issue, whereas mobilization over the fate of workers in general means defending a cause. Both levels of action resort to ideology as a legitimating frame of reference, but each is usually attuned to a different wavelength in terms of the mode of expression.

Pattern-preservation/pattern-retrieval

Up to now, our discussion of mobilization has concentrated upon pattern-formation. For the sake of clarity in the exposition, certain nuances which might have clouded the discussion have been deliberately avoided. At this stage let us take them into consideration.

Between pattern-maintenance and pattern-formation, two other types of collective action upon patterns can be distinguished, both propelled by mobilization and subject to ideologization. I call these two types of collective action pattern-preservation and pattern-retrieval.

Pattern-preservation – or, if one prefers, pattern-retention – is a process whereby existing patterns are systematically reinforced by a legitimating discourse, that is by ideology. Culture indeed furnishes justifications for social actions. It does not emphasize, however, the consistency, among themselves, of all roles and patterns, though there may exist, as Claude Lévi-Strauss claims, an inner logic (of opposition or otherwise) linking, for instance, signs and symbols. Pattern-preservation is impelled either by a counterpattern movement or by a threat of extinction; it works as a reaction or a response to a change, real or apprehended, in pattern-maintenance. Pattern-preservation provides explicit legitimization for values and roles from which patterns are derived. When values and roles no longer come as natural or normal, when they cease to be taken for granted, they are from then on submitted to some form of logical structuration. In a defensive move culture gives way to ideology. But seldom if ever are all cultural values at stake; therefore it would be more correct to say that chips off the old cultural block are called upon the become parts of a new whole, this time contrived in more intellectual terms. Pattern-preservation is undertaken as if the set of patterns, roles, or values formerly accepted had to be set up anew. In this respect, it proceeds as pattern-formation does, but with the difference that it is on the defensive; it reacts to change.

As for pattern-retrieval, it corresponds to a reactionary move in a literal sense, that is, an aspiration to the *status quo ante*, an aspiration to recover former values that got lost for one reason or another. Pattern-retrieval is not solely the lot of 'conservatives'; it may, in some instances, be a mobilization towards values that have been thwarted in their progress. The Portuguese return to liberal institutions is a case of pattern-retrieval involving the call to election for the legitimation of rule making.

Pattern-retrieval and pattern-preservation follow, so to speak, the same dynamics as pattern-formation; they proceed from mobilization and ideological representation, and there are no basic differences in the way the processes are carried on. Any move to restore cultural control patterns on the wane or already in disuse is bound to start anew a procedure of diffusion very like pattern-formation. The fact that the patterns were widespread and largely accepted in the past may work for or against their preservation or retrieval in the future. There is no way, in the abstract, to predict their fate. In most cases progress is understood as the denial of some controls qualified as traditional in favour of more progressive controls, but some traditional controls are recaptured for reasons that have little to do with their first manifestations.

Mobilization = conflict
Mobilization, as has already been mentioned, points towards change in role structures, without necessarily propping up new ones. But whoever calls for changes in roles automatically prepares for conflict. Mobilization evolves within a state of conflict which is either actual or potential. In a potential conflict mobilization works to foil any attempt on the part of frustrated interests to draw back.

Conflict is the other face of control. It comes out of a refusal to accept controls, whatever form they take. The controls to which some people are opposed may be those in actual operation, as is the case of women's liberation movements which express opposition to controls which currently remain in men's hands; or conflict may emerge from the anticipation of potential controls, those that are, through mobilization, proposed as desirable and which precipitate adverse movements as a counterweight. Medicare in the United States stands out as an issue which, from the end of the forties onward, has galvanized the medical profession against any move in this direction. Mobilization usually involves both sides, for and against, each resorting to ideological arguments to legitimate its position.

Conflict also tends to produce and strengthen solidarities. Georg Simmel, for one, expounded the whole of his sociological disquisition from the hypothesis that social ties are born and kept alive through confrontation with outsiders.

Conflictual situations certainly help to develop images of in-groups in opposition to out-groups. From the 'we' sense emerge ideologies which purport to act as justificatory devices, stimulating solidarity within the group and trying to accredit the group in the eyes of outsiders. The 'business creed' as expanded by Sutton et al. (1956) exemplifies the conflictual and polemical aspects of ideology: the way the system and its achievements illustrate the advantages of capitalism over communism is, by and large, an exercise of legitimation directed at an out-group.

It seems that Marx understood classes to have little meaning when they were not opposed to one another, so much so that in his mind one could hardly talk of a class as a singular entity; it had to be tied to its conflictual counterpart to find its full meaning in politics (Poulantzas 1973). An intention to reveal the dialectical interplay of contradictory forces is evident. Without necessarily adhering to the Marxian identification of classes, we can note with interest both the important part played by conflict as a catalyst for group actions and the conception classes have of themselves as opposed to others.

Ideologies are articulated around the idea of the in-group doing away with the out-group and thereby creating a relative state of harmony; communism and fascism are formal in their goals of conflict denial. For the former, after the transition to the proletarian dictatorship, society becomes classless; for the latter, society subscribes to subordination to the fittest, under the effect of a morally voluntaristic *élan* of ther whole collectivity. As for the liberalism of the *laissez-faire* tradition, it lets loose the idea of the interdependence of economic aspirations, which are construed as external to any conflictual pressures. These general types concur in suppressing conflict by introducing new controls or putting an end to existing ones. Ultimately, ideology is called upon to become culture, after the struggles are over and the domination of ideology is overwhelming.

Conclusion
In this framework pattern-maintenance has been associated with socialization as a process for the transmission of accepted rules of action. Culture, which is the product of consensus, provides for the acceptance of role allotments. Pattern-formation, on the other hand, proceeds from conflict and mobilization, which are the counterparts of consensus. Ideology provides legitimization for the proposed changeovers unless these are imposed by sheer force. Finally, pattern-preservation and pattern-retrieval are assimilated with pattern-formation, which generally constitutes, though, the basic process in opposition to pattern-maintenance. All the processes unfold in an arena of interests in action. Agencies of socialization and mobilization introduce mediating factors which are also submitted to the subordination of controls.

3

The structure of conditioning

Conditioning is seldom exclusively devoted to either socialization or mobilization, in other words, to either pattern-maintenance or pattern-formation. In most cases conditioning works in both directions, for the distinction between the two is made for analytical rather than practical purposes. Almost any discourse, conservative as well as progressive, offers a mixture of cultural and ideological propositions. It is hardly conceivable in modern times that anyone can be entirely respectful of accepted values or be entirely innovative. Few interests can be connected exclusively with either. Conservatives may have a propensity to suggest the retrieval of patterns or their mere preservation, which amounts to an ideological orientation, while progressives usually give a radical extension to values already shared by most. No one these days is entirely cultural or ideological in his discourse. Apparatuses of conditioning easily provide for both: few media are inherently cultural or ideological, even though some of them may be more appropriate, at a given time, for the expression of either a traditional or a progressive outlook. Consequently, the problem does not rest so much in the orientation given to values but rather in the whole operation of diffusion. Referring to an ideal framework of political socialization in general, Kraus and Davis make the following comment:

The linear model of parent to child, teacher to child, peer to peer and media to child is too simplistic an approach for understanding the complex phenomena inherent in the political socialization process. This model places too much emphasis on determining the unique role of discrete agents. Future models should focus on the interrelationships among various socialisation agents and, in particular, identify the relationship between media and other socialisation agents. (1976, 28)

It is therefore possible to go further in two directions: the first calls for the intro-

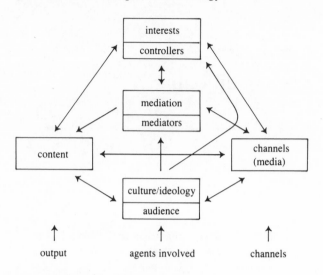

FIGURE 5 Structure of conditioning

duction of a few more factors covering more than mere agents; the second attempts to provide a framework accounting for the simultaneous interactions of these factors. All the factors so assembled could be identified as forming a structure or, if one prefers, a system. I am using 'structure' to refer to a set of elements in a situation of interrelationship such that a change in one is most likely to have repercussions for at least one of the other elements, if not all of them. Ideally a structure should be so conceived that a modification in one of its components engenders a modification of the whole. The future tells whether the model reaches its ideal functioning in this respect.

Conditioning involves, first of all, interests which act as controlling agents in the shaping and content of it. Secondly, mediators are usually called upon to intervene as actual conditioners, under the direction of the controller. Thirdly, the channel used certainly imposes a style as well as certain inherent limitations. Fourthly, the content to be transmitted calls for adaptations to the channel and the way it is put in operation. Finally, the audience itself induces or prohibits the adoption of certain types of media and contents. This setting is certainly not oblivious to the classic categories already put forward by Harold Lasswell, who had a knack for synthetic catchwords: 'Who says what in what channel to whom with what effect' (1948, 37). Five sets of analyses, as Lasswell states, are involved here: control, content, channel, audience, and effect analyses. I retain the first four as constituents of the structure and the fifth as the result of these four interacting to give that product that we may call the outcome (Figure 5).

INTERESTS/CONTROLS

Apart perhaps from hermits confined to the desert or other isolated places, everyone is saturated by all sorts of overt and covert signs, from the explicit messages of newspaper editorials to styles of clothing, cars, architecture, and so on. But not everyone is in a position to act upon others in this way. The right and the ability (financial, informational) to condition others is severely limited for most people. Conditioning is subject to controls which channel, to some extent, the flow of signs in given directions. Roles are allocated that foresee, within any social circuit, the area of possible intervention.

Controls over conditioning refer to those controls exerted over the channel, the content, or both, either directly or through a mediator. Controllers exercise their control directly whenever they are in a position to use some medium in person or to assign content to the conditioning. Some face-to-face relationships of socialization and mobilization fall into the category of rather simple cases of direct control over conditioning: parental inducements to conformity, door-to-door canvassing for causes liable to change accepted values. Peer groups of any age, from the little leaguers to the old-timers playing on bowling greens, usually act as a stimulant or deterrent in the adoption, maintenance, or refusal of identified patterns. Such groups are in part simply people mingling together who, consciously or not, ventilate ideas throughout the course of multiple informal meetings, which seldom have as their purpose the circulation or transmission of these patterns. The same applies to the enlarged situation of everyday life which involves the personal conditioning of others by conformity or nonconformity to common life styles. Manners especially elicit the acceptance or rejection of given sets of values: the way employers and employees address each other accounts for daily conditioning – except at weekends – which registers compatibility or incompatibility in the mutual interaction of the two parties.[1]

Also on a face-to-face basis, but at a more macroscopic level, are all those producers of signs and artefacts who, on their own, act as conditioners; they may be priests, artists, narrators, actors, writers, designers, or architects, who singly or collectively produce signs, symbols, or designs liable to induce conformity or

---

1 One might invoke the situation whereby an employee, for instance, is obliged to conform to a code of etiquette that is meant to show deference towards the employer. In such a case, the employer is implicitly exercising control over his employee. It should be remembered, by the way, that patterns must not be judged from singular events, but from their common acceptance, whether voluntarily or by rule.

nonconformity to given patterns. Their productions are here appreciated in terms of their likeliness to have an impact of great or little significance on control behaviours.

All these components of socialization and mobilization do not operate at random – or at least I presume they do not. Their capacity for intervention and their share of the 'burden' are restrained by a series of factors. The parents, peer groups, parsons, and intellectuals just referred to for illustrative purposes act within given frameworks of action which provide for specific roles which differ from one social network to another. A parent's legal capacity may be great in one society and highly limited in another. Children brought up on kibbutzim are institutionally more exposed to peer group pressures for conformity than those raised in an American middle-class family (Bettelheim 1970). In fact, the peer group's ability to influence may turn out, in many cases, to be a controlled conditioning emanating from above. Similarly, religious proselytism has to submit to a diversity of accommodations depending upon where it is taking place. So, whatever the collectivity, there are interests dedicated to the transmission of values, old or new; they act through roles which allow them to work in this direction. The allocation of these roles provides for controls over conditioning. We shall soon note that this allocation may be considered as part of the structure of conditioning. But before embracing the whole of the dynamics of conditioning interests at work, one important factor must be explored which provides for the sharing of control owing to the introduction of a division of labour.

MEDIATION

Mediation involves the presence of third parties in the relationship that initially implied solely a conditioner and an audience. This addition introduces a higher degree of complexity. Hence, controls are shared, since the recourse to mediators is largely due to the inability of any controller to act on his or her own. Conceptions about the use of a channel, for technological but also for ideological or cultural reasons, often impose the presence of mediators. Mediating agencies of conditioning come as a screen or a filter having interests liable to be discrepant with the interests of the original controllers, and the controllers may frequently have to make concessions regarding the content. The fact that mediation is introduced is likely to have a bearing not only on content but also on the use of the channel and on the conditioning the audience will receive.

Usually, ownership entitles controllers to determine to a large extent the use of a given channel, be it a school, a newspaper, a publishing house, or a radio or television station. From this status, controllers may frequently want to enjoy a corresponding position so far as content is concerned. But this is where the shoe pinches, for mediators, usually professionals in the field, may request some freedom of action deriving from their own expertise. So new interests, which may not necessarily be compatible with those of the original controllers, find their way into the process, and a *modus vivendi* has to be arrived at.

The controls exercised over mediators' initiatives are stringent or flexible depending upon the setting. The French educational system, for instance, requires strict curricula which are to be closely followed through regular inspections and standard examinations. Michel Crozier (1964) has drawn an extreme illustration from a Second Empire minister of education who took pride in being able to say, from looking at his watch, what precise page of Virgil all French students of a given grade were labouring over. In a spirit not entirely divorced from this nineteenth-century anecdote, education at university level in France still remains faithful to some of these rules, where the members of the faculty – the mediators – pursue a hierarchical tradition worthy of the Ancien Régime. The state's presence is evident in the organization as well as in the drawing up of curricula.

Following an entirely different tradition, the American system of higher learning has rather been vulnerable to criticism that it is too closely associated with the business world. Thorstein Veblen's (1957) strictures dating from 1918 have not dissipated; some, like David N. Smith, still underline the strict reproduction of business patterns in the decision-making process of higher echelons: boards of trustees modelled after boards of directors such as exist in private corporations. The efficacy of the trustees' control is still, as a matter of fact, variously assessed by different analysts. While Jencks and Riesman (1968, 15–17) tend to minimize their control by distinguishing between formal powers and actual controls, David N. Smith (1974, 64), on the other hand, emphasizes cases drawn from Berkeley's recent history. This debate and the French situation described above exemplify the part taken by mediators whose degree of autonomy from upper controls is liable to be a constant preoccupation for them. Conversely, the state, trustees, or regents may well harbour suspicions about the faculty. Unless the former entirely give up their controls to these mediators, relations between the two groups are bound to remain in a state of flux.

The process of diffusion through mass media lends itself to the same type of shared responsibilities and controls. Proprietors of newspapers usually want to have a say in editorial policy and in the management of news as a whole. Without getting into details, they may insist upon imposing a general perspective. At the stage of selecting their staffs, they make sure that those chosen conform to these goals. Content is supervised and certain coverage may well be imposed or suppressed. There was, for instance, a rumour in Paris in the fifties to the effect that one of the morning papers had a policy of omitting any reference, good or bad, to Pierre Mendès-France: he was, so far as the newspaper was concerned, non-existent. High circulation newspapers, which often rely on heavy advertising, may also be less prone – *ceteris paribus* – to sensitizing their readers to price fixing, trust fixing, advertising abuses, and so on. Because of high costs, newspaper chains have become more and more widespread, especially in North America, raising the problem of a lack of diversity in news coverage and the imposition of set policies in editorial writing. In his *Review of Sociological Writing on the Press*, Denis McQuail notes that interference by publishers is probably more common in the United States among local independent newspapers than among national groups or chains, though he adds, 'There is little doubt that, in the United States, proprietors do try to influence content ... and often succeed' (1976, 24–5). In Canada in 1981, the Kent Commission on newspapers set out recommendations intended to thwart the growth of chains and to provide fiscal means to encourage excellence and discourage mediocrity.

David White's classic conception of 'gatekeepers' suggests a 'chain of communication' from the reporter up to the service editor who is expected to make the final and most important decisions (1950). Seen in a much wider perspective, controls must be considered in a more inclusive fashion, covering the whole process of diffusion: the selection, shaping, displaying, tuning, withholding, and recurrence of messages (Donohue, Tichenor, and Olien 1972, 42). While initially gatekeeping was meant to shed light on occupational roles and individual preferences, it has since been used to account for organizational and institutional aspects of control (Hirsch 1977, 21). News agencies are to be included here; although limited in number, they have an important say in which events of national and international significance are thrown into the limelight. News agencies exercise, in terms of quality and quantity, a right of pre-emption on the newsworthiness of events, and a fair number of mass news media have to rely almost exclusively on the dispatches of such agencies.

Regulative controls
Because of high costs, and thus the limited number of stations possible in any one place, radio and television are particularly subject to a variety of controls. To start with, the state usually intervenes to establish its right to determine norms, often taking over management of the whole system itself. For a long time Great Britain excluded competitors to the BBC. France tolerates independent stations that broadcast specifically to the French population although until recently they were doing it from outside her immediate frontiers. Canada has willingly accepted a mixture of both public and private broadcasting, while the United States has stood aloof from any direct state intervention in the steady diffusion of diversified programs intended for a domestic audience. Newscasts and programs of a political nature, whether debates or comments, are usually followed very closely by any

administration. A convincing example may be drawn from Alain Peyrefitte's volume *The Trouble with France* in which the author, a former minister in a number of cabinets under the Fifth Republic, describes the rights he had as minister of information over the radio and television networks:

It was April 15, 1962, and Christian de La Mâlène, whom I was succeeding as minister of information, showed me a battery of buttons on his desk. 'This one is for calling the reception desk, this for your principal private secretary, and that one is for the director of the RTF (the government-operated French radio and television network), the news director, the radio and television program directors ... '

'Every day around five P.M. you call them in to decide on the main lines of the evening radio and television newscasts ... Don't leave your office before one-thirty in the afternoon and eight-thirty in the evening. After the television news program, your colleagues will call you to reproach you for what displeased them.' (1981, 59)

Peyrefitte later notes that this procedure dated from before the war and had been blessed by the well-known writer and dramatist Jean Giraudoux. Everybody knew that the communications system was working hand in glove with the party in power, but few suspected that they were quite so close.

Although they do not have a public sector as such, the Americans are very aware of government rules emanating from the Federal Communication Commission (FCC), the object of many studies.[2] It has already been established that the FCC is the focus of a diversity of interests. Staffed by the White House, the commission has to deal with the broadcasting industries and their lobbies, with citizens' groups, with all three branches of government (the President, Congress, and the courts), and with members of its own bureaucracy who sometimes hold back information to commissioners (Kranow and Longley 1978), who figure to some as 'reluctant regulators' (Cole and Oettinger 1978). Some rules at least are bound to have a direct effect on the content of programs. In order to respect the commission's norms regarding the national character and the impartiality of news coverage, the stations have had to confer on events a national and 'dialectical' status. There had been, in other words, a strong incentive to create the illusion of truly national coverage encapsulated as 'national stories,' as well as a propensity to dichotomize issues, to look at them from only two sides – the pros and cons – and to keep aloof from news content which is too controversial (Epstein 1974, 63ff., 103; Adams and Schreibman 1978, 16). As a consequence the content deviates from what it would have been had rules never been introduced. This does

2 American experience in television broadcasting has involved the strong vertical integration of networks (Litman 1979).

not mean, however, that the result would necessarily have been better or worse.

The American experience in the field is only one among many, for most countries have felt the necessity to submit the use of broadcasting to some control. The Canadian Radio-Television and Telecommunications Commission, for instance, performs this function in that country.

To sum up, intermediates introduce a reduction in the amount of control vested in the strict right of property. Limitations may be imposed from above, by the state, and from below, by mediators. Controls are shared, and shared very differently from one country to another. The family, the church, the school, the recreational association, the firm, and the mass media are vested with different roles allowing or forbidding the interference of mediators that may add an element of complexity to the conditioning process. These various groups, mediators included, make up a set of interests at work. The question is to determine the degree of coherence among the various groups, as well as the degree of conflict. The set constitutes a whole of which both integrative and disruptive aspects are parts.

CHANNELS

Effects on controls
By the term 'channel' I mean the material apparatus or support, as well as the setting, used in the transmission of signs and symbols. Common media spring to mind: radio, television, newspapers, books, and so forth. But the concept is here given a wider acceptation; it takes in all means collectively resorted to for conditioning purposes. It includes, of course, all the mass media just referred to plus other modes of expression we come across in our daily life: all printed matter such as billboards and posters falls into this category; any product derived from any other means of reproduction, such as recordings or tapes; and material arrangements used for any expression which is likely to lead to conditioning, for example, theatres and architectural designs. Apart from the physical aspect, the channel also designates any setting conducive to conditioning purposes. The setting refers to the manner in which the audience receives the content – on an individual basis, in a face-to-face relationship, or as part of the common experience of a large group. Each means of expression usually requires a distinct organization to put it to work: one does not control a publishing house as one would a school, a radio station, or a newspaper. So in some respects the channels have an immediate bearing on the way controls have to be shared with mediators. Conversely, controllers and mediators determine to some extent the use to be made of any channel.

Effects on contents
Channels also have a direct effect on content; as material intermediates they

facilitate or even maximize the transmission of some contents, while at the same time they impose limitations on the transmission of others. Some channels are better adapted than others to the diffusion of certain types of signs and symbols. Since in order to reach their audiences socializers and mobilizers are in many instances forced to adopt the most popular media, the content is likely to be affected thereby. Politicians and propagandists have not taken long to realize that televised messages are not to be delivered with hustings eloquence. Modes of conditioning stemming from technological as well as cultural or ideological changes are likely to effect modifications in content.

Newsmaking is a good example of a mode whose content is modified by conditions inherent to the mode, conditions imposed by the obligation to provide daily coverage of a diversity of national and world events. Production constraints actually limit the journalists' potentialities for originality and rigour. Back in the early twenties Walter Lippmann laid out the general conditions which led to journalistic standardization, stereotypes, and routine judgments.[3] The press is often likened to a sort of machine designed to manufacture news by selecting events and then perpetuating their relevancy by furnishing further details to keep them before the eyes of the public. Using a more organizational approach, Gaye Tuchman (1973) shows that to function properly newsmen are bound to cope with the unexpected by submitting it to a sort of routinization treatment which results in the preconceived typification of events. This way of transmitting events, which submits itself to organizational requirements, is also part of a conception about the appropriateness of swift diffusion of facts that are considered of public interest. Here we reach the audience which shares this mentality of immediacy.

Pressure is constantly exerted to select data swiftly and to handle the data in a limited amount of time under technological constraints which also contribute to routinizing the treatment of events (Roscho 1975, 111–12). Technical devices at the disposal especially of televised news seriously hamper mobility and partly explain the 'geography of news,' which is concentrated on big cities so far as the American experience is concerned (Epstein 1974, 105ff.). In fact, the recent introduction of lighter instruments may reduce this tendency (Adams and Schreibman 1978, 16).

Probably more common than direct intervention are the indirect effects on content which are becoming more and more evident as a result of studies of the so-called organizational constraints imposed upon newsmakers (Epstein 1974).

3 'Without standardization, without stereotypes, without routine judgments, without a fairly ruthless disregard of subtlety, the editor would soon die of excitement.' He added that 'the thing could not be managed at all without systematization, for in a standardised product there is economy of time and effort, as well as a partial guarantee against failure' (Lippmann 1960, 352–3).

Certain authors in search of greater precision have contended that the organizational constraints should be more appropriately labelled 'budgetary concerns' (Paletz and Pearson 1978). To this objection it should be pointed out that organizations are above all working dispositions intended to cope with a state of scarce means. It is true, though, that credit appropriations derive from a hierarchy of the importance assigned to different activities.

Immediate concern for reduced costs is manifest in cases where, for instance, the number of correspondents is intentionally limited, and they are called upon to cover predictable events such as the Speech from the Throne in Britain,or to gather foreign news that is not liable to date too rapidly, such as war sequences that offer a sort of timelessness. More closely associated with organizational concerns can be ranked all the conflicts and bargaining which take place among reporters on the beat, among newsmen inside the organization, between reporters and their news sources, or between any of these different levels. Editors may arrive at solutions which have little to do with the importance of the events themselves but are rather the result of close bargaining. The 'three way split' frequently apparent on the front page of the *Washington Post* and the *New York Times*, which chops reality up into three pieces, foreign, domestic, and metropolitan, may be attributed to a 'balance' reached between the three desks concerned with the production of news (Sigal 1973, 5, 28).

Information sources too have developed standard means for offering ready-made pieces of news. They have evolved along an organized method of providing news through agencies that specialize in shaping events (Fishman 1980, 44ff.), and on which reporters rely. Selectivity and screening operate here before newsgathering takes place. This bureaucratic adaptation and the media's organizational constraints contribute to the imposition of a conception of diffusion whereby those events which are to become newsworthy are fixed in advance.

It is not my immediate concern to evaluate the degree of accuracy reached by some media compared with others. Certain media are not at all devoted to the transmission of knowledge: artistic expressions frequently have no pretension to any veracity whatsoever. Those who diffuse so-called information are more liable to be accused of distortion. Newsmakers are usually the first to be called on the carpet. David L. Altheide (1976) refers to the 'meaning' and 'significance' of events which are superficially covered by television news (27) and thinks in terms of the 'objective characteristics' of events (173); he calls for 'more truthful and complete accounts of the social world' (196). Though it may sound naïve, this preoccupation is still widespread among scholars of journalism. Without getting involved in a philosophical discussion of the possibility (McQuail 1976, 48–9), or more likely the impossibility, of producing a faithful account of any event, through any means or groups of means, I think it worthwhile to note that media produce a new output out of the diversity of input that they marshal. In reference to the news-making world, I may add that 'the act of making news is the act of constructing reality itself rather than a picture of reality ... Newswork transforms occurrences into news events' (Tuchman 1978, 12).[4] The same could be said of any medium, though the point seems more obvious when applied to the transitory world of newsmaking.

Any transmission of an event corresponds to a 'selective encoding' which introduces *per se* what some have called an 'inevitable bias' (Frank 1973, 7–8). Factors of bias are legion: the news encoders are influenced by their peer groups' socialization as well as by their own. When regrouped into common patterns of cognition, interpretation, and presentation these factors make up a frame of reference.[5] The media frame directs news to deal with events rather than conditions, individuals rather than groups, conflicts rather than consensus.

The channel should always be seen as part of the product itself. Be it a group of two neighbours around a cup of tea or a more official means of transmission, the impression which emerges through the channels may well have a greater bearing than that which emerges from direct witnessing.[6]

Singling out an event or an aspect of an event is already a bias which stems from assigning to happenings a hierarchy of importance. When CBS used to end its evening news with the statement 'That is the way it is on this *n*th day of captivity for the Americans in Tehran,' it was a reminder of a fact which, through repetition, came to be understood as more than a fact reminder. Part of a news report in the *New York Times* of 1 June 1980, very like news items which can be read in any newspaper at almost any time, shows two aspects of news production:

President Carter today praised his rival for the Democratic Presidential nomination, Senator Edward M. Kennedy, as a 'loyal Democrat' who had waged a determined campaign and said that their contest had strengthened the party for the fall.

Mr. Carter, who suggested 12 days ago that Mr. Kennedy was campaigning on 'empty slogans,' 'false promises' and 'distortions of issues,' said today that he had 'no doubt that

4 The way foreign events are covered is a good indication of the inner bias which presumably slants their coverage right from the outset: from the selection of events to their processing as diffused news (Galtung and Ruge 1970). 'The public is not necessarily wrongly informed through television's news broadcast; it is only, at least potentially, inadequately informed' (Batscha 1975, 236).
5 'Media frames are persistent patterns of cognition, interpretation, and presentation, of selection, emphasis, and exclusion, by which symbol-handlers routinely organize discourse whether verbal or visual' (Gitlin 1980, 7). The concept is borrowed, as the author states, from Goffman (1974).
6 'Media may not be more "real" ... but very often they are unmistakably more powerful than the events and people in the real world that they capture and transform' (Monaco 1978, xi).

Senator Kennedy and I can work harmoniously' to defeat Ronald Reagan in the fall. He offered concessions on the campaign platform.

The first paragraph states facts that have been selected from the event being covered, whereas the second paragraph recalls a former event that is used as a contrast and to pose a question about the consistency or the good faith of the president. The whole piece is news and news comment under the guise of neutral reporting. I am not trying to evaluate, here, whether this form of journalism is proper or not; I am describing a conception of newsmaking. The Parisian daily *Le Monde* is basically oriented towards this type of journalism, yet its standing is very high.

The aim of the present discussion is to show the relationships between elements that should be understood as a whole and not as detached pieces. The reliability of the messages is not my concern, at least for the time being. This leads us to the effect of media on content which has to conform to the conditions of its transmission.[7]

Effects on audiences

Some media will have greater impact on their audience than others. Lazarsfeld and Merton (1948, 497) have underlined the effect the mass media have in conferring status on public issues, persons, organizations, and social movements. While contributing to the consolidation of social norms, the media are also likely to induce their audiences to believe that some sort of consensus has already been reached on new values being talked about, or on the setting of agenda when issues are submitted for public debate (DeFleur 1966, 136; McQuail 1976, 48). In the sixties the media acted – willingly or not – as links for events which had a meaning only in so far as they were recognized as part of the same movement: the student upheaval throughout the American universities was a merging together of actions that were physically taking place miles apart and needed the solidarity provided by the media to survive. The same might be said of the demonstrations in favour of civil rights at somewhat the same time.

Without getting too McLuhanesque, one also has to recognize the conditioning built into the medium itself: the message is indissociable from the medium. Reading an illustrated edition of *David Copperfield* is different from reading it in a more austere presentation. Culture and ideologies are probably affected, in the long run, by the extensive use of some media rather than others, for modes of

---

7 'The content of radio and television does not consist of culture that exists independent of media; content is either created by media or tailored to fit media format' (Altheide and Snow 1979, 23). This idea can be developed much further by showing that the structure extends beyond culture, media, and content.

diffusion are bound, as stated earlier, to determine to some extent the content itself and by so doing have a bearing on the whole outlook on values to be shared within the community. Socializations and mobilizations in the living room, through television, are likely to have built-in effects that are different from those inherent in other modes of transmission. These effects contribute to the constitution of a media logic: 'Since people perceive, interpret, and act on the basis of the existing media logic, that logic has become a way of life' (Altheide and Snow 1979, 237). It should be added that since all signs and symbols are diffused through channels, all cultures are part and parcel of the means used at a certain time in the transmission of values. Obviously our societies think widely in terms of images and messages contracted into nutshells, since the content is generally couched in such terms.

The built-in effects may also take the form of patterns of behaviour transmitted through the socializing process itself. The way the channel is effectively put to work is likely to have a bearing upon its audience. The actual structure of controls involved in the diffusion relation implies a conditioning to patterns of control: the structure of controls in the family and the classroom, for instance, have been recognized as models for behaviour in other activities of life. The school serves as a model for society, not so much from the content of its teaching, but rather from the very composition of the teacher-student relationship that implicitly defines the terms in which authority at large should be exercised (Grannis 1970). Michel Crozier (1964) has tried to demonstrate the intimate consistency between the bureaucratic functioning of the French social system and its equally bureaucratic mode of education, the latter being a mere reflection of the former. Bourdieu and Passeron (1970) have developed the concept of 'habitus' which emphasizes the high degree of automaticity reached in the internalization of principles throughout any educational process. Working from the notion of patterns of authority, Eckstein and Gurr have expounded on the homology of patterns which are to be found in different units of societies, notably those that socialize citizens as well as those that recruit and train political cadres and élites; the authors see congruences or non-congruences between the patterns as good indicators of the probable performance of the political system (Eckstein 1966, 234ff.; Eckstein and Gurr 1975, ix). These authors and others (Dawson and Prewitt 1969, 158) underline the replicating effects of prime socializing channels which impose patterns of controls that are apt to be reproduced thereafter in other social settings.

CONTENT

Content, as a concept, refers to the signs, symbols, designs, and sounds sent through any given channel. The common use of the term generally designates written or spoken signs, but in the present context it also includes less obvious elements: architectural as well as pictorial and sculptural designs; orchestral or vocal sounds; any other display of elements within the capacity of a channel. As a result, the content is not necessarily reducible to a logical proposition. For example, the Nuremberg meetings under the Nazis had as their channel the gathering of people in an arena; the content included speeches but also, and even more important, an impressive display of flags, banners, and military forces in perfect array. One has to see and hear documentaries of the time in order to have at least an idea of the content involved in such shows of collective commitment, even though the documentation is still only a reproduction of the original events.

In its most common expression, content aims at values which have a direct impact on roles. People are shown how to behave in conformity with accepted sets.

Types of content
Content may be of one type only, or a combination of any or all three types according to the effect it produces: informative, contemplative, or normative. Informative content aims at facilitating some action; it has a utilitarian purpose. Information amounts to a code that is efficient for the achievement or the evaluation of an action.[8] Technology is basically an informative system of signs, a system of efficient signs. Information also covers signs whose transmission constitutes data or facts likely to have a bearing on the other two types of content, whenever information is conducive to a new evaluation of contemplative or normative contents. Techniques of painting, for example, are basically utilitarian; they are of the informative type although they affect the contemplative type. Information also involves the emergence of facts that may upset a normative discourse.

At the opposite end of the spectrum is contemplative content, which appeals exclusively to disinterestedness. Arts and religions are certainly contemplative; mathematics and many sciences are too, being for the most part expressed in speculative terms. All these disciplines share an aesthetics which provides for beauty for the sake of beauty or knowledge for the sake of knowledge. Some expressions may be very rational, like mathematics, whereas others may evoke feelings and have little to do with logic. But all are directed to a pure satisfaction of the mind at different levels of its expression.

Finally, normative content is identified by the values it implicitly or explicitly carries. It contributes to a moralization of human behaviour and also furnishes an

8 Schramm proposes the following definition of information: 'It is any content that reduces uncertainty or the number of alternative possibilities in a situation' (Schramm and Roberts 1974, 13).

ethic for aesthetics and knowledge in general. Normative discourse is the discourse of the conditioners; it states how to behave in conformity with a code of ethics.

Whatever its composition, the content here examined is considered exclusively in its social aspect or, in other words, as a collective discourse. We are not dealing here with individuals, but with types of content that are social recurrences. It would be futile to pay attention to the intentions of individuals in the production of such sounds, symbols, signs, or designs. All three types of content are gauged by the use people put them to: the content may be directed at actions, at pleasing the mind, or at furnishing moral guidelines.[9] Truth, or more precisely what is believed to be truth, can be found in any of the three types depending upon the field of application. Truth, as such, adds nothing to the tryptych.[10]

Some discourses may adhere to a pure form, remaining throughout strictly either informative, contemplative, or normative. Some may remain unchanged and yet be diverted to other uses: the Koran is normally used for contemplative and normative purposes – most Islamic countries understand it in these terms. On the other hand, recent developments have caused western nations to analyse its content carefully as predictive of further moves on the part of these countries. In this case, the content becomes solely an informative device for the elaboration of further actions. Information in disuse falls into other categories, mostly contemplative, providing historical matter for scholars, for instance.

Mixed contents are, of course, quite common. Four combinations may be derived from the initial three categories, as Figure 6 suggests. Instead of exhausting these four possibilities, one may draw from the social sciences a synthetic example which partakes of all three categories. The 'Public Choice' school stands as a discourse which first elaborates in the abstract a theory of human behaviour within a social context, then outlines prescriptive propositions built into the theory, and finally formulates conclusions which may well serve decision-makers in their action for a freer market. Whether the discourse is more

9 Fritz Machlup quite rightly believes that an objective interpretation according to what is known is less likely to be satisfactory than a subjective interpretation relying on the meaning ascertained by the 'knower.' His approach, though, is exclusively oriented towards individuals – '*Who* knows and *why* and *what* for' – while mine is more sociological (1962, 21).

  Wilbur Schramm furnishes a distinction from the sender's objectives of communication – which may be to inform, teach, please, or propose/persuade – and from the receiver's – to understand, learn, enjoy, or dispose/decide. My own typology comes close to the distinction made from the receiver's objectives (1974, 19); sociologists are already familiar with Parsons and Shils's distinction (1962, 162) in terms of cognitive, expressive, and evaluative symbols, where the actors' intentions are primordial.

10 Expounding upon his former work (1962), Machlup remains significantly aloof from truth as a notion to be opposed to or distinguished from knowledge (1980, 114ff.).

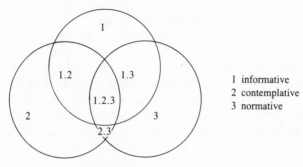

1 informative
2 contemplative
3 normative

FIGURE 6 Types of contents

normative than, say, informative or contemplative is not here our concern. It fills three functions at the same time, at a particular moment in the development of social science, especially in America.

The aspect we are looking for when discussing the content of conditioning is, of course, the normative aspect. The informative and contemplative aspects are referred to solely to make it clear that normative content does not always stand by itself but can easily be coupled with content of either or both of the other types. Our daily life is fraught with norms for behaviour engrained in aesthetic and informative contents. The task is to extract only the part that belongs to some social valuating processes.

Content: illustration of roles
For the purpose of conditioning, content aims at two social types of value-laden realities: roles and collectivities. It describes or simply implies ways for individuals or groups to behave and legitimizes or extols the existence of given groups or communities. However, content may just as easily call for the suppression or modification of these same roles or collectivities.

Content frequently suggests models of behaviour, and most roles are learned in this way. Textbooks, newspapers, television programs, and advertisements show how one becomes a man or a woman, a boss or an employee; how the role entitles one to impose controls or, alternatively, how one should submit to accepted controls. People are constantly exposed to patterns of controls that are taken for granted. These contribute, in the long run, to determining traits that become more or less essential to the achievement of individual identities. Dominance, for instance, will generally be prescribed for male identity and absent, if not literally proscribed, for females (Stoll 1974, 79; Tuchman, Daniels, and Benet 1978, 55). Certain studies on the roles ascribed to men and women on television are illustrative of biases surreptiously introduced into programs and advertisements. One of these studies (Manes and Melnyk 1974) suggests that although female achievers are widely accepted as models, their financial independence is shown as incompatible with successful marital relations. Another (Courtney and Whipple 1974) reports on analyses which demonstrate that television commercials still tend to show men in positions of authority as major announcers or voice-overs. In the latter case, the role ascendancy of men over women is subtly rather than overtly confirmed: the sponsor's expectation is probably that the audience will attribute more credibility to a man than to a woman.

Role acquisition, which is first and foremost a sociological approach to socialization in general, has frequently been turned into a psychological process of role internalization. The emphasis is then put on the individuals' personality development, which varies according to the very personal experiences they have been submitted to. A good illustration may be drawn from Stanley Renshon (1975, 51–5), who enumerates the following factors in personality formation in the family: degree of autonomy allowed, allocation of decision-making authority, nature of rule enforcement, trust in parents, parental empathy (that is, the degree to which parents were perceived as understanding the children's emotional needs), and parents' level of personal control over life space. Granted, these factors belong to different levels of socialization. But the point to be made here is that, instead of focusing on individual processes, a more sociological approach, while keeping the same items for the sake of the demonstation, would have directed its interrogation to common patterns of family upbringing within a given social network. Societies, classes, and religions certainly have a bearing that is more interesting for my analysis than the strict cumulative effect of atomized units observed along the lines of individualized processes. Sociologically speaking, individuals are of significance in so far as they adhere to roles – sets of patterns – whereas personalities as such are of little relevance.

Apart from the above patterns, there are roles transmitted by face-to-face relationships, or through mass media, which are less intimately linked to the immediacy of daily life. Roles associated with regulation also have to be integrated as recognized sets of patterns even though the roles are somewhat more distant from those who have to comply with the regulation. The legitimacy of the patterns has nonetheless to look as if it had the sanction of at least a segment of the community. Explicit content comes into play here, such as the ideological eulogy of the regulatory roles, as well as more subtle calls to adhere to the importance of the role, such as the pageantry surrounding gestures which are to be understood as the role's externalities.

Political socialization as elaborated by most political scientists has been tied to regulatory functions or their symbols. There are innumerable studies which analyse the progressive apprehension, from childhood to youth, of the levels of authority vested with different degrees of regulatory capacity; as the first step towards political sensitization, the child takes note of the police at one end of the spectrum and the president (in the United States) at the other, and then progressively proceeds to more differentiated apperceptions of authority (Easton and Dennis 1969, ch. 7). Likewise, British children will more spontaneously attribute the role of ruler to the queen than to her prime minister (Greenstein et al. 1974).

Closely linked to the regulatory roles understood as necessary or desirable is the community which in large part legitimizes not only authority roles but a good number of the others as well. Almost all news media put a strong emphasis on domestic events, which becomes the object of detailed coverage and heavy editorializing. Since they expect their audience to be domestically oriented, the media conform to this inclination and in return reinforce in so doing a sense of belonging. The effect is thus circular: the audience imposes a content which acts as a reinforcement to request more of the same. Most people have the feeling of living in society, or perhaps rather of living in a given society. This latter reality is even discernible among social scientists, who usually make sociological pronouncements that translate as profound ethnocentricity. American studies on development, for instance, have for a long time used the United States as the ultimate reference: it stood as the omega of the whole process.

Content: cultural and ideological

Content may adopt the exhaustive form of a didactic discourse, appealing through demonstration to the opportunity of sustaining a given set of values or, on the contrary, the opportunity of going counter to it. Most of the time, however, the content is implicit rather than explicit, proposing values in a rather dispersed fashion, while, for instance, entertaining a relaxed audience. In the United States, magazines are said to have a tendency to universalize upper-middle-class practices as if they were shared by all Americans (Gans 1979, 27). In such conditions, the values are more intertwined into a way of life that is deemed to be common to the society as a whole.

Content is usually a mixture of traditional and innovative components. It often upholds basic values while proposing the adaptation of new ones. It then stands as a cultural discourse calling for the integration of ideological additions, mixing a light pattern-formation content with an already strong pattern-maintenance content. Socialization easily teams up with mobilization; the same agent simultaneously moves on both registers, being at once favourable to the reproduction of some values and the alteration of others.

In a wider scope, content also refers to the mental structures imposed upon a long process of collective internalization of values and, even more, the internalization of a way of conceptualizing. In this connection, the French culture is frequently mentioned: the deductive character of its way of reasoning insists that principles be first laid down and that one then proceed to evolve the logical consequence of the principles. This method of reasoning satisfies a so-called Cartesian necessity for clear thinking while at the same time adding to it a moralistic twist (Crozier 1964; Wylie 1963; Debray 1979, 104). Values are thus shaped within modes of thinking that pre-empt, so to speak, their formation; in other words, modes of thinking stand as basic mental values which preside over the production of further values. Conversely, it is plausible that the new values might affect their incipient mould, modifying the mode of thinking itself.

As we have seen, content is multifarious in its forms, and it does not even have to be conceptualized as content: a picture in itself constitutes its content. Content runs the whole gamut of products furnished by media in so far as they act as conditioning for some people. This leads us directly to the determination of the impact such conditioning is likely to have.

AUDIENCE

The audience is an integral part of the whole structure. It has an effect on the other components, and it is also affected by them; all the components submit to such dialectical dynamics. The audience is not different from the other components, even though it serves as an indication of the success or failure of certain conditioning endeavours.

The term is commonly used to designate the people for whom messages are intended. My acceptation of the term is a bit more limited, however, for its use is meant to fit into a strictly sociological approach. I take the term to refer to people as vehicles who, as an existing network having in common either cultural or ideological values, are sensitized to new beliefs or reinforced in their common beliefs, or are being conditioned to accept or refuse certain values such that a new network is formed. The concept applies to people already acculturated or ideologized, as well as to people who, under the pressure of signs, symbols, or designs, are induced to make up a new group.

Let us start by examining the effect of the audience, as a cultural or ideological entity, on the other components of the conditioning structure. Culture (or ideology) defines status and roles which enable some people and not others to express views. The right to express oneself through writing, speaking, drawing, parading, singing, or otherwise is determined within confines that vary depending upon place and time. In traditional settings, the right to speak, especially in public, is by rite limited to the happy few conditioners so entitled. In other settings the financial capacity to put out a newspaper or a magazine is just about all that is required. Most of the time regulation merely reinforces an already accepted state of conditioning. In the Middle Ages, for instance, the clergy almost captured a monopoly of the overt transmission of values, whatever the society concerned (in Europe). The acceptability of the conditioners or, if we prefer, the communicators, is in this respect a matter of status and role: it states whether one is entitled to the function in question and whether the function entitles one to diffuse a given set of values.

Culture (or ideology) also affects the use of channels. In some cases the use may be entirely forbidden, or at any rate severely limited: theatre has long been regarded by the church as a very questionable mode of expression. Intellectual activities are not equally appreciated in all societies: books, for example, may be looked upon as almost subversive. So culture and ideology stimulate but also limit the use of media: apart from an informal type of censorship, they canalize media potential. It seems, for instance, that in the United States television is widely accepted as a medium mostly adapted for the transmission of experience rather than information (Epstein 1974, 262); events are *felt* by the audience rather than analysed.

Being part of culture, or at least ideology, free enterprise as an ideal and a practice must be considered as a way of managing pattern-maintenance and pattern-formation; the use of media is thus bound to be affected. Audience maintenance, which belongs to the inner dynamics of free enterprise, dictates, from a reading of the culture of the American public, that news transmission be entertaining. Hence the popularity of the story format whereby the news is structured as an action which unfolds in terms of a beginning, a climax, and an end, the whole having to exhibit exciting scenes that legitimate the necessity of displaying the most violent moments. This brings up the question of when and to what degree people expect to be entertained by the medium. Nevertheless, commercial mass media will by nature avoid offending audiences and by so doing act as social reinforcing agents (Klapper 1967, 51).

It is possible to investigate further and note that, being mental structures first, cultures fix the general framework of expression and understanding to be applied to given media. McLuhan (1962, 36–9) draws from John Wilson's experience the illustrative case of non-literates in Africa who could not see films or photos without a good deal of training. As Wilson points out, a picture is a convention: it is meant, in western culture, to be looked at first as a *whole*; African non-literates on the other hand scan the picture and retain only aspects that passed unnoticed by the very people who made the picture. The same principle could be applied to realism, which is also a convention (Goodman 1969); the bison, deer, and horses in the caves of Lascaux in France dating back to 15,000–10,000 BC probably looked very realistic to the Stone Age observer.

When culture is confronted with the notion of channel, the concept of content is involved automatically, for the channel is necessarily gauged by the content which is its product. This explains why all the instances furnished above put the channel and its content in relationship. But if both are necessary in evaluating the impact of culture or ideology on the media, such is not the case in the observation of cultural effects strictly on content.

As expected, cultural values readily prohibit some types of content, labelling them libellous, reprehensible, blasphemous, or simply shocking. But, as just mentioned, cultures shape ways of expression and comprehension while also imposing forms that have more to do than mere styles. Cultures and ideologies determine to some extent what is meaningful and worth mentioning. As stated in the discussion on content, there exist mental structures that mould the way people think and express themselves. Schooling reflects the reproduction of such structures; the same applies to the way events are reported. Coverage of the same event by the London *Times* and *Le Monde* will be different in many respects. Ideologies too filter journalistic selection of meaningful events and their hierarchy of importance in the same fashion.

OUTCOMES

Mediated effects
Since we have been dealing with a structure that is formed by a confluence of elements working in some sort of interrelation, the outcome, in order to be consistent, also has to be looked at from an integrated perspective. Bernard Berelson's concern in the forties is still serviceable even though we are not bound to arrive at the same conclusion: 'Some kinds of *communication* on some *issues*, brought to the attention of some kinds of *people* under some kinds of *conditions*, have some kinds of *effects*' (1948, 531).

The emphasis here is obviously on the diversity of factors or conditions that delimit the actual process of communication. With Lazarsfeld and Gaudet (1968), Berelson was among the first to question the rectilinearity of former approaches and to experiment with new paths. The two-step flow model as applied to communication has since been severely contested. It suggested that ideas flowed from mass media to opinion leaders, and from them to less active portions of the population. It is not my purpose to exhaust the gamut of comments that these hypotheses generated; it is rather to use an example from the field of mass communication as an illustration of how the structure can be put to work in terms of outcomes, which are the effects of the entire structure on the audience.

The two-step flow model banks on the pervasive influence of interpersonal relays to provide for the diffusion of values.[11] Though the model claims not to overlook the cultural aspect (Katz and Lazarsfeld 1966, 132), it nonetheless gives greater importance to attitudes that are shaped by dynamics introduced from the psychology of groups. The model stresses the power of primary groups, and informal and interpersonal relationships in *Gemeinschaft* types of ties (Robinson 1976, 304), while contenting itself with sociometric connections among individuals along the lines of education, social status, age, and sex as explanatory factors. It may be seen as a reflection of the mid-twentieth-century society which in the United States was still under the influence of locally based groups and traditional leaders (Kraus and Davis 1976, 123); perhaps today's expansion of federal functions in the United States and the growth of television – especially with its national news, which served as a catalyst for large-scale movements in the sixties, have contributed to attenuating the impact of face-to-face relationships. More recent followers have been inclined to make the model more complex. Lloyd R. Bostian (1970, 110) for one argues that early researches did not actually measure a two-step flow process but rather showed the absence of a one-step flow: what was demonstrated was that the media did not influence its audience directly. Right from the early sixties the model was considered too simple for so complex a process (Robinson 1976, 314–15; Bostian 1970; Rogers 1973, 294–6; Rogers 1962, 214– 15). A multi-step flow model became a necessity, a model which left room for more relays of opinion leaders working on a vertical as well as on a horizontal basis: opinion leaders affect each others as peers while at the same time keeping in contact with their followers via a direct line or chain.

Both the two- and the multi-step flow models stress the mediation between, on the one hand, the controllers of the mass media and content and, on the other, the audience. In this respect these models shed light on a relation that was formerly taken for granted as unilateral, the media being considered as acting directly upon their publics. Conditioning is not the preserve of the mass media; in order to reach their audience, the values the mass media elicit have to be managed by conditioners in the field.

In the meantime, scholars have been progressively more attentive to the audience's capacity to select and filter values transmitted to them by mass media.

11 There is little necessity here to toy with the distinction between strict information and influence. Events in themselves are likely to be influential anyway, and their selection as food for news is already value-loaded (Berelson 1948, 534; Robinson 1976, 306–8). As my interest lies solely in the normative effects of communication, I am only concerned with the outcome, no matter whether the original intention was to inform or influence.

Formerly regarded as a passive entity, an object of influence, audience as capable of reacting is nowadays so well recognized that communicators take great care in casting their messages in acceptable terms (Bauer 1973, 141–5). Though at times the distinctions are not perfectly clear, receptive behaviour may be broken down into four stages: selective exposure, selective perception, selective retention, and selective recall (Rogers 1962, 252; Bauer 1973, 143–4). It is a commonplace that people pay attention to messages that are in accord with their own views and have a propensity to interpret and remember them afterwards in their own way. Mass communication would, under these circumstances, be an instrument better suited for the reinforcement of norms than for conversion to new ones (Klapper 1967, 50). But the 'sleeper effect,' which is known to produce changes in values through a long-term process of surreptitious internalization (Catton 1969, 297; Bauer 1973, 145), acts as an undertow current and depreciates sweeping presumptions about the audience's capacity for selectivity.

The group as basic referent
All these models, which are frequently prolongations of the two-step flow, are more often than not grounded on a 'groupist' approach. The group, which develops a sense of belonging, serves as a screen between the communicators and the public. Following a dynamic of its own, the group presumably stimulates the emergence of opinion leaders whose high degree of information, cosmopolitanism, social participation, social status, innovativeness, and the like – to take Rogers's categories (1962, 237ff.) – put them in a situation of influence. It is most likely that groups act as barriers to mass conditioning. But the main criticism that may be levelled against this approach is that it has a propensity to single out the group as the sole explicative factors: the group is *the* social system of reference (Bauer 1973, 149), and only lip service is paid, once in a while, to the consideration of a wider field. Interestingly enough, group dynamics, as an analytical focus, fulfil certain deep-rooted expectations: the possibility of safeguarding the individual's parameters of age, sex, education, and the like, and of mixing these with psychological considerations (the psychology of groups); the ideological undertones of group protection against the devastating effects of mass societies, as described by William Kornhauser (1959) and Edward Shils (1956, 159), for instance.

A sociological perspective can hardly satisfy itself with a theoretical framework which by and large adheres irremediably to the group, without feeling obliged to go further. The intention is not to claim that groups' reactions are not worthy of study, on the contrary But, to be significant, the analysis must be given its full heuristic dimension. The notion of opinion leadership, which is central to the 'groupist' approach, should really be situated within a social context. With the present models leaders seem to emerge largely from nowhere (in practice, that is) or from resources that as individuals or personalities they have managed to muster together. The title of Katz and Lazarsfeld's work, *Personal Influence*, is certainly no coincidence, though even there, it should be added, group influence, especially that of small groups, is stressed as well as outside norms (1966, ch. 4).[12]

These authors, especially the trail-blazers, are conscious of an outer world but don't really take it into consideration. Opinion leaders, and followers as well, are measured according to social characteristics which are dealt with as given. A more embracing scope of observation would analyse such data in relationship with other aspects of social life. Age, sex, education, and profession remain of limited significance if they are not matched with a structure endowing them with some sense. For example, we might say that conditioners and conditionees are provided with resources – some with more, some with less – and animated by values both of which (resources and values) are differently allocated depending upon age, sex, education, and profession. The allocation within these categories is bound to vary according to the social network. Opinion leaders are so called because of the expertise or prestige attributed to them – whether polyvalent or specific, polymorphic or monomorphic, to use Robert K. Merton's terminology – not only by their followers, but also by a more embracing community which consciously or unconsciously defines, by and large, these leadership roles. Social networks determine what are perceived as requisites, in terms of resources, for the achievement of a given status. One can imagine a group defining its own idiosyncrasies in a unique format, such that the group could be accorded a character of singularity as compared with similar groups. A family, for instance, may develop on its own features which evoke values at odds with those of all other families. The uniqueness of the sample may be of interest to the analyst, but only in so far as the norms of the sample are examined in conjunction with the norms adopted by others; in other words, the interest lies in the sample's difference, and what is significant will be decided on the basis of what is different. To sum up, opinion leaders arrive at a status and accomplish a function by virtue of norms, controls, or regulation that permit them to do so – hence the necessity of integrating these processes in a set of relationships that go beyond the limited frontiers of group dynamics. I hypothesize that group activities vary even within the same network, and for this reason we can examine the economy of the whole

12 'We must, as a matter of fact, learn to distinguish the role of the small group in *generating* idiosyncratic norms and the role of the small group in *transmitting* and maintaining norms which vary only with larger social categories-social-class, for example' (Katz and Lazersfeld 1966, 132).

without labelling as outmoded those efforts which have been made on a more atomistic level.

The use and gratification approach
Another 'activist' school suggests that the audience participates by using the mass media to fulfil needs. This school counters the common propensity to attribute to media content a one-way effect on the audience. The receptors, conceived of as 'goal-oriented,' determine the use of the instrument and the gratifications to be derived from it. More often than not the 'use and gratification' approach is largely inspired by psychological assumptions. Some proponents of this approach derive, avowedly, from the Maslow tradition of needs (Rosengren 1974). But in most cases provisions are made for more sociological interpretations, even though the interpretations are developed only to a very limited extent. The state of the art offered by Katz, Blumler, and Gurevitch is quite illustrative.[13] In principle, there is no difference in the degree of attention which ought to be paid to either the psychological or the sociological origins of needs. The authors even complain about the absence of a theoretical bridge that would provide a link between the two.[14] As a matter of fact, the approach in general has not been immune to criticism, especially of the loose treatment of functionalists, who are criticized for relying on a 'vague conceptual framework,' a loose utilization of major concepts, and a perspective that emphasizes the audience's intentions and omits to show what the audience actually does with the media (Swanson 1977, 214; Swanson 1979). The model has also been credited with a liberal-rationalist slant that is quite deserved.[15] In practice, it has leaned towards psychology, drawing jauntily from psychological concepts and apparatuses of interpretation. Katz, Gurevitch, and Haas make reference to the need 'to be connected' as a central notion: mass communication is used as an instrument to connect individuals with themselves, their families, their friends, the nation, and so forth (1973). Significantly, the treatment of this need, as proposed by the authors in question, leaves little room for a sociological interpretation. One could, of course, ask oneself, from a sociological perspective, why people want to be connected with themselves, their families, and their friends, but this does not seem to be the point of view adopted by Katz et al.

13 Recent studies 'are concerned with (1) the social and psychological origins of (2) needs, which generate (3) expectations of (4) the mass media or other sources, which lead to (5) differential patterns of media exposure ... resulting in (6) need gratifications and (7) other consequences, perhaps mostly unintended ones' (Katz, Blumler, and Gurevitch 1974, 20).

14 The authors add: 'It is not so much a catalogue of needs that is missing as a clustering of groups of needs, a sorting out of different levels of need' (ibid. 1974, 24).

15 The stress on audience selectivity 'stems from liberal-rationalist beliefs in human dignity and the potential of the individual for self-realization' (Blumler 1979, 13).

Agenda setting

Recent developments in the analysis of mass media impact on 'political' behaviour have emphasized what is being called the 'agenda setting'effect. The determination of which issues are relevant for public discussion is attributed to the media, in lieu of the audience: the media, by the degree of importance they give to events, decide what is worth debating. Along these lines, mass media are not necessarily expected to succeed in telling the audience what to think, but they may well succeed in telling people what to think about and talk about (Cohen 1963, 13; Becker, McCombs, and McLeod 1975, 38). The reception of these hypotheses has not been without calls for caution. In the beginning, the 'agenda setting' effect may have been treated as a more or less 'mirror image' hypothesis of a mechanical registering of issues submitted to the audience (Erbring, Goldenberg, and Miller 1980). But recent analyses have contributed to a weaker conception of media impact, stressing its limitations. One such analysis notes only a 'modest congruence' between television content and audience preoccupations (Oyengar 1979), whereas another relies on influence in the long term (Shaw and Clemmer 1977). Another author has drawn an interesting distinction between the world experienced by people and the world produced by the media (Zucker 1978). He comes to the conclusion that audiences are likely to be influenced by news issues that are far from their day-to-day life or experience and that have only recently been given coverage: the closer an event is to the audience's experience, and the longer the issue has been covered, the less the capacity of the media to impose it on the agenda.

Some go further in suggesting that issues are largely the product of the audience's latent preoccupations which surface when they are triggered by the stimulus of media. They claim that media effects are essentially 'audience effects,' 'exposure to media content [being] a necessary but not a sufficient condition' (Erbring, Goldenberg, and Miller 1980).

On the whole, the audience is looked at in a less 'massified' perspective these days. The 'mass audience' is being progressively dissolved in favour of more specialized and sophisticated audiences. This fragmentation may easily lead to premature conclusions about a pervasive individualism – sufficient reason to begin to think in terms of more complex interactions at work.

The structure as a whole

Returning to the four components of the conditioning structure – interests, channels, content, and audience – it is now possible to consider their interactions in terms of the determination of the outcome. In order to enjoy a status of communicator, the controller, to deliver his or her message, has to be legitimized. The idea of credibility and trustworthiness (Klapper 1967, 129; Kraus and Davis

1976, 143), often treated on a psychological basis, may be considered acceptable here – together with other psychological based notions – so long as it refers to an attitude collectivity shared, that is, founded upon social values (which may, as has been said, be of a psychological nature): a Catholic priest addressing himself to a group of Orangemen would certainly be rather ineffective. Along the same lines, communicators are expected to diffuse their messages in determined settings: audiences are not indifferent to the settings chosen. One, if not the sole, piece of advice given by the colourful mayor of Montreal, Camilien Houde, upon relinquishing the office in the early fifties to his successor, Jean Drapeau, was never to appear on the ice of the Forum during hockey games. This example illustrates perhaps that in some cultures politicians are better appreciated in the stands than on more slippery matters. Likewise, not all contents are equally agreeable; the communicator, the medium being used, and the audience must all be taken into consideration.

Raymond A. Bauer's contentions that the audience takes an active part (1973, 142) in determining what it will pay heed to and that different people react in different ways are likely to be more rewarding if they are not kept within the confines of an atomistic or groupist approach. Kraus and Davis come quite close to this goal when they write: 'The social order produces patterned uses of the media system and in this way grants the media a certain sphere of influence within the nation. The media system in turn gives the nation certain new capacities for social change' (1976, 143).

The open reference to the 'nation' is perhaps inappropriate, but the idea serves well to illustrate the general perspective of interrelationship between active components. The audience's relationship to values transmitted through culture and ideology is as dynamic as that of the communicator.

The structure being proposed draws attention to the interaction of components in relationship with the whole that they constitute. It seems that the recent trend in discussions of socialization has been to concentrate almost exclusively on the study of processes (Schwartz and Schwartz 1975, vi; Froman 1962), whereas formerly, as in the analyses developed by Easton and Hess (1961) and by Fred I. Greenstein (1969), the emphasis was on outcome. My intention is not, as I have mentioned earlier, to discard these contemporary efforts but to integrate them into a more comprehensive model. Processes may very well account for the way different components interact. In this respect they are undeniably of great use. Nonetheless processes have to be integrated into an explicative framework if we want them to be of any significance.

Generational cleavages
The outcome is derived from a structured set of actions which thus far in the

discussion have been looked at as more or less synchronic events. Patterns have been dealt with as if they were acquired in a static context. Of course, the structure provides for cleavages in the resources being controlled; all classes, for instance, do not follow the same process of pattern internalization. However, the model has ignored, up to now, the impact of events as they unfold historically in the process of pattern acquisition. Some recent studies in socialization (Cutler 1975; Cutler 1977) have applied themselves to demonstrating the relevancy of a generational approach, as opposed to the lineage analysis which stresses the role of intrafamily interaction in terms of parent-to-child transmission of values. Without rejecting the latter, it is certainly desirable to focus on the discrepancies in socialization which are due to events which shape successive generations. The cohort[16] approach, as it is commonly called, rests on two orders of human reality, psychological and sociological, and both hold about the same degree of importance. So thoroughly integrated as to be indissociable, they are both considered explicative. In order to achieve maturity human beings must follow the course of a biopsychological development and are submitted along this course to events which vary from generation to generation and contribute to the making up of cohorts moulded by experiences that have been shared at a given stage of their development. The whole argument is obviously based upon the premise that human beings are more easily influenced at some moments of their life than at others. A more pervasive sociological or anthropological outlook would surmise that stages in life are also experienced differently depending upon time and place. Adolescence, for instance, could be considered as typical of youth which is prolonged for social purposes ingrained in industrial societies. Nonetheless, the notion of the cohort offers the advantage of taking into account a diachronic aspect in the composition of cultures and ideologies. In addition, it provides for the understanding of cumulative effects at work on specific cohorts. For example, people who lived through the world wars, and therefore the depression years and the advent of Nazism in Germany, are bound to share values that are specific to them while, of course, having other values in common with the younger part of the community. Karl Mannheim's 'generation unit' adds much to the notion by having concentrated on the identity of response shared by a number of people from the same generation, owing to other social determinants (1952, 304ff.).

The diachronic mode of analysis introduces the notion of change, which constantly challenges static instruments of observation. With regard to the structural approach, change may affect at least three of its basic components:

16 Cutler (1975, 264) proposes the following definition using Ryder's phrasing: 'A cohort may be defined as the aggregate of individuals ... who experience the same event within the same time gap. In almost all cohort research to date the defining event has been birth.'

controllers, channels, and the audience's culture or ideology. New resources will affect controlling patterns, new techniques will facilitate the emergence of new channels, new values will be registered at the cultural level; modifications in any one of the three components produce an entirely new set of interactions. These modifications refract, so to speak, a more basic phenomenon: change, which will be developed later. At this stage it is well to note that structures of conditioning vary not only from one place to another but from one time to another as well, and that the time factor has to be accounted for and not dismissed among environment outcasts.

CONCLUSION

Controls over conditioning are usually objects of contention. Interests vie for either the maintenance of patterns already in use or the production of new ones. Thanks to exclusive resources, some agents maintain the privilege of monopolistic or oligopolistic domination of certain media. Interests frequently coalesce in such a way that a diversity of sources does not translate into a diversity of messages.[17] From time immemorial the maintenance of patterns has not been left to chance. Among bands of hunter-gatherers who embody one of the most incipient types of social life, socialization is usually vested in elders who become the official holders of myths, legends, and traditions. In industrial societies the control over pattern-maintenance easily becomes an issue. Family socialization is usually the first, together with the church (former pattern-maintainer), to be limited in its scope of intervention, compulsory school taking over its functions.

Opting for a 'radical view' which would allow for the consideration of how potential issues are kept out of the political arena, Stephen Lukes elaborates in these terms:

The most insidious exercise of power, is to prevent people, to whatever degree, from having grievances by shaping their perceptions, cognitions, and preferences in such a way that they accept their role in the existing order of things, either because they can see or imagine no alternative to it, or because they see it as natural and unchangeable, or because they value it as divinely ordained and beneficial. To assume that the absence of grievance equals genuine consensus is simply to rule out the possibility of false or manipulated consensus by definitional fiat. (1974, 24)

17 As Denis McQuail (1977, 84) writes: 'Here what matters is less the monopoly of ownership and control than the monopoly of attention and the homogeneity of content. Uniformity and repetition establish the important result of monopoly without the necessity for the structural causes to be present.'

Expressions such as 'insidious exercise of power' and 'false or manipulated consensus' are by and large objectionable, because they impute to agents intentions they might not have, and because they couch the argument in ethical terms, which is not the most convincing or the most operative way to proceed.[18] But this aspect aside, the excerpt has the advantage of summing up what effect conditioning may have. Basically, the role of socialization is to shape perceptions, cognitions, and preferences in conformity with a given order of things, whatever the community. The role of socialization is obviously not to offer alternatives, but rather to create a consensus in favour of a definite option. Acting counter to this movement, mobilizing ideologies often try to create a new consensus which can hardly be said to be more or less genuine or manipulated than the consensus which comes through socialization. Lukes's opposition to the naïvety of the pluralists (Dahl, Wolfinger, Polsby, and others), which leads them to focus exclusively on the decision-making process, is certainly well founded. And also well founded is his criticism of the 'reformist view' (Bachrach and Baratz), which stops short of considering the whole conditioning arrangement. Of course, socialization transmits more than explicit ideas or norms that can be readily identified as such by the receiver. Socialization does even more: it provides for the reproduction of a frame of mind from which stem most of the other values. This process escapes, in large part, the transmitter's as well as the receiver's awareness.

On the other hand, the structure purports to gauge the degree of compatibility or incompatibility among the different sources of conditioning. Perfect compatibility is plausible within limited networks like communities of hunter-gatherers which have small populations. Diversified communities are bound to produce a variety of conditioning elements which, unless severely censored and muzzled, display areas of overlap, thus of reinforcement of one source by another, and areas of discordance, thus of conflict among communicators. Opposing interests may be assumed to evolve according to a social logic that puts them in a state of confrontation. The dynamics of mobilization are definitely those of competition.

The same agency may readily combine the role of socializer and mobilizer, that is, may act at once as a perpetuator of accepted values and an introducer of new ones. What is commonly referred to as 'socialization' (which has a different connotation from that used in the present framework, where it is intended to designate only pattern-maintenance processes) has been enlarged from its incipient formulations which postulated that it acted solely as a mechanism for the reproduction of accepted values. For some time now, the meaning of socialization

---

18 It is interesting to note that Lukes uses the same terms as Alain Touraine (1971) did in describing how technocracies manipulate post-industrial societies.

has been enlarged to cover a process of mixed diffusion, embracing devices both of confirmation and of invalidation of traditional norms. Dawson and Prewitt see the task of 'political socialization' as threefold: maintenance, transformation, and creation (1969, 27). These authors follow in the line of many other scholars in the field (Easton and Dennis 1969; Schwartz and Schwartz 1975). Educational institutions, for instance, are not entirely and exclusively devoted to the cause of pattern-maintenance, nor are they solely geared to conversion to new patterns. An analysis of the whole structure of conditioning should furnish more information on the reasons for such cleavages. Further consideration of social classes should shed some light too, as it clarifies the positions of controllers and their pronouncements by looking at them from a dynamic perspective.

The purpose of the exercise so far has been to explicate two notions: control and conditioning. Each was examined first as a solo instrument, then as part of a duo, in preparation for the entrance of the third component, regulation. But to have regulation of any sort there has to be a collectivity of reference, a non-fortuitous effect of both interests and conditioning at work.

4

Collectivity:
a product of interests

Socialization and mobilization do not elicit values in the abstract, out of the blue. Cultures and ideologies constantly refer to collectivities of which they are themselves, in part, manifestations. Cultures imply collectivities; ideologies usually create them or bolster them. Besides, no control enjoys an existence of its own. Being derived from values, it stems from a collectivity of reference. A controller acts in his own right only in so far as his role is socially accepted, that is, recognized as such by a group of some sort.

The purpose is not to try to explain human gregariousness. Aristotle presumed that human beings were political animals. For Hobbes and Locke society rested on some form of rationality – for the former *vis-à-vis* the fear of violent death, for the latter *vis-à-vis* so called natural rights. Rousseau preferred relying directly on ethics which would explain man's turning astray into a society of greedy proprietors. Being more down-to-earth, the younger Marx interpreted society as a response to basic needs. While human beings may or may not be intrinsically moral, for these authors, they become involved in moral considerations whenever they make up a society.

From an entirely different perspective, the new generation of sociobiologists has relied on the existence of inner social urges which are dictated by prolonged genetic adaptation; they inevitably end up with moral considerations on altruism and other inclinations of the sort that they see human beings as having in common with animals.

Whenever causes are attributed to the foundation of society, the propensity also to attribute to society a purpose, or end, is all too frequent. The 'why' becomes an 'ought,' with appropriate remedies prescribed to correct failures found along the course of society's evolution. At least for the time being, I propose to consider social relations as given and to analyse them as such, granted that further inquiry into the origins of social relations may be undertaken at a later date. I am therefore concentrating on the actual interplay of elements contributing to the workings of social life.

ARE COLLECTIVITIES CONCRETE ENTITIES?

Collectivities may, of course, be looked at as concrete entities. Common sense dictates that they are so, and cannot be otherwise. After all, statements that collectivities are abstractions will be greeted as the height of absurdity. Italy, Singapore, Harvard, and Macy's are surely as real as you and I. Many prominent social scientists, after Emile Durkheim, have not steered clear of this reifying trap of considering societies as more or less real things. Talcott Parsons has remained the most positive in maintaining that, beyond any doubt, collectivities stand as concrete entities (1961, 34ff.).[1] He goes even further in referring to 'concrete' roles. His preoccupation is obviously to root his theory on empirical ground. The intention commands respect, but the application leaves something to be desired. Behaviour, I posit, is the sole referent for any empirical recognition of social facts. Networks of exchange, control, production, and conflict are also amenable to some form of identification, so long as one can follow a thread of behaviour in process. When submitted to this treatment, the networks become constructs, very like Parsons's extraction of his different systems. These networks are only parts of a reality. The sum of these constructs (if it were possible to add them all up) would not, for all that, create a state of greater reality. The networks are likely to overlap the frontiers intended to circumscribe collectivities. All they can show is that the belief of constituting a group and, in most cases, the application of rules have brought about certain networks of behaviour which are more or less confined to a number of constituents.

Whenever collectivities are assigned a concrete status of reality, they are likely also to be assigned goals. Analysts begin with a reification of society, only to find they have fallen into psychological interpretations in which a sort of collective conscience, a volition, motivates actions and sorts out meanings for the whole of society. This procedure comes close to the Ancients' preoccupations with ends; it is implicitly teleological, following a rationale akin to Aristotle's search for the ultimate objectives of beings. It is not accidental that Parsons drew the bulk of his quadripartite construction of social action from a close reading of Robert Bales's psychosociology of small groups (Devereux 1961, 54–5). The slide is obvious

---

1 More or less following Parsons's distinction between societies and cultures, Karl Deutsch furnishes a good illustration in the same vein: 'Societies,' he writes, 'produce, select and channel goods and services. *Cultures produce, select and channel information*' (1966a, 92; italics in original). We are here close to a double case of reification coupled with an animist approach to culture.

from psychology to sociological analysis: societies are coped with as if they were psychological entities. Just because collectivities are composed of psychological entities, it does not follow that the whole should be observed with the analytical instruments used for the observation of its components. Parsons's ambition was to submit all levels of human reality to his quadripartite grid, thus following Bertalanffy, who was eager to generalize systemic isomorphisms and make them applicable to a series of disciplines.

The humanist bias is the strongest when it feels most threatened, and at such times collectivities are liable to be identified with the same parameters that serve for the identification of individuals. Persons have goals; collectivities do not. Conferring on them an ethos of any sort is an abuse of language. Cultures account for the provision of goals, but both culture and goals are analytic constructs created by the observer.

When collectivities are broached in terms of concrete entities and goal orientation, they are also frequently looked at as if they were built in the fashion of Chinese boxes that fit into one another. Collectivities are thus broken down into sub-collectivities embraced by a larger whole. Having construed society as tangible and set goals for it, we find it very hard to avoid the all-embracing perspective that once again Parsons systematically exemplifies.

Parsons has always been a keen exponent of the plurality of affiliations individuals are nowadays involved in. He also accepted, but with more restrictions or less enthusiasm, solidarities that transcend national confines (1972, 254–5). But, whatever the pluralistic state of societies, in his mind they form an all-embracing dome which serves as *the* unit of reference. This is a must, if the functionalist mode of explanation is to be applied. Functionalism is based upon the assumption of a single whole that accounts for all the activities (of a given natutre) which take place within its autonomous dynamics. This led to Parsons's adamant opposition to any attempt to fragment the unity; he was conscious that frag-mentation would have meant the end of his theories.[2]

Collectivities in reality overlap, frequently defying boundaries designed to limit their extension. A few examples will suffice. From the Middle Ages up to our times the church has stood as a community that maintains a culture that overlaps national boundaries. Multinational companies today cultivate a 'we feeling' that purposely transcends national frontiers, developing a corporate solidarity that is expected to take the place of national solidarity (Barnet and Muller 1974, 89ff.). The Diaspora stands dramatically as the best instance of strength of perpetuation

---

2 'We have argued strenuously that a university should *not* be conceived as a microcosm of a society; on the contrary, it should be conceived as a functionally specialized subsystem' (1972, 257).

without even, for long periods of time, a strict regulatory device to pull together its dispersed membership. The next chapter on regulation will make more explicit the factors of mobility that impose more or less stringent barriers on given collectivities.

TYPES OF SOLIDARITY

A collectivity usually responds to two opposite types of solidarity, one of a strictly rational and utilitarian nature, the other emotional.[3] In the first instance, it may be seen merely as an organization for the attainment of specific goals.[4] As a whole it is conceived as an abstraction, an artefact, couched in terms of a division of labour which corresponds to a structure of status and roles, a complex of production. From this aspect, the collectivity is reduced to its utilitarian usage, efficiency being the criterion for evaluating its performance. Almost all collectivities are to some extent submitted to this imperative: few are not committed one way or another to some determined output. Even families cannot be considered exempt.

Controls allotted through the distribution of statuses and roles respond to the rationale of efficiency with regard to the expected output. In this respect the collectivity may be called functional. The endeavour may not be rational, however, in view of other more embracing goals or values. For instance, an industry may exhaust human resources within a short period of time and, in spite of costs incurred within the frontiers of other networks, be considered efficient. So while they may at times appear indisputably rational, controls can be considered such only with respect to accepted goals.

Collectivities respond even more strongly to emotional solidarity, the feeling of togetherness. Endeavours of any magnitude will look for this second type of adhesion from its members, even if its main purpose calls for a rational solidarity. Firms, for instance, are by definition bent on profit making, but they strive to create among their employees and officers an environment which is meant to be conducive to profits in the long run.

Rational solidarity tied to imposed goals is reliant on emotional solidarity for the achievement of its goals. Emotional solidarity rests upon feeling, not upon

---

3 This distinction is the most common since Tonnies, although my treatment does not necessarily follow the same logic.
4 It does not follow that organizations really do have goals, nor that their activities are all focused on them. Organizations are conceived as goal oriented by the different agents, but this does not mean that they actually work this way. Many objections have been levelled at the rationalistic approach to analysing organizations (Hall 1977, 67ff.; Benson 1977; Salaman 1979, 84ff.; Silverman 1970, 9ff.).

calculation, as is the case for rational solidarity. Emotional solidarity is a 'we feeling,' a sense of community, which is presumed to be shared to different degrees by all the community. This feeling, in turn, stems from a common belief (which does not have to be shared by outsiders) in the existence of a whole of which they are constituents. As a matter of fact the existence of such a whole is just as uncertain as it is elusive. Emotional solidarity imposes itself through the unspecified character of its goals. The collectivity as a whole no longer stands as an idea, as is the case for the organizational arrangement of rational solidarity, but as a fictitious entity lodged in its constituents' imaginations. In its organizational aspect, a collectivity is recognizable in the abstract, since it is actualized by agents who fulfil the roles it prescribes and in so doing serve as tangible manifestations. In its communitarian aspect, the collectivity as such can only be evoked but never expressed, and therein lies its mystery and also its galvanizing properties; it responds to R.M. MacIver's conception of myths.[5]

The same rationale applies to events or actions which are the manifestations of the collectivity without being the collectivity itself: signs, symbols, and goods will be produced, exchanged, controlled, or fought for in the name of collectivities, whether these are nations, social classes, political parties, trade unions, or firms. There is no doubt that manifestations account for the strengthening or weakening of the members' morale, since they may affect the components' ability to keep their *raison d'être*.

Collectivities may appear to some people as systems of signs, as systems of production and exchange of signs and symbols, or simply as systems of communication. But are they really? Individuals exchange or produce goods and services. Whenever they act as a group they do so in the name of the group, as provided by its organizational dispositions. The community as such never acts except through all or some of its agents.

As an organization, a collectivity is an idea, a blueprint, a set of roles to be actualized.[6] As a community, a collectivity is a product of the imagination. Both are forms of abstraction. They are no more concrete than culture, though they are

5 Myths are 'the value-impregnated beliefs and notions that men hold, that they live by or live for. Every society is held together by a myth-system, a complex of dominating thought-forms that determines and sustains all its activities' (MacIver 1947, 4). The term is meant to hold no pejorative connotation.

6 Berger and Luckmann (1967) cherish the idea that society is an objective reality. Such a proposition may be misleading for it introduces confusion by attributing the same analytical status to two types of social products: language and community (which they call society). Language amounts to a code whose signs are real in the sense that they are usualy recognizable at all times, from their rules. Communities are only identifiable from the actions which derive from their presumed existence. Communities are real so long as people believe they are. Dead tongues still exist so long as the code is not lost, but such is obviously not the case for communities.

different. Culture stands as a conscious construct of the observer, whereas collectivity is lodged in the constituents' minds.

COMMUNITIES

In order to form a community, a collectivity must necessarily show traits or activities that induce people to believe in their togetherness. Students of integration at the level of macro-communities are familiar with factors that have been advanced as exerting a unifying influence upon people, factors such as geographical proximity; homogeneity in wealth, education, status, religion, race, language, and ethnic identification; knowledge of one another; and shared functional interests (Jacob and Teune 1964, 11). Karl Deutsch has emphasized on many occasions the impact of communication which is revealed as the prequisite transaction for the emergence of nationalities (1966a). He even proposed to quantify aspects which up to then had remained at a qualitative, not to say descriptive, level (174). All these components are only conditions for the development of a community; they are not meant, in themselves, to furnish explanations. There must be material on which the community is based, but it should not be confused with the community itself. In other words, the community is built up out of these features.

The community resolves its unity in a fictitious entity which is unamenable to rational treatment that tries to circumscribe its exact meaning. It is not conceived to be understood, but rather to be felt and shared. Referring to the nation, Ernest Renan could write a century ago that it is a 'spiritual principle,' a 'moral conscience' (1887, 305, 310), adding that its essence rests on the fact that all its members have many things in common and that they all have forgotten many things (286). Without accepting the concepts used here, one may agree with the level of reality they convey. The community is *par excellence* of an allusive and evocative nature; it can only be apprehended from what we perceive as its manifestations, never by direct contact. This being so, the community possesses an impressive capacity to attract. Its rallying value is not to be compared with that attributed to organizations, which always have to produce a definite output in order to be kept working. The type of solidarity derived from the community is loyalty. Using Albert O. Hirschman's triad, we can say that 'exit' and 'voice' may be expressed in organizations while 'loyalty' and 'voice' find their way into communities. Naturally, communities may be found at all levels of human interaction, just as organizations may: from families to the concert or cacophony of nations. Churches and religions stand at the apex of the rallying capacity, the loyalty attached to them being rooted in the accepted intangibility of their reality. In other words, members of a church identify the whole community in elusive terms, seldom having to feel its materiality. Other communities may be endowed with such a sacred status and thus become quasi-churches. Nations and political movements sometimes come quite close to this stage. Collectivities, more immersed in day-to-day contingencies, are frequently referred to in more mundane terms, so much so that people may easily be led to believe them tangible entities.

In-groups/out-groups
The 'we' identity, whether limited or widely extended – 'We the Tikopia' or 'We the People of the United States' – can hardly be thought of without reference to the 'out-group,' that 'they' which symbolically acts as a foil. Identity is stimulated by opposition to, or at least distinctiveness from, other collectivities. The symbols of belonging are, after all, geared to what distinguishes the group from the outside. Georg Simmel would go much further, assessing the group as fundamentally determined by its opposition to others. Opposition is no doubt the essential ingredient of ideology, and it is even tautological to say so, since ideology is basically conflictual. Militancy revolves around an opposition axis which produces a mobilizing effect upon the group. One may wonder whether the statement applied by S.M. Lipset to the United States is not applicable to any emergent community: 'Born in a prolonged struggle for independence,' he writes, 'the United States defined itself from its beginning in ideological terms ... Americanism' (1970, 71). Is it possible to imagine the birth of nations, states, parties, and the like in other terms?

Ethnic and national groups in their formative years have to strongly delineate their distinctiveness in order more or less to legitimate their *raison d'être*. This is likely to lead them to emphasize characteristics of exclusion from others, characteristics that show to what extent they are *not* the others (Armstrong, 1982, 5).

Inherent to ideology, 'out-grouping' is carried on in a more subtle fashion once it is absorbed into a culture as prejudice. Still of interest despite its age, Berelson and Salter's study (1946) shows how discrimination against minorities can be surreptitiously maintained through magazine fiction, which serves as a vehicle for the transmission of stereotypes: the sly and shrewd Jew, the Italian gangster, the ignorant black, the emotional Irishman. These are cases where the community reinforces its homogeneity to the detriment of its minorities, creating an inner community of, for instance, true Americans. Negative perceptions of outside collectivities are also common in cultures, but whenever such perceptions turn into a conflict over values, the whole setting becomes ideological.

Communities rely heavily on the past to legitimize and consolidate their existences. We are all familiar with the creation of heroes who perpetuate a mythology common to almost all communities: the cult usually runs in favour of individuals, as if the individuals epitomize in their persons the search for unity performed by the whole community. But even more, history contributes in fusing traits to form a composite which describes the evolution of a whole. In this respect, history sanctions the existence of a community as one and distinct. Events are so selected as to serve as illustrations of the community's existence and importance.

Inasmuch as a collectivity is usually a community – that is, is bound by emotional as well as rational solidarity, and is thus more than a mere organization – it implies a number of people who through communication of some sort come to consider themselves as constituting in some respect a distinct entity. This body may be a couple or a family, as well as a corporation, a trade union, a political party, a church, or ultimately a nation. The amplitude of the bonds will vary from rather limited ties to very embracing ones. The community as an entity resides exclusively in the minds of those involved, outsiders as well as insiders, who come collectively to believe that its members belong to a whole which is recognized as distinguishable from any other whole.

Community consciousness
The problem of consciousness must be considered. The community, maintaining its existence through emotional adhesion, postulates a degree of awareness on the part of its members. Drawing from his study on the Nupe people, S.F. Nadel states that consciousness is indispensable for the existence of a community. He shows that, though the acceptations of Nupe people, language, and country do not coincide, the Nupe have no difficulty in recognizing each other as Nupe, although no external symbols serve to identify them as distinct. For Nadel, social unity is based upon an awareness of unity (1961, 12, 17). The opposite view contends that, first, the concept of awareness is too volatile to be of any theoretical use and, second, consciousness should be discarded as a condition of identification since people are frequently said to belong to a community without being aware of it themselves (Ladd 1959, 274–7). Of course, the term is open to question for its polysemic character. But such an objection constitutes an easy way out of the utilization of almost all notions in the social sciences. The war of words is here to last. The second objection is more substantial. What do we do with members who do not share the saving grace of awareness? Are they considered to be in or out of the community? Wasn't it established at the beginning that consciousness was null and void in the present discussion?

The notions of consciousness and awareness imply a referent. One is conscious or aware of something. It is this something that makes all the difference. The proponents of consciousness usually claim that the referent is an objective entity which, in other words, exists without and before its being thought of. The notion of class interests usually falls into this category of consciousness. Workers' awareness is not a condition of their class interest; class interest exists even before it is apprehended as such. Class interest awaits adhesion to itself. Awareness of the national can be discussed in a similar manner. Nationalist thinkers will claim that one is a Frenchman, an Italian, an American, or a Canadian before anything else; the problem lies in becoming conscious of one's own national identity. When the concept of consciousness or awareness is understood in these terms, it is, from the present framework's perspective, of no interest. In such a case, consciousness purports to account for the reflection of an already existing entity. Consciousness is quite a different thing if it means accepting a conception as an entity in itself. The term 'belief' is probably more appropriate in this instance.

Collective beliefs are of interest. Whether members think that their reference group is concrete or not does not *per se* affect the analyst's concerns. In fact, most people are probably convinced that their families, social clubs, towns, and countries are as real as the print on this page. The notion of awareness is to be dealt with from indications of adhesion. The concepts and representations that serve to identify adhesion are precious constituents for the analyst's understanding of what the communities are meant to be. Communities are fictions to be reconstituted by him or her, fictions that are worthwhile for the analyst in as much as they are shared by the agents they are supposed to pool together. Beliefs and representations are considered in term of collective conformity. Cleavages are of interest so long as they are grouped together according to significant categories of social behaviour: sex, age, class, education, profession, and so forth. Sex and age are appreciated, in this instance, as social products, socialization accounting for differences in perspective. We may expect that every Frenchman has 'une certaine idée de la France,' as any Argentinian probably has a distinct idea of Argentina: yet the landscapes vary from one street to another. What counts is the common denominator among these representations, or the basic differences along social disparities. The same reasoning applies to smaller aggregations – a town, a firm, a family – in which cases the analyst has to use greater care in distinguishing social factors from merely psychological ones.

Solidarity is difficult to gauge; the frequency of its manifestations is easier to evaluate than the intensity that sustains them. Solidarity can be measured from the extent of support given, in terms of costs incurred by the members. The expression of some signs and symbols requires little effort: the exhibiting of flags on a national day requires minimal expense. Exhibiting the same flags when an occupying force overruns one's country is a lot costlier. In most cases the ultimate cost is one's life for a collective cause: the nation, the class, the religion, or the family. Some communities manifestations may well be very apparent, not to say noisy, on minor issues and rather discreet on major ones, while the converse is true of other communities.[7] What people say they are ready to do belongs to a set of manifestations which we call signs and symbols; what they actually do is another set, which covers signs and symbols as well, but also loss of resources.

The collectivities considered here are those which exhibit the greatest social impact in terms of pattern formation or maintenance. For this reason, emphasis is put on macro units which offer the most potential for socialization and mobilization. Today, the nation is still held in high esteem and widely accepted as the most embracing unit. Let us look at this sociological reality in order to relativize its impact later.

Since Antiquity, at least, the most embracing communities in the western world have taken the shape of cities, empires, states, and nations, which left the tribal mores of the past far behind. The Athenian city, the Roman republic, the feudal setting, and the nation, to take the most prominent forms of macro units, refer to communities whose imaginary contours are distinctly different. Being an Athenian, a Roman, a Frenchman under Saint Louis, an Englishman under Victoria, or a Russian under Stalin refers to representations of the mind that have very little in common; and despite appearances, the latter two, the Englishman and the Russian, probably offer greater points of resemblance in the confection of their respective collective images than any of the others.

NATIONS

Nowadays, the fiction of the nation still prevails. No community is viable without a fictitious entity which, at a given time and for a number of reasons yet to be discovered, imposes itself as the most satisfactory social attraction. The nation is frequently confused with the state, with which it is associated, and the hyphenated pleonasm 'the nation-state' is employed. The nation is recognized as the basic unit entitled to hold legal sovereignty. Apart from this widely accepted competency, the rest of a nation's attributes are swallowed up in a maelstrom of ambiguity.

One point, at least, on which most scholars would agree when broaching the concept of nation, is its intrinsic equivocalness (Emerson 1962, 90). Nation is readily confused with race, language, religion, territory, common history, and the state (Snyder 1972, ch. 2). General de Gaulle opens his memoirs with that classic and ominous sentence, 'Je me suis toujours fait une certaine idée de la France' ('All my life, I have thought of France in a certain way'). As people come to feel that the territory they occupy is a homeland about which they have had a say, a capacity which was not recognized in aristocratic eras, patriotism for the defence of the land develops and progressively evolves into exaltation of those who people the

7 Manifestations under duress will be dealt with in a later chapter.

land. Interestingly enough, connotations of the concept vary from one language to another, which accounts for the diversity of ways in which patriotism is expressed. It is an easy exercise to compare the way global communities have at times come to be defined or described by their instigators: Barrès's France, Kipling's British Empire, Mussolini's state, Hitler's race. Communities are extolled in terms that distinguish them from others, so much so that they become incomparable: they are made to look as if they had nothing in common with any other community, as if they were unique and irreducible in their essence. All communities, from a couple or a family upwards, are likely to create such representations, whose purpose is to convince people of the communities' unique character. For a Frenchman, there is nothing like being a Frenchman, for an American, nothing like being an American. The analyst may easily come to the conclusion that by comparing communities he is thereby depriving himself of something essential. Communities are, so to speak, very good at inducing any observer to respect their complete integrity and eschew rational interpretations that might work as 'disenchantments' of their worlds.

The community's entity, as it is evoked by its members, is probably more interesting to observe in terms of its bonds with the rest of the structure to which it belongs, than in comparison with other communities. Comparing conceptions about the nation or the state as they are circulated in the different countries' school textbooks, newspapers, and other media is most likely to produce, at its best, a classification reminiscent of botanical taxonomies, a treatment which always stands at the threshold of scientific explanations without ever getting further. Instead of comparing fictions, is it not more instructive to analyse the dynamics to which a community belongs, and only thereafter indulge in comparing it with other communities?

Community-makers/nation-makers

Communities seldom exhibit the interests that lie behind their beginnings, or those which still maintain them. It is of course tautological to infer that interests bring about the creation of groups, in so far as a motivation is necessary for any human endeavour. But the point is that, generally speaking, not all community members have the same degree of interest, and some may have none at all at the beginning. Small communities may, in some circumstances, show a comparable degree of utility shared by their founding members: groups of hunter-gatherers, for example, as well as other types of collectivities oriented towards equal implication of all members. But even then controls are not equally distributed.

Since most collectivities are designed for production of some sort, they are conceived as useful devices for marshalling human resources. Though more complex, macro-units may be viewed in this same perspective. This does not mean that they are bound to espouse the cause of massive industrialization. The production sought may be, from their founders' point of view, aimed at religious or similar symbolic activities. This is only to say that the collective objectives proposed at the beginning do not necessarily have to be carried out afterwards. Such objectives are promoted by interests which see an advantage somewhere in the emergence of a community.

The Marxist tradition has very aptly underlined the coincidence of nationhood and capitalism, the emergence of the former finding its explanation in the latter. Nationhood meant – through the uniformity of language – grouping in one entity, one government, one code of law, and one national class interest and consequently the establishment of one market (Emerson 1962, 173). Nations certainly look like products, or by-products, of industrialization; this does not imply, however, that industrial interests which have taken full advantage for a time of, say, tariff barriers, might not at some future date be less inclined in favour of national entities.

Max Weber (1968, 921) was among the first to question Marxist tradition in this respect, by putting the emphasis on the impact of the petty bourgeoisie, which harbours feelings of prestige in direct connection with the attainment of national power positions. Is it in fact necessary to discard the economic factor, as he does in this case? Both industrial and intellectual interests may at a given time derive common advantages from a given state of affairs.[8] It is not my intention to furnish a definite interpretation here, but simply to ventilate the question briefly.

Apart from the capital versus prestige polarization stands the vexing problem of precedence: which came first – the nation as a cultural entity or the state as a political entity? Emerson's classic *From Empire to Nation* adopts a moderate stance which leaves room for both eventualities (1962, 114ff.). Undeniably the state fashioned out most European nations, with the exception of Germany and Italy. Medieval England was moulded first as a territory whose inhabitants then progressed to forming a distinct entity. The introduction of the Circuit Court under Henry II as a means to guarantee some uniformity in the land largely favoured the emergence of the common law, which later acted as an important factor in the establishment of homogeneity. Nineteenth-century France was, deliberately or otherwise, submitted to a policy of nation building: roads and railways converging on Paris, uniform public schooling, and the military service accounted to a large extent for the formation of national cohesion. One should not forget that before the Revolution of 1789 only part of the population spoke French and that even in 1863 about a quarter still did not speak it (Weber 1976, 67). On the other hand, it is possible to imagine communities considered as nations which, although never in

---

8 In his *Protestant Ethics and the Spirit of Capitalism*, Max Weber was more fortunate in trying simply to attenuate the Marxist economic approach, without putting it aside altogether.

their history conceived of in any regulative terms, later become states. But in most cases, even those of Germany and Italy, at least some regulation did occur. Both Germany and Italy each finally emerged as a set of unified former provinces. The same rationale applies to colonies in their achievement of complete autonomy. Entities which are solely cultural are not easy to imagine, even though legend would, of course, have us believe they exist. With hindsight, nations are seen as the legitimizers of states, but in reality a nation is, to a large extent, the product of regulative endeavours.

Intellectuals and the search for identity
Policy makers have had to rely on conditioners to extol the entities they planned to bring about. As Edward Shils says, nations, whether in Europe, America, Asia, or Africa, have been created out of tribes thanks to 'intellectuals' (1972, 5). Julien Benda (1965, 55ff.) used to lament the national partiality, not to say the fanaticism, of the learned whose works, whether artistic or scientific, were tinged with that spirit conducive to an affection for the particular at the expense of the universal.

The great feat of some 'intellectuals' has certainly been to market the notion of identity, which has come to be applied to collectivities as some psychologists have applied it to individuals. One may dare to throw doubt upon the value of identity in psychology, asking among other things if it is ever possible to arrive at the true identity of a person. But these considerations are out of the present field of observation.

Writing in defence of the Occitany (the southern part of France), Robert Lafont stands as a good example of a nationalist who believes strongly in the identity of people: language, he says, enables people to become conscious of their collective identity (1968, 44). Medieval France, in his mind, triggered an imperialist policy which progressively rounded up her neighbouring 'nations' into one country. Occitany, Provence, Britanny, Burgundy, Béarn, Alsace, Lorraine, and Corsica were thus victims of a colonialist intervention which later extended to more remote areas.[9] Lafont strongly believes that the conquered 'nations' were all animated by an identity of their own.

Few analysts would indulge in such extremes, for most, especially those of the North American tradition, would be careful to ascribe the identity process to individuals, and not to collectivities. Consequently, the problem of identity tends to remain, on the whole, within the confines of a strictly psychological approach. Scholars of nationalism (Kohn 1945, 4ff., Smith 1971, 28) have shed some light

9 This is a process that is not alien to the interpretation of 'internal colonialism' attributed to Britain's expansion in Celtic lands (Hechter 1977).

on the belief shared by many that human beings need to join groups for reasons of solidarity or security. Kohn would say that this purportedly natural tendency is one 'which, having been produced by social circumstances from time practically immemorial, appears to us as natural' (1945, 4). And more specifically he says about patriotism: 'This love of the homeland, which is regarded as the heart of patriotism, is not a "natural" phenomenon, but an artificial product of historical and intellectual development'(8).

The question as to whether human beings are 'joiners' by nature or not does not rule out, as many authors have noticed, the problem of determining the limit, if there is one, of their 'natural' inclination for larger units.

Identity crises
Lucian Pye, who is mainly preoccupied with the question of development, has probably been the most explicit exponent of the 'identity crisis' as a stage in the achievement of a five-stage process (1966, 63). Inspired by the task-oriented works of Erik Erikson, Pye borrowed the idea of 'identity crisis' and, by analogy presumably, transposed it from its original psychological setting, applying it to political science. Pye uses the expression initially to apply to individuals as members of the community: 'They [the people in a new state] must[10] feel as individuals that their own personal identities are in part defined by their identification with their territorially delimited country' (1966, 63). But at times there is a slide from the individual to the community itself, which happens to undergo, as a whole, a similar process: 'An identity crisis occurs when a community finds that what it had once unquestioningly accepted as the physical and psychological definitions of its collective self are no longer acceptable under new historic conditions' (Pye 1971, 110–11). The 'resolution of the identity crisis' as expanded by Pye (1971, 124) is bound from then on to imply the community as such.

The notion of identity itself is conducive, in any case, to deceptive treatments (Mackenzie 1978). Already disputable when used in its original psychological setting, it is even more open to question when it is meant to apply to collectivities, or to individuals as affected by their belonging to collectivities. The only satisfactory usage would be in reference to collective acceptance of a set of values, in which case the notion becomes coterminous with the concepts of culture or ideology and therefore loses any utility it might have had pretensions to. Whenever cultures are challenged, it is by ideologies, and the result may be a mixture of cultural and ideological values. This composite product is easily identified as a 'crisis of identity,' since neither set of values is entirely accepted

10 The interventionist intention here is obvious.

or refused. 'Intellectuals' especially are keen to detect such 'soul-searching' situations as ideal grounds for intervention. On this ground, almost all contemporary societies would fall into the category of entities ridden by inner conflict; few could claim that their values are entirely consistent. Historical development, which is the fate of societies, imposes the emergence of contradictions which are bound to affect their so-called identity.

Canada offers an interesting example of 'intellectuals' in search of national identities. French Canadian 'intellectuals' of yesteryears used to be quite at ease in defining French Canada in terms of its belonging to France's Ancien Régime, whose values, among others, embraced those of catholicity and rural life.[11] The sixties smashed this conception to smithereens, so that nationalists of that generation had to look for an entirely new community of reference. One route of access was recourse to psychoanalytic devices which were deemed to facilitate the emergence of Quebec's identity (Bélanger 1977, 155ff.). Canadian anglophones on the other hand, have found themselves in a quandary of a different nature (Bell and Tepperman 1979).

Crises of identity are fuelled by incompatible interests that put forward arguments likely to arouse a divided perception of the community, which seems, as a result, at a loss to find a 'definition' of itself. Crises derive from discordant discourse among mobilizers who come to believe that the collectivity is on the verge of collapsing (which in reality is exceptional) or is confused in determining its most basic values.

The recognition of the community as something concrete emerges as the first step in the achievement of a regulative network. People come to believe that they existed as a tangible whole before being submitted to any authority. Such an accomplishment is probably the greatest feat of 'politics': subjects become convinced of their collective being as the primary mover in the regulative process. As a result of this fiction, conceived as real and eternal, the rulers are ready to pronounce their legitimate right to rule.

11 Canon Lionel Groulx epitomizes this traditional nationalism (Bélanger 1974, 191ff.).

5

The structure of regulation

We have established that controls follow patterns of behaviour whereas conditioning provides for the recognition of the patterns through socialization and mobilization. All controls correspond to rights which legitimize them. The rights, in turn, stem from norms, some of which are more binding that others. Rules are simply more clearly specified norms. They stand as principles of behaviour (like norms), but principles whose status implies, in case of nonconformity, the recourse to official sanctions from the collectivity or its presumed representatives. Rules refer to a more collective and institutionalized mode of intervention than ordinary norms. Feuds among hunter-gatherers, which often degenerate into the killing of the protagonists, may very well remain within the realm of norm infraction, so long as officials are not called upon to arbitrate. In contemporary societies, norm deviance, or simply nonconformity, may very well trigger a collective response psychologically harder to bear than official sanctions which translate into fines or even imprisonment. In a literary form which may have overstated the case, Alexis de Tocqueville wrote:

The master no longer says: 'You shall think as I do or you shall die'; but he says: 'You are free to think differently from me and to retain your life, your property and that you possess; but you are henceforth a stranger among your people ... You will remain among men, but you will be deprived of the rights of mankind. Your fellow creatures will shun you like an impure being; and even those who believe in your innocence will abandon you, lest they should be shunned in their turn. Go in peace! I have given you your life, but it is an existence worse than death.' ([1875] 1953, 264)

CONTENT

Rules
Most controls nowadays are entrenched in rights that are derived from rules

accepted within a social network. The rights may be explicit or implicit. They are explicit whenever they manifestly correspond to a rule – or set of rules – which either belongs to an oral tradition or has been laid out in writing; they are implicit whenever the action undertaken is permitted or tolerated because there is no rule against it. The French legal tradition could be caricatured as illustrating the extreme in the non-existence of implicit rights, since all that is not formally permitted can be considered forbidden; conversely, the British legal tradition can be submitted as the opposite extreme, where all that is not expressly forbidden is permitted. Such statements, of course, are mere exaggerations of both systems. The point to retain is that many important rights, especially in modern western tradition, rest on an absence of law. Liberalism, especially the British variety, relies on the non-intervention of the state or, in other words, on the absence of regulation. *Laisser faire* produced all sorts of controls, some of them unexpected, by leaving the economy on its own. Laws which intervene in labour relations and market transactions have frequently been intended to reduce or suppress controls enjoyed in a free economy. Child labour laws in nineteenth-century Britain are examples of actions intended to thwart what were interpreted at the time as abuses of the system. The right to pollute the air has been interpreted as a similar abuse. So, rights may rest on open rules, but they may also be exercised through an absence of rules. From David Easton's systemic perspective, values[1] which are not explicitly allocated can hardly be accepted as part of the political system, since they do not derive originally from demands – or withinputs. In this respect, the framework encompasses sets of non-decisions which happen to amount to decisions, conscious or unconscious policies of non-interference that validate types of controls.

Rights are obviously claimed by people either for themselves or for others. Children's rights, for instance, are taken care of by adults who act as the children's defenders. All rights act as legitimizers of controls, authorizing the patterns followed by controllers. Rights cover the whole spectrum of controls. They may be, for our purposes, classified according to the objects over which control is sought: people, things, or signs. Rights over persons predominantly affect labour relations, from slave-owning societies to industrial civilizations, whether capitalist, socialist, or communist. Levying troops through conscription also means exercising a right over persons, a right generally vested in the authorities themselves. Finally, rights over people apply when the controllee is considered incapable of acting properly by himself: children and mentally deficient people, for example, are subjected to the control of parents or tutors who insist that their subordinates conform to values their caretakers expect them to share.

---

1 'Values' is used here in the Eastonian sense.

Rights over things fall into the wide range of appropriation. The right of property (which is here understood as excluding property rights over people, such as slavery) extends to all material goods considered to belong either to an individual or to a collectivity. It may be summed up as the right of exclusivity to a given object, in accordance with rules that may limit the time, the space, or some other aspect of the exclusivity enjoyed. The exercise of this right obliges others to keep out, or away, and thus implies negative control. Outsiders are forbidden access to the goods, and in so far as the rule is abided by, we may say that a control is being exerted.

A third type of right, which is more abstract and quite diversified, involves the circulation of signs and symbols. The right of censure – barring free access to ideas – is what is usually called to mind. But in fact this right is a great deal more inclusive. The right over the circulation of signs certainly involves a recognized prerogative to intervene in the diffusion of ideas and representations. No society accepts that anybody is entitled to express whatever crosses his mind. We are also quite familiar with patent rights and copyrights which preclude the use of some knowledge or the reproduction of signs whose exclusivity is recognized as vested in its proprietor. To this extent, rights to the circulation of signs and symbols may be likened to the right of property, but here control is over abstractions, especially the use to be derived from them. Furthermore, this same category of rights sees to the distribution of honours and titles and, more extensively, the distribution of status. Professional recognition is frequently founded on official acceptance of this privilege: physicians, lawyers, and engineers practise through a right formally granted to them after they have satisfied conditions laid down by those in control of granting such rights.

Finally, rights over signs also involve the right to establish, correct, overlook, or interpret rights – in other words, the right over rights.[2] In traditional societies, only the right to oversee the exercise and interpretation of rights exists. The introduction of new rights as such is not accepted although rights may be introduced surreptitiously, since in the long run judicial interpretation can affect the allocation and exercise of existing rights. In modern societies the right over the determination and abolition of rights, whatever their nature, is recognized in principle.

All the above instances illustrate rules directed at defending and legitimating rights which support controls. Apart from supporting controls, rules are also devised to forbid certain types of control. If rights are necessary to validate certain controls, they may also be used to invalidate others. Rules provide, as well, for what are called 'rights of action,' the claim to be freed from restrictions

2 What H.L.A. Hart (1967) calls secondary rules.

in the performance of some conduct.[3] Freedom rights are expressed in these terms.

Rules establish rights and their limits, together with the obligations that are their counterparts. The latter refer to compulsory submission to controls legitimated by rules. Rules determine the conditions of access to status (*who* is entitled to positions of control); they also define roles (*which* controls, among other actions, may be exercised from a given status). Who, for instance, may claim to be employers, and from their of employer what rights may they claim over those whose role designates them as employees? Rules reinforce the controls enjoyed by some roles to the detriment of others, even when they provide for counterpart controls. Some interests emerge better served than others. No rule may claim to be neutral, objective, or well-balanced. Those adopting the rules may think them neutral or well-balanced, but no measure exists to verify a hypothetical state of equilibrium. For example, the amount of control put in the hands of the consumer in his dealings with possible sellers depends upon a conception of strict duality or, more likely, comes in reference to other cultural aspects. Any attempt at balance will nonetheless amount to an approximation whose criteria rest on values which are relative by nature and also likely to change with time. This is why rules, which are normally designed to endure, easily outlast the interests that first saw to their inception, such that the originating interests may even eventually turn against the rules they have created.

Within the present framework, all rules put into practice in given social relations are looked at from an amoral point of view. There is no intention of determining to what extent the rules respect natural, democratic, or ethical principles. Of course, rights intrinsically involve a moral dimension; they correspond to the acceptance of values which legitimize courses of action and give rise to specific controls. I do not intend to make value judgments about rules or rights. They are accepted as facts of social life, with no intention of making comparisons with some hypothetical just or ideal life.

Rule making
Regulation involves the process leading to the establishment and enforcement of rules. It amounts, in other words, to the institution and implementation of rules in the conduct of controls within a given collectivity; in an Eastonian paraphrase, it could be summed up as the authoritative allocation of controls. Regulation provides for the imposition of new rules, as well as for the maintenance of existing ones.

Two aspects must be distinguished in order to bring out the different com-

---

3 D.D. Raphael (1967, 56) distinguishes between 'rights of action,' as understood here, and 'rights of recipience,' which rest on a claim to oblige others.

ponents at work. Regulation may be seen as proceeding in two steps: rule making and rule application.[4] Rule making establishes or modifies rules setting status, roles, or patterns. It determines who is entitled, under what conditions, to what function, and how that function is to be accomplished. Rule making sets rules in general or universalist terms, in the sense that it purports to fix conduct for categories of people. The rule may even single out a role which is one of a kind, for instance the functions of a king.[5] Whatever their scope, rules are understood to hold for at least a while. They are meant to last. Hence the necessity for some form of proclamation or diffusion.

Rule making unfolds in a variety of settings. The juristic tradition posits that it is accomplished by what is commonly called the legislature. This is certainly the case in some western countries, but 'executive' or 'governmental' decisions are of sufficient import to set rules in their own right or by delegation. The same applies to the judiciary: the 1954 judgment on race relations by the Supreme Court of the United States certainly set rules of the same character as legislative decisions. The discussion above draws on the experience of modern states; in mcre traditional settings, as in the Middle Ages, the judicial functions furnished incremental changes in the interpretation of customs which, in the long run, produced the same effect as rule making.

But rules remain of no consequence if they are not put into use. Governments may, for instance, postpone indefinitely the application of some rules: laws on combines are frequently ignored and sometimes put in abeyance, right from their inception. Rules may also be challenged and submitted to adjudication, which is part of rule application; court decisions can reinforce a rule, attenuate it, or invalidate it entirely. In sum, rule application furnishes a testing ground for the impact of rule making. It is geared towards direct intervention: from principles set by rule making, rule application outlines what specific actions fall under categories earlier established (at least analytically) in universal terms and ends up designating people and their obligations on an individual basis.

4 In this matter positions as well as traditions vary. The juristic schools may be categorized as the dualists, triadists, and quadrialists. Hans Kelsen emerges as the most convincing dualist, distinguishing between legislation (*legis latio*) and execution (*legis executio*). More common are the triadists who, following what is thought to be a system derived from Montesquieu, posit the legislative, executive, and judicial 'functions'; Almond and Powell, incidentally, have extended these 'functions' into a classical 'sextet.' Finally, some have differentiated the executive from the administrative 'function,' a more explicit function of governance being attributed to the former; widespread among some jurists, this tetramerous conception has found one adept in political science (Bergeron 1965).
5 The generality of rules becomes intricate at times, especially when, under the guise of universality, it is in fact directed at one or very few individuals.

Rule application

Rule application works by command, that is by summons to abide by a rule. It can be visualized as unfolding through an escalating process of steps, each of which is a bid to compliance. The first step towards enforcement of rules takes place in the day-to-day dealings of our lives. We are all involved, whether as controllers or controllees, in relationships that call for controls. Routine commercial transactions involve controls from both parties, sellers and buyers, who keep records of their transactions. Collectivities provide for the rights and duties of both sides. Command comes whenever one party makes a request which derives from his rights: a request for a receipt, a request to be furnished with information on the quality of products, and so forth. Most commands come from individuals who demand that their rights be respected, but they may also come through officials who act as spokesmen for a whole, whether the state, the tribe, the band, or a trade union.

Should the first bid fail, should, in other words, command be met by refusal to abide by the rule, recourse to enforcement will reach a further step, common to us all – the implication of authorities, that is, representatives of the collectivity who, through threat or bid towards the courts (adjudication), make more explicit the consequences of non-compliance. The right to wield a control is submitted to the collectivity and its officials for implementation. While strictly private in its first bid, the exercise of control takes on a public character when entrusted to official hands.

It was established in the first chapter that deprivation and ultimately force are parts of the control arrangement. The ultimate resort of force is mostly enshrined in the regulative process, specifically in rule application. No command, it has long been recognized, can function without the possibility of recourse to severe deprivation as a consequence of non-compliance. Command works through threat. Whenever it works through reward, it involves exchange, which will be discussed later, and not control. Sanctions are meaningful so long as they are integrated into the cultural setting. There is no such thing as the most severe sanction, in the abstract. Death appears to be the ultimate, but it is not *per se*. Excommunication from the church may be felt to be more depriving than death itself. Hunger strikes leading inexorably to death are used to support causes which are seen as surpassing the value of life itself.

Recourse to physical force serves as an excellent device to prevent people from following a given course of action. Its forbidding impact is obvious. Withdrawing people from circulation, by execution, imprisonment, or otherwise, is unrivalled as a means of obtaining immediate results in terms of preventing people from doing things. The long-term impact may turn out to be the spawning of a counter-movement, but that is another question. Physical force is not as efficient when it is used to serve positive purposes, to make people do things. It will work in many instances, but not in all.

The use of force to impose compliance is, then, conceived as the ultimate sanction, the last resort. It is not meant to be the common means of obtaining compliance, but is rather a possible recourse if a command is not complied with. There is no command without threat, and the threat of physical force is commonly understood as the ultimate means. The possibility of resorting to force stands as a reserve, a residual means in case of need. Its use has to be plausible. So, any command rests on it as a last recourse. The capacity to employ force remains fictitious to the extent that the use of force could hardly apply to all cases at the same time. The police and the army could not enforce the rules on a collectivity that decided to ignore all rules at once. Thus, the capacity rests on an implicit understanding that a general showdown will not happen, otherwise the system would go bankrupt, just as a run on all savings accounts could not satisfy all claimants.[6]

Those eager to reduce the import of force in the make-up of societies spontaneously emphasize the distinction to be made between rule infractions which result from deviancy or nonconformity and those that result from defiance of the regulative arrangement. The distinction offers the advantage of marking a neat differentiation between resorting to force to suppress crime and doing so to quell manifestations of insurgence. Societies in the throes of criminal violence are thus distinguished from those shaken by civil disorders. Such a differentiation ultimately rests upon an evaluation of the offenders' intentions, whether according to the analysts the offenders were acting against the rule or against the regulative device that instituted the rule and provided for its implementation. The offenders themselves are no better judges of their own demeanours or misdemeanours. As already stated, social events should not be interpreted through the agents' feelings. Britain's hot royal wedding summer of 1981, for instance, opened the way to a diversity of interpretations, from blatant 'thuggery' or hooliganism to full social disorder. What these interpretations have in common is an attempt to furnish answers by gauging the transgressors' states of mind.

Resorting to force is a social and official event. Whatever the cause, it puts to the test the collectivity's ability to impose commands derived from rules. Thus, the point of interest at this stage of the discussion remains the real capacity to sustain the whole network of controls which take place in the collectivity's name.

Regulation works as a compound of conditioning and control; it is partly conditioning and partly control. There is a great temptation to make a simple

6 Parsonians will have readily recognized aspects borrowed in this paragraph from the master, while also noticing the limited usage made of them (Parsons 1967, 264ff.).

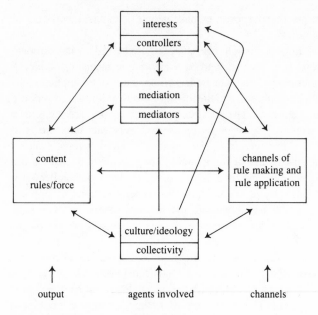

FIGURE 7 Structure of regulation

distinction establishing rule making as following a conditioning pattern and rule application as the controlling aspect. Reality is not that simple, as we shall see, for rule application too borrows from conditioning. The demarcation line is elsewhere, that is, between the universal character of conditioning which imparts general standards and the specific nature of control.

INTERESTS

Regulation displays a structure of functioning that shows many affinities with conditioning (Figure 7). It relies heavily on communication, but with a greater emphasis on mediation, and contributes to an output which is expected to lead to controls. Inasmuch as it belongs to conditioning, regulation reproduces a combination that exhibits many points in common with conditioning. Distinct from conditioning, though, is the extensive use of mediation which is basic to regulation's functioning. Regulation is fundamentally a process of representing interests that are defended and interpreted.

Any regulation is instituted by interests that see an advantage in setting it up. It aims at consolidating existing controls or providing new ones. In some instances, especially in small units, the interests may be collectively shared by all the members of the community. But even in face-to-face groups there emerges a leadership of some sort which contributes to providing greater controls to some within the group. Regulation must be seen as a product and an instrument for the achievement of purposes that lie outside the mechanism itself. At least in its foundation, regulation is conceived of as a device, not as an end in itself.

Parsons's functionalist approach dictated a goal-attainment function for the 'polity' of a community; like Durkheim he conceives of society as endowed with a sense of purpose. The introduction of cybernetic considerations (Deutsch 1966b; Easton, 1965) later contributed to consolidating a belief in the political system as the dynamic centre. Granted that Easton attributes a triggering effect to demands that put into action, so to speak, the whole system, the basic reference still remains the steering role devolved to authorities that convert demands into output. In fact, the classic feedback loop is intended for the authorities who are expected to adapt to the environment. However, attention is drawn to the authorities' ability to keep the system working, while the environment remains a secondary concern.[7] As a consequence, the feedback dynamics are kept outside the major field of observation. If there were to be an examination of feedback I feel that what should be looked at is the interests that are at the steering wheel of controls and that use regulation to adapt to the social environment at large. The authorities acting as mediators come to develop interests of their own and for the community they say they represent, but I see such a reality as secondary. Whenever a regulative device is set up, it comes first from interests which derive, or at least expect to derive, a pay-off from the use of the device.

MEDIATION

Regulators stand as the official mediators, and their role generates a chain of mediating processes. Official mediators do not always have decision- making powers; in some cases they merely act as rubber stamps or puppets. Nevertheless, they are indispensable in conferring collective recognition on a given set of controls. Rule making and rule application unfold in the name of an abstraction – the collectivity or the community. Whether among hunter-gatherers, tribal groups, or contemporary states, whether among small face-to-face groups, associations,

7 The biological import inherent to the systemic approach has often been underlined, but it is not the import itself that is to be criticized but rather its limited capacity for explanation in the present case.

firms, or political parties, rules are derived from a presumed right of intervention in the affairs of people designated as members of the unit in question. Regulation introduces the notion of roles designated to take regulators in charge, whether for a short while, intermittently, and with limited competences, as among hunter-gatherers and informal groups, or for longer periods and with a wider range of possible intervention. Monarchs who may concentrate the exercise of regulation in their own hands and express in their own name the making or application of rules, still do so as part of a given role which operates within an abstract entity that is often designated merely in terms of territory. Some pieces of land in Europe are known to have changed hands according to the fortunes of war without the people concerned feeling particularly alienated. Territories 'nationalized' since then would by no means lend themselves nowadays to the same treatment.

For purposes of clarity in the discussion, regulators can be set in a category of their own. For while they serve as mediators of the collectivity's presumed interests, they hold the privilege, or advantage, of being in control of certain stages in the channelling of rules-in-the-making. In this process, as we shall see, the work of the regulators themselves is more often than not mediated by an array of experts and bureaucrats.

Legitimacy: a serviceable concept?
These days, any extensive treatment of politics in general will more or less take for granted the notion of legitimacy. Usually the reference is incidental, since legitimacy is an accepted value. Contemporary classics usually still devote a few paragraphs to the notion, adding little to earlier formulations. The notion as it is understood today stems from the liberal tradition that originated with *monarcho-maques* and other authors of the sixteenth century, established its foundations with Locke, and has pursued its course to the present day with the seminal impulse of Max Weber. Who is not familiar with Weber's triad? Underlying the concept of legitimacy stands the cherished idea of consent, which is often opposed as the alternative to naked coercion; consent endows a dignity on those who submit. Weber points out that leaders will make claims to legitimacy, but the realization of such claims rests in the hands of their followers, who must give their agreement. Legitimacy corresponds to a belief on the part of the followers, a voluntary compliance in conformity with Weber's comprehensive perspective of sociology. Legitimacy is meant to account for the population's motivation. It amounts to a consensual perception of regulation, an implicit form of contract entered into within a traditional, charismatic, or legal-rational frame of mind. In fact, it is no more than an analytic device to keep out of the picture factors that in reality are here to stay: force, coercion, fear, opportunism, defensive conformity and the like. The Weberian approach is a way of sounding out the followers' dispositions in the abstract, without other considerations, and from a liberal perspective on

)ciety.[8] In Weber's mind 'domination' is a composite of coercion, conformity,
nd legitimacy, the latter being an aspect that is extractable from the rest.

Most authors, Weber included, recognize the part played by elements that
ondition people to compliance. Compliance under duress is considered invalid by
ome but acceptable by others, the Hobbesian fear of violent death being the
ltimate illustration. The list is standard: obedience may be obtained through fear
f sanctions (including death), 'manipulated' minds, effects of expediencies,
nreflective habituation, custom, apathy, indifference, conformity with the
nvironment, unconscious socialization, opportunism, self-interest, deliberate
noice, and so on (Bryce 1901, 6ff.; Weber 1968, I 312; Laski 1957, vii; Easton
965, 285; Partridge 1971, 32ff.). The interest of authorities in converting force
nto consent has long been recognized. The argument is drawn from the rationale
nat authority cannot stand on violence alone.[9]

Notwithstanding moral connotations, many scholars consider legitimacy as
serviceable concept, despite problems raised in circumscribing it in reality.
arsons sets it as a condition for his conception of the exercise of power, while
aston puts it to use as a basic component of support.

I consider legitimacy solely as a construct designed to record some sort of
dhesion to authority. Does it constitute, under these conditions, a satisfactory
evice for analysis? It should be borne in mind that, as such, legitimacy can only
e posited, never proved beyond any doubt for any length of time. Referenda are
ften thought of as the perfect means of expressing legitimacy, especially when
upport is strong. Referenda are consultations of momentous effect, but of
nomentary value. Who can assess their worth even when they take place under
hat some would call the best of conditions? And what is their weight as time goes
y? Legitimacy works from a presumption on the part of the observer that, left to
nemselves, that is without any constraint, the constituents would adhere to the
node of authority they are at present submitted to. Some authors, like David
aston, incorporate legitimacy with other factors of compliance: apart from fear of
orce, he mentions habit and expediency. He insists, with reason, that whether the
asis for acceptance is any of these, including legitimacy, is irrelevant. Practice
roduces a combination of these elements, and of others as well (1965, 285). In
aston's mind, it still remains possible to consider legitimacy, on its own, as a
omponent of 'support.'

'Weber used the concept of legitimacy primarily to focus upon the emergence of rational-legal
orders of domination, particularly bureaucratic, and upon rational systems of law emerging out
of traditional ... and charismatic regimes' (Bensman 1979, 45).
J.-J. Rousseau sums it up well in his *Contral social*: 'Le plus fort n'est jamais assez fort pour être
toujours le maître, s'il ne transforme sa force en droit, et l'obéissance en devoir' (book I, ch. 3;
'The strongest is never strong enough to be master all the time, if he does not convert force into
right, and obedience into duty').

Obedience should be understood as part of the structure of regulation which includes sets of conditions, not merely dual entities formally opposed in a rationalist dialectic of ruler and ruled. Reality is not served by analytic reductions that purport to compress it into a contract-like organization or legitimation of society: the rulers on one side operating, under fictional conditions, with a sort of mandate from their followers on the other side. All these constructions have as their purpose to legitimate or to confer a status of acceptability on present or future arrangements. Whether derived from the classics, along the lines of Hobbes, Locke, or Rousseau, or taken from more contemporary proponents, the contract still ends up with a moral adjustment to the rude reality of regulation. Compliance should therefore be contemplated as a social product which emerges in conjunction with other parts of the structure itself. All components have to be discussed separately for analytical purposes and yet still kept in constant relationship with the whole.

Legitimacy is of legal import and should remain so. It serves as an abstraction to validate a right to regulate. Any regulation derives from a *raison d'être* which supersedes the exercise of the regulation. Intervening in the name of a collectivity requires a principle of authority: the wish or the impersonation of the gods, natural law, the divine rights of kings, the expression of the will of the majority, or some utilitarian or supernatural purpose. This principle endows the role with the necessary aura of respectability, if some are to speak for the whole. Authority will in some instances be confined to ruling on feuds like the Nuers' 'Leopard-skin chief' (Evans-Pritchard 1947), or to the leadership so common among the bushmen. In other instances, the field of authority's control will be elaborated to the point of conferring on authority an abstract identity. Such is the case for the state, which acts as a juridical device contrived to depersonalize the exercise of authority to the point of dissociating it from the collectivity it is expected to rule. The state can be contemplated as an abstract entity in whose name institutions or structures are established to rule over a collectivity or a community within the bounds of a given territory. In this perspective, institutions should not be confused with the state, nor should the collectivity or the territory. All are subjected to a fictitious entity, the state, which is put to work as the fountain of authority. Even when authority is more or less identified with a person and confined, as in restricted groups, to a narrow field of intervention, its principle remains as an abstract reality permitting the exercise of regulation; it stands as the ultimate legitimating value.

Regulators' interests

The principle of authority, from which the right to regulate derives in the abstract, should be considered as a social product, and not as a pre-existing idea designed to preside over the ruling of given collectivities. As already mentioned, the principle varies depending upon the size of the collectivity, the times, and the place. But in all cases it endows regulation with a character of universality within the collectivity whose existence it is intended to confirm: the fragmentary nature of interests is meant to be ignored in favour of supposedly common purposes. However, even in what are called interest groups or pressure groups, inner interests are at work behind the promotion of the common cause. In the same fashion as communities are furthered by the socialization and mobilization of interests, the introduction and maintenance of regulation serve a number of interests.

The right to regulate within a given collectivity, according to a given set of rules and by given individuals, is a product of culture and ideology. Claims to legitimacy are common currency; they are part of the efforts engaged in by rulers. Charles E. Merriam coined the tandem of the '*credenda* and *miranda* of power' – authorities surrounding themselves with a host of artefacts to be believed in and admired (1950, 102). Hence the necessity for rulers to furnish followers with symbols to impress and signs to rationalize their status. The demonstration is not devoid of cynicism about what is commonly called 'politics.' But in fact the rationalization of status takes place within a framework of mobilization and socialization which transcends the strict frontiers of a leader-follower relationship. The emergence of regulation is to be considered a social event. It permeates the life of all constituted groups while at the same time confirming the access of some interests to positions of control – control over resources as well as control over regulative devices.

'Rulers' do not appear as from a Jack-in-the-box; it may at least be hypothesized that they cannot make it by themselves. All of them need followers who share the same set of values or interests.[10] Abrupt changes of personnel seldom mean changes in the principles of authority and in the rules of the game; *putsches* and *coups d'état* are routine in some countries. The stability or instability of the controllers of regulation is of limited interest as such. Changes implying major modifications in norms and roles, however, are more significant, as well as major modifications in the instruments used for the consolidation of norms and roles. Mobilization and socialization are constantly in process. The making of

---

10 David Hume expresses the same idea in other terms which are more intimately linked with the institution of government and which refer to consent: 'It is ... on opinion only that government is founded; and this maxim extends to the most despotic and most military governments, as well as the most free and most popular. The solan of Egypt, or the Emperor of Rome, might drive his harmless subjects, like brute beasts, against their sentiments and inclination. But he must, at least, have led his *mamalukes* or *proetorian bands*, like men, by their opinion' (1854, 28).

regulators, as well as their maintenance at the wheel, is the work of conditioning coupled with control, which, like most controls, engages the use of force as an ultimate means of achieving compliance. The establishment of an order of regulation, commonly called a régime, will require a massive investment in terms of mobilization to put it to work and to keep it working. Afterwards, a process of socialization takes over maintenance.

Representation: the functional approach

Up to this point in the discussion regulators have been by and large treated as representatives of the whole, mediators whose position is due to a combination of interests in favour of the regulating device, regulation legitimizing controls and, in so doing, reinforcing the controllers' position. But regulation should be understood as basically a phenomenon of mediation and representation for the promotion of diverse interests.

For the last two decades, the most common approach to representation (although the actual term is not necessarily used) has been the functional approach. Its most valuable contribution has probably been of a negative nature. The functionalist school may be thanked for having debunked the tradition, of institutional character, which long plagued the discipline with unfruitful attempts to propose typologies for the study of political parties and pressure groups. Yet the substantialist school is not dead; recent studies still long for a definition of a political party (Sartori 1976, 58ff.). Besides, it is thought possible to start from the notion of party and thereafter proceed to a multi-functional prospective, by asking oneself what functions a party fulfils. Roy C. Macridis (1967, 17) has provided a list of those functions most commonly proposed in the field: representation, conversion, aggregation, integration, persuasion, recruitment, and so forth. It is obvious from this series that the concept of function is given a variety of meanings. In some instances the suggested functions have connotations of contributions to a whole, whereas in others the functions amount to mere effects. With its more systemic objective, Almond and Powell's classic *Comparative Politics* has avoided too 'structural' a mode of explanation in favour of a processual approach. Demands are seen in logical succession, proceeding along a continuum from interest articulation and aggregation to mediating stages of decision making. Within this processual approach, 'structures' are sought *after* identification of the process itself, and not the other way around, as is still done at times. Attention centres on actions considered significant within 'structures.'

Representation qua mediation

Considering processes instead of institutions is already a step in the right direction. But representation as such needs further investigation. Representing interests or, more precisely, acting in the name of interests amounts to more than articulating or aggregating demands; it means expressing what is or is not advantageous to these interests. It is a role of mediation of a specific nature involving the determination of purposes and their degree of possible achievement by agencies who act as mandators – whether or not they have a mandate in reality. This role usually implies mobilization in two directions: towards the interests themselves as well as towards the outside, the outside being the collectivity and the regulators.

Representation extends from the least formal forms of leadership to the most organized ones. We are all familiar with actions undertaken towards administrations by representatives of a group: students dissatisfied with a teacher or property owners angered over increases in tax rates or evaluations. In some instances the whole group may be present, but usually delegates represent the group. With or without officials to represent it, the group is bound to have been activated from within, in which case leaders have emerged to mobilize and activate the group. A mob is seldom a mob. Revolutions as well as city riots are galvanized by representatives who act as inspired leaders, and who may well oppose each other, diverge, or coalesce. The French revolution, to take one example, unfolds as a series of strategies amongst rival representative groups stimulating their own troops and trying to impose their views upon outsiders.[11] In fact, almost any demonstration exhibits different levels of representation. Heading the march are often the leaders who have emerged as spokesmen; they act, whether they have been designated formally or not, as the demonstrators' representatives. But the demonstrators themselves usually serve as spokesmen for others of their condition, or whose condition they represent, for selfom are all who share the same interests present at these gatherings. Demonstrations are commonly left to the few, even if they look numerous – in other words, the vanguard.

Whereas they may have been mandated one way or another to do so, representatives may also take it upon themselves to defend interests that have not yet been expressed formally. They will pose as spokesmen, waiting for more support afterward. Trade unions, especially in their beginnings, act with the official expectation of rallying worker backing in the future.

11 Neil J. Smelser (1963) establishes a clear distinction between collective and institutionalized behaviour, the former preceding and transcending the latter. I do not see, at least for the time being and within the present framework, the necessity for this distinction, for I am more interested in the mediating role of representation, whether formally organized or not, and in its connection with the whole, than in the conduct of movements as autonomous in their own dynamics. Any social movement is more or less represented and organized at any stage of its development; it is a question of degree.

Organized mediation

Although representation may be transient or intermittent, it is also amenable to organizations of great stability in time. Trade unions are among the best examples of mediation of interests, since they are directed at the controllers – the employers – as well as at regulators in general. The other side, through chambers of commerce and other more specialized associations, also holds its own, but in a more dispersed fashion, many of its members remaining loyal to their own specific organizations.

Organization is meant to provide for efficiency and expertise in representation. At the same time, it introduces new devices of mediation: speaking in the name of a given set of interests becomes a whole enterprise and, in so doing, opens an arena for conditioning and conflict for control of policies and strategies, not to speak of the offices to fill within these units. Any organization takes the form of arenas where activities are negotiated and fought out, some agents enjoying a better position for managing uncertainty than others (Crozier 1964).[12] Scholars in the field are familiar with these conflicts where expert is pitted against bureaucrat, staff against line – the former wielding control through information, the latter through hierarchy. In passing, the term 'bureaucracy' should be here understood as neutral; it identifies, as far it can, the administrative aspects of organizations, which amount to a device contrived to look after routine tasks and made up of a hierarchy of roles, ranks, procedures, limited authority of office, and so forth (Blau and Scott 1963, 8; Perrow 1972, 5). The bureaucratic phenomenon is interesting because of its impact on final output: it may progressively lead, in some organizations, to the displacement of goals in the bureaucrats' favour (Merton 1951, 155).

If bureaucracy is liable to be heavy in some representative units, such as trade unions, the impact of expertise is likely to be prominent in most of them. The prominence of experts accounts for a widespread propensity for organizations, whether private or public, to resort to the knowledge of specialists to determine the main guidelines of policies – a phenomenon sometimes dubbed technostructure or technocracy. This tendency is likely to produce a widening gap between the administrations and their members: shareholders being estranged from the executive board, and workers feeling aloof from their union leaders. This trend was noticed long ago in mediating groups. Robert Michels's 'iron law of oligarchy' is familiar to most students in the field. Even though his discussion was specific to the situation of socialist parties in Germany at the beginning of the century, some elements of his rationale are still worth considering.[13] Whenever an

12 Graeme Salaman's remark is quite apropos: 'Organisations are, essentially, structures of control. The question is how is control exercised, by whom and for what purpose' (1979, 107).
13 His considerations on the 'incompetence of the masses' may be put aside.

association or a group of some sort designates a number of persons to devote themselves, on a full-time basis, to the management of their organization, there is likely to emerge a set of leaders who, from the position they hold in the organization, impose their views on the grass roots: their superiority derives from the higher degree of information they can muster and retain, and from their formal network of communication with the membership that gives them a better vantage point. Interests specific to the leaders are thus bound to develop, the leaders perpetuating and enlarging their control through co-optation. There are, of course, exceptions that are worth mentioning, but such exceptions should be analysed from a global perspective that would probably explain these cases of control dispersion. The 'stratarchy' noted by Samuel J. Eldersveld (1964) in the American political parties falls into this category: if controls, as is shown, are diffused along layers or echelons of authority called 'strata commands,' it is most appropriate to reset the phenomenon into its own structure of explanation. Eldersveld's thesis was aimed at cutting the theory of élite control down to size. A fuller perspective which takes the rules of the game in general more into account would probably have revealed a more circumscribed field of application for Eldersveld's stratarchy. So, whatever the distribution of controls within these groups, whether they are centralized or widely dispersed, organizations emerge as combat grounds for the maintenance or extension of controls.

As a relation of mediation, representation readily produces a sense of responsibility and purpose for those leading the process. As regulators themselves, whatever the size or goals of the groups subjected to them, leaders tend to develop ends for the benefit of the whole as such, which at times may turn out to be of very limited benefit to the individual constituents and only have significance for the collectivity as a whole. It is in this line of thought that some propound the idea of a national interest being elaborated for itself, and not for the sake of any segments of society (Krasner 1978). It might be postulated that the more organized a representative device becomes, the heavier the bureaucratic and technocratic weight is likely to be and, hence, the greater the autonomy we can expect the bureaucracy or technocracy to have. The interplay between bureaucrats and politicians in the elaboration of policies would show a merging tendency growing at the top (Aberdach, Putnam and Rockman 1981, 209ff). These public officials, it is argued (Nordlinger 1981), develop from their own expertise and experience and conception of what is best suited for specific groups in society or for society as a whole. Conditioned to this governmental outlook, decisionmakers are less likely to be responsive to public appreciation. Likewise, monarchs, as representatives of their kingdoms' interests, came to develop strong enmities with their dukes or barons whose interests were often divisive.

Mediators' interests

Mediation is part and parcel of regulation, which is impossible without it. There is always a need for somebody to represent the wishes and interests of the whole, whereas segmentary interests will also produce representatives to defend their causes. Introducing representation thus affects the expression of interest management. Regulators, the first managers of representation, do not always respond to the interests that set them up. Representatives, as mediators in direct relationship with regulators, also add a dimension of complexity. The multiplication of mediating relations through administrations, associations, parties, and regulatory bureaucracies entails the cropping up of interests particular to the mediators as a whole. For apart from defending others' interests, which they may also share in some cases, representatives are almost always bound, at the same time, to push forward their own interests as mediators, mistaking one for the other. The process of mediation is conducive to the building up of mediating interests which later strive for survival and expansion. Such a trend has already been diagnosed in bureaucracies, providing in France for the consolidation of state-created élites which are expected to fill the major executive institutions, the 'grands corps de l'Etat' (Suleiman 1978). But the trend can be found in most mediating situations. Unless the representation is circumscribed, especially as to length of tenure and number of interventions, it is likely to turn into a fairly permanent device of mediation. Representatives seldom claim on their own initiative that their usefulness is over; in their minds there is always a job to finish or to continue. The Soviet Communist Party serves as a good illustration of a supposedly temporary representation which is not on the point of ceasing, since the communist stage which was expected to spell the end of it has had to be postponed indefinitely.

History provides many examples where the mediating function of regulation is deeply ingrained with interests that are associated with the role. In days gone by, the monarchs' interests were closely linked to their positions, from which privileges and advantages were derived. This meant, at times, significant withdrawals from the state's coffers. The splendour of Versailles exemplifies an extreme which nonetheless had the effect of lessening the monarchy's real influence in favour of the more state-oriented views of certain commoners.

The next chapter will enlarge upon the extent to which mediation may become the main role to be played by a given class in society. But mediation is first and foremost a mode of defending interests for a given set of authorities.

CHANNELS

Rules of the game

Any regulative device implies formal rules for access to the status of regulator. The function may be concentrated in a single agent, but it usually provides for a distribution of roles set up with limitations on the control the holders of the role may exercise in the rule-making and rule-application process. The rules of the game, so to speak, may in some cases, such as in some hunters' bands and associations, allow all members of the collectivity a say.

The rules of the game trigger a dynamics of their own comprised of both cultural and ideological traits. Once established, the rules are expected to channel and select demands which come from the interests that set them up. For instance, liberal institutions were thought of, in the beginning, in terms of rights held by property owners or people sufficiently well off to vote 'responsibly.' However, in the long run they turned out to favour a much wider audience, at least so far as voting is concerned. When they are set, the rules of the game are never innocent or objective. But most of the time rules outlast the interests they were made to benefit, and they often end up working counter to the originating interests. As a matter of fact, the rules of the game are often the result of compromises arrived at after negotiations between divergent interests. Federalism is a good example of a bargaining product which can turn out, in some cases, to run contrary to the wishes of its founders, who often get more than they bargained for. The Canadian 'constitution' of 1867 is a good illustration; it provided the provinces with a sphere of responsibility that did not exceed by much the competences traditionally vested in municipalities: roads, welfare, education, and so on. And to help finance these items, the constitution restricted provincial fiscal competence to direct taxation on income and property, a type of taxation which at the time was unpopular and in limited use. Later history revealed the more than strictly civic character of such competences and fiscal capacities. If the founders had realized this, they would probably not have placed so much power in the hands of the provinces.

Scholars of political institutions are familiar with the comparison constantly made between the American system of government and the British parliamentary system. From Tocqueville to Laski through Bryce, the American institutions have been examined in the light of systems from abroad. It is unnecessary to take up these learned considerations once again. Suffice it to notice in passing the extent to which regulators become accessible or vulnerable to pressures depending upon the rules of the game. Actions undertaken to influence deputies will have very different effects depending upon the degree of autonomy accorded the deputies. Members of Congress are important targets for pressure groups, while in the parliamentary system it is cabinet members who are the objects of pressure tactics.

Rules dictating the selection of candidates for regulating functions are interesting to compare. Some involve multistep procedures starting with primaries, while others involve much less. The French system seems the least costly and the most open to a wide variety of candidacies for the presidency.

The Canadian system for designating party leaders betrays in its effects the importation of a procedure alien to the parliamentary dynamics. In this system, the leader is elected at a convention by delegates selected at local levels (for the most part) who are called upon to determine who is best fitted to lead the members of Parliament on a personal basis, as well as the most capable of winning the next election. This mode of selection is conducive to the election of leaders with strong momentary charisma, but it also leads to tensions between the victor and his vanquished colleagues. Long, open, and public campaigns certainly leave indelible scars; hence the almost inevitable series of resignations or dismissals that follow leadership campaigns and take their toll in terms of public image and internal cohesion. Conventions are thus best suited to candidates who will not be forced to work together afterwards. In Britain, by contrast, the selection process has for some time been limited to a period of a fortnight, and only the members of the Commons have a say.[14]

These examples, drawn from different national traditions, are only intended to illustrate that procedures whose effects can hardly be fully foreseen before they are put into use may be significant later on.

The effects of electoral methods on the emergence of parties, their numbers, and their types of platform have been widely discussed in the past. Studies comparing proportional representation with the simple-majority single ballot system have come to the conclusion that the former is more likely to result in a multiplicicity of parties which will, in turn, be prone to develop elaborate programs; the simple-majority single ballot system, on the other hand, seems to favour, at least at the constituency level, two parties competing on pragmatic issues (Katz 1980, 40ff., 115ff.).

Arenas

Rule making provides for channels: some of the channels are formal, set as official rules of the game; others are consequences or adaptations of the former. Rule making follows processes of representation which unfold in a state of conflictual conditioning. Mobilization is served by mediators who, acting in the name of interests, try to convince regulators of the legitimacy of their requests. Ideology works at its best here, and rule making supplies selected channels for its expression.

Channels determine the steps to be followed and thus have an effect on the arenas of debate. Arenas may be considered as instrumental loci where mobilization over issues has a bearing on whether or not these issues are converted

---

14 Recent development within the Liberal Party and later in Labour have led to 'democratic' selection by party conferences, with the results that might be expected.

into rules. An institutional or juridical approach usually concentrates solely on aspects provided for by the rules. The notion of arena extends the field of application to any stage where the outcome of mobilization has an impact on decisions made through regulation. Official rules may invest in only one person the capacity to decide on some or all occasions; this capacity will nonetheless give way to mobilizing steps not formally provided for by these rules, should it be only advice lavished on the person in authority. Seldom are arenas entirely confined to the regulating apparatus. Usually, a discussion which takes place within its confines undergoes a spillover effect, with interests prolonging the discussion outside the confines of the regulating apparatus. Debate spreads to the press or elsewhere. The British system of governmental consultation with representative groups offers a good example of covert discussions leading to rule making (Stewart 1958; Finer 1966). It works through advisory committees where both parties, government agents and representatives of specific interests (agriculture being a privileged interest), exchange information and views conducive to the elaboration of rules affecting the interests in question. The arena breaks down and becomes more open when representatives are unable to meet their constituents' expectations or when, failure having been registered at the covert level, open campaigns and parliamentary pressures signal the impasse. A clientelist mode of functioning develops when bureaucratic agencies come to consider specific groups as natural representatives of given sectors of activities and provide for these privileged channels of access (LaPalombara 1964, 258–60).

Corporatism (Schmitter 1974; Panitch 1980) offers a similar approach towards the regulation of conflicts, but by acting along a more institutionalized mode of consultation. Specific associations are granted monopolies of interest representation in given fields of activity, thus, often instituing official hierarchies within associations, imposing compulsory membership to the *de facto* exclusion of other forms of representation, and introducing a channel for the implementation of public policies (Schmitter 1982, 260). In other words, the regulatory rules of corporatism provide for controls vested into privileged groups over resources (in terms of subsidies and other facilities), representation (areas of decisions), organisation (relationship with members) and channels of decision-making (rule making and rule application) (Offe 1981, 137). The system may adopt different forms. The 'hegemony' enjoyed by the FNSEA (Fédération nationale des Syndicats d'Exploitants agricoles) in France in the sixties and seventies is a good example of sectorial corporatism whereby the Federation held exclusive access to decision centres, grants and devolved authority (Keeler 1981, 188).

Another illustration of covert arena is furnished by the Dutch mode of accommodation, as described by Arend Lijphart (1968), where this time political parties come out as the locus of compromise within an otherwise non-consensual society. 'Summit diplomacy' among leaders of different parties acts as the ultimate, albeit covert, arena, followed by formal parliamentary approval.

At the other extreme, open arenas in the press or in public demonstrations may well sound the knell for any future mobilization on a particular issue at official levels by the House of Commons or Congress. Some arenas will be perceived as decisive enough to anticipate the decisions of following arenas: the election results of 1945 which brought the Labour Party to power after a campaign over massive nationalization meant that massive nationalization was on the way. Interestingly enough, such conclusions can hardly be drawn from election results in the United States at any time, voting being more the expression of tendencies than of actual commitments.

Access to channels and, in some cases, the faculty of imposing an arena upon others stand out as two important aspects of representation and mobilization. The right of access depends upon the acknowledgment of certain agents as representatives of given interests. The mass media will, in some instances, contribute to the accreditation of some movements as more representative than others and of some people as their leaders. In this way, specific groups obtain a form of recognition, to the exclusion of other groups, and some of their leaders become representatives of the whole movement from a newsmaking perspective (Gitlin 1980, 128ff.). In this dynamic, movements may be seen as being at the mercy of the media, who are in a position to make and unmake them, sanctioning some form of leadership in conformity with media norms, but not necessarily the leadership desired by the rank and file of the movement.[15]

Regulators are greatly concerned with recognizing some group representatives as opposed to others. In the example mentioned above of the British operation of advisory committees, accreditation or non-accreditation makes or breaks the mediating capacity of an agency. Unrecognized entities are reduced to mobilization from the outside. The same applies to interests – some are permitted to express views and be listened to in the different rule-making committees of legislatures and some are not. Throughout the process of representation, some issues will be 'organized into' the regulating arenas while others will be 'organized out,' to adopt E.E. Schattschneider's well-known conception (1960, 71).

Mediating channels introduce a bias into the regulating structure as any rules of the game will, whatever the context. Some interests are bound to be better catered to and some representatives to find more welcoming accesses than others. The setting of arenas opens the door to some organized interests and closes it in the face of others. Those already in control of procedures will readily select those issues

15 The effect of mass media coverage may also be to inflate membership in a direction unforeseen and unwanted by the original group.

they consider worth debating, and will sidetrack others. The bias, for there always is one (and this should not be taken pejoratively), is to be found in the channels of regulation as well as in their management.

Regulating channels do not only affect the expression and representation of interests; they themselves also have a bearing on the capacity of agents to achieve their goals. American institutions are interesting in this respect since they show a multiplicity of possible stumbling-blocks. The federal system, merged into a device of checks and balances, offers a good illustration of a system conceived to hold up, rather than hasten, any proposed intervention. Rule making, from the liberal perspective of its founders, is strewn with conditions that render it precarious in itself. In principle, minorities are likely to be well served by attempts to curb different majorities. In turn, these majorities turn out to be volatile aggregations of minorities (Dahl 1967). Being the product of multiple bargaining arenas, rules are liable to inconsistencies which are revealed once the rules are applied. The introduction of whole programs necessitating a series of legislative measures, like for instance a social welfare plan, is bound to be dispersed into 'log-rolled' bills exhibiting little consistency as a whole. The parliamentary system, on the other hand, is better suited to the production of consistent regulation. Both systems illustrate the built-in effects of channels on rules and, indirectly, on controls. In sum, channels, like the official rules of the game, are never innocent, objective, or neutral.

Regulation: a conflictual process
Arenas are meeting places or, more generally, channels for the process of mobilization which triggers any rule making. This process leads inevitably to conflict unless the whole collectivity, having been properly conditioned, agrees with the change or refrains from any countermove. Controls over conditioning itself, or over means of access to the arenas, often account for lack of open resentment to new controls which are introduced through regulation.

Until now the discussion has revolved mainly around the phenomenon of control, which, supported by conditioning and regulation, is always apparent in all collectivities. Already noted when dealing with mobilization – although merely in passing – conflict arises with greater intensity when it is attuned to regulation, of which it is part and parcel. Mobilization, which operates in conflictual situations, reaches its fullest expression whenever it stretches its action to the regulating apparatus. In such cases it battles for or against the introduction of new controls or the suppression of existing ones.

Many definitions of conflict have been furnished in the past (Fink 1968), but in the present discussion the concept almost flows from previous developments; conflict is a social interaction derived from the insupportability of a control, either present or future. It occurs whenever there is a refusal to accept any particular control, a control already in operation or one about to be introduced. To a large extent, the conflict originates with dissenting controllees. Conflict is in many instances the counterpart of controls which stand as the causes, and also as the effects, of conflicts (Caplow 1968, 16).

Any student of conflict is familiar with the notion of scarcity with which it is usually associated. As a social event[16] conflict has scarcity for a condition, as does economics. Whereas the economist takes scarcity as a given, the sociologist will inquire into its significance – for scarcity, to be of any use, must be interpreted. Needs, wants, and desires have meaning, in terms of the present discussion, when they are construed as social products. Hunger, for instance, will give rise to collective discontent in some societies and none in others. Controls, conditioning, and regulation stimulate, permit, or forbid the expression of some desires. Scarcity in one country is plenty in another, as we are accustomed to hearing. It is more interesting to analyse scarcity in terms of the whole structure, and not as an isolated fact.

In a conflict, the contending parties are ready to forsake scarce resources they already control in order to acqurie more of these resources, or resources of some other nature. Those that already have easy access to resources are likely to use them in order to stabilize their position or improve it. This activity implies costs and risks. If information is perfect, as in the liberal model of economics, there is no room for conflict, since all parties know the issue in advance.[17] Uncertainty is inherent in conflict which evolves through a process of exchange of signs or messages that are meant to fill in the lack of information and show superiority in obtaining coveted resources. The information furnished is supposed to impart either that there is worse to come or that the conditions for achieving the goal are fulfilled, such as the results of a vote on a bill in a legislature. Conflicts are prone to inflations of signs and thus are hard to understand as a whole, because so many actions take place at the same time. The French revolution is an excellent illustration: the decade from the General Estates and storming of the Bastille of 1789 to the 18th Brumaire is filled with a plethora of sign exchanges open to a variety of probable interpretations.

Considerations provided by the theory of games are welcome here, for they typify positions whose rationales can be, at least in part, explained from the logic

16 Some conflicts derive from psychological clashes between incompatible personalities, or from unilateral initiatives undertaken by naturally aggressive persons. Scarcity is of little use in explaining the origins of such conflicts.
17 A party will fight a lost cause when the struggle is valued for itself – the 'better dead than red' of the fifties, the last-ditch struggle, or martyrdom are examples – or for its consequences: some causes need martyrs.

of situations, be it the classic prisoners' dilemma or other situations. The same applies to the logic governing the formation of coalitions (Riker 1962; Caplow 1968) or the strategy developed by political parties in given circumstances (Downs 1957). Mancur Olson's work *The Logic of Collective Action* formalizes the contradiction that exists between individuals' rational self-interests and the achievement of common goods. Following an economic approach, the model relies on the actors' strictly rational mode of behaviour. The case is one of perfect rationality whereby individuals logically stay aloof of collective endeavours since such activities would imply for each one taken individually higher costs as compared with total inaction. All I can say from my perspective is that the better a culture abides by the rules of enlightened individualism, the closer it is likely to get to the behaviour exemplified by this model. Again, Olson's argument must be situated within the bounds of a specific culture. These partial models certainly have much to add, especially when the aspects considered as givens are reinterpreted as part of the whole structure of regulation. Preferences, for instance, stand by themselves in economic reasoning, whereas from our point of view they have to be integrated with the structure to have any meaning.

It is well understood that the elaboration of rules which lead to success falls into a prescriptive type of reasoning. It thus falls outside our field of observation, our interest being focused on what people actually do, rather than on what they ought to do to be efficient. But should some be more astute as social beings than others, and have developed this quality, we cannot ignore it, because then their propensity towards efficiency does not depend upon mere chance. F.G. Bailey's distinction between pragmatic and normative rules describes the difference between those rules followed in order to win, and those followed in order to conform to ethical imperatives (1969, 4). The latter respond to personal as well as cultural standards. Although Bailey does not say so, it should also be borne in mind that pragmatic rules do not come out of the blue: some cultures develop this sense of strategic efficiency more than others. The Florentine environment of Machiavelli is no mere coincidence. When sociologically analysed, both types of rules, pragmatic and normative, are largely the effect of the community's culture on the unfolding of rule making.

Political styles and personal preferences of individual regulators are likely to vary depending upon the elbow room provided by the rules of the game. But even dictators need a following, and no successful experience of authoritarianism happens without a favourable social environment. Indeed there remains a part played by personal factors, and they may be of great weight at times in accelerating or slowing down certain mobilizing movements. Nonetheless the present perspective aims at extracting the social factors in collective actions including the social circumstances of leaders' emergence.

REGULATED COLLECTIVITY

Regulation is undertaken for a collectivity, and in its name. Not all collectivities need to be capped with a rule-making device, but most do in one way or another, for otherwise controls will hardly be respected. In especially large collectivities, such as countries in the way they are thought of today, borders are usually the result of wars and strife. Regulation may also apply to a collectivity composed of parts of other communities. Belgium, for instance, is composed of two ethnic entities whose unity is, or was, to be found in aspects other than ethnicity. In the past, force has succeeded in some cases, like the Roman Empire and the Islamic conquests, whereas in others it has failed. The Chinese, however, even managed to assimilate their Mongol and Manchu rulers. Systematic displacements of population may well lead to problems in the long run: for example, the Scots in Northern Ireland or the blacks in the United States.

With this reality in mind, David Easton insists upon a distinction between what he calls the 'political community' and the 'social community,' the former being more restrictive than the latter since it is supposed to include only those bound by a 'political division of labour' (1965, 177, 184ff.). The distinction is interesting; it is easy to replace 'political' with another term and talk about a 'regulated collectivity' and a 'regulative division of labour.' The only weakness which must be underlined is the way that 'political community' works in terms that translate into adhesion on the part of its members. His starting point is representative of the liberal tradition which counts first on the collectivity in order to elaborate afterwards on the whole mechanism of regulation. A sense of belonging induces people to recognize themselves as part of the regulated community: 'We are subjects of the king' or 'We are the citizens of this democracy' (Easton 1965, 185) serve as expressions underlining what others would call a 'sense of identity' (Verba 1965). There is, right from the start, a commitment, strong or weak, to the 'political system.'[18] Solidarity and loyalty, as in the liberal classics, stand first in the discussion.

The discussion takes another tack when one adopts the more realistic approach of postulating that the community was first told '*You* are subjects of the king' or '*You* are the citizens of this democracy,' exactly as the Americans were told by their delegates that henceforth they should be that 'we' to be found in the introductory sentence of their constitution. A good number of associations are founded on these premises: a mobilizing minority institutes itself as representative of given interests. The more embracing a group is to be the more likely, we may

18 The same rationale is followed by Parsons's notion of commitment to values as a generalized symbolic medium for the activation of obligations (1969, 448).

presume, that it will be processed along these lines. So, there is, first, a presumption against the consensual approach which banks on a form of assent. This does not necessarily lead to the espousal of the conflictual approach. Political sociology is too prone to impose a single choice: one is expected to side either with the consensualists, Parsons et al., or with the conflictualists, Marx et al., as if there were only two antagonistic social relations to 'explain' society, a 'love or hate' alternative, co-operation or conflict. Control, as such, does not belong to either. It derives from a conception of normative necessity, a world of obligations. Ideology and culture generally rationalize this situation in terms of co-operation, but they do not, for all that, 'explain' or shed more light. Conflict shows up in the picture but as a counterpart of control. Therefore, collectivities of any proportions are not likely to be the happy effects of innocent or spontaneous endeavour; they are more likely to be the products of conditioning and controls, whose failure prompts conflict.

Thresholds of tolerance

The aim of regulation is to impose a set of rules on a collectivity. Whenever the imposition is achieved, whatever the means, regulation is said to exist. From our point of view, this situation must be taken for what it is, and not for what it ought to be. Introducing the notion of legitimacy would be to use a moral measuring rod and to be brought to question most if not all regimes, depending upon the rigorism of the observer.

Instead of coping with the collectivity's effect on the other parts of the structure, in terms of consent – which amounts to a positive approach – it is probably closer to reality to contemplate instead a negative approach, one that construes the collectivity's reaction in terms of thresholds of tolerance. People are no longer thought of as supporting the 'system' in the sense of giving strength to it, but rather in the sense of having to bear it, to endure it, to put up with it. Indeed, the whole spectrum would range from enthusiasm to opposition, with indifference as the neutral position. But few situations show consensual effusiveness for the regulating apparatus. Postulating levels of tolerance does not exclude, *per se*, positive attitudes, but nevertheless applies itself to registering degrees of grievances. The progress in tolerance thresholds may be conceived as in Figure 8.[19]

Grievances are generally levelled first against the agents, then against the rules of the game, and finally against the upper layer. Opposition grows from dissatisfaction with immediate levels and moves to dissatisfaction with more universal sets of constraints. Discontent with, for instance, the rules of the game,

19 The sequence combines some elements already present in Easton (1965) and Smelser (1963).

3 spirit of the rules
   principles of regulation

   ↑

2 rules of the game
   procedures, distribution of competences

   ↑

1 authorities/agents

FIGURE 8 Thresholds of tolerance

as in France when the Third Republic gave way to the Fourth after the war, and when the Fourth gave way to the Fifth in 1958, almost necessarily entailed a severe setback for some politicians. Revolutionary changes which mark the adoption of new principles in regulation mean the downfall of the two lower levels and their replacement by new rules of the game and a new set of authorities. By spirit of the rules or principles of regulations, I mean norms that set ways of conceiving the managing of regulation in general; such norms affect the conduct of state affairs as well as the conduct of associations.

On the whole, the collectivity's impact on mediating channels is one of prevention. Its position is one of potential intervention against one of the three levels already outlined. Elections seem, at first glance, to be exceptions whereby indications of adhesion are expressed towards the happy few elected agents. A closer look will at least temper this optimism. For one thing, most elections result in a person being voted in by a limited fraction of the electorate – President Mitterand was elected by 43% of the electorate in 1981, Mrs Thatcher's conservatives by 31% in 1983, and President Reagan also by 31% in 1984; indifference, inability to vote, or hostility are the lot of the majority 'others.' Even if one were to obtain the assent of more than 50% of the electorate, it does not follow that the assent would be elicited from an enthused majority; the assent is more likely the result of a choice among limited alternatives or strong opposition to a badly regarded rival. Indeed, preventive or latent opposition is most apparent in cases where force has been widely resorted to and remains in extensive use.

Mobility/compulsory membership
The collectivity's propensity to strengthen its opposition to regulation is liable to be, *ceteris paribus*, in direct relation with the constraint exercised upon the members' ability to withdraw from the collectivity. Mobility is a determinant in relaxing tensions. If exit is made impossible through force or severe deprivations of a material or symbolic nature, it is to be expected that voice (to take up Albert O. Hirschman's concepts again) will take over and even put the solidarity, that is, the

loyalty, of the whole to the test. It is unfortunate that political science has made so little use of a notion that is much exploited in economics, and with such happy results. Conversely, non-mobility enhances the intensity of scarcity, and in so doing aggravates conflicts.

Collectivities under state governance offer a convincing illustration of limited mobility. While among bands of hunters and gatherers membership fluctuates (though along norms that extend to the community of hunters and gatherers at large reducing the degree of mobility in reality), such is not the case in the communities that have succeeded these bands. Political anthropology commonly acknowledges as state systems the ancient, medieval, and Renaissance city-states, the Meso-potamian and Mesoamerican settlements, Ancient Egypt, and the Mongolian, Persian, and Chinese empires. Long discussions of a philosophical, juridical, and anthropological nature still argue the definition and delimitation of state societies. For some, the distinction between state and non-state societies is not that obvious.

There is a wide divergence of opinion over the causes for the growth of states. Which were determinative – demographic pressures, trade, conquests in warfare, internal strife, or a combination of these (Cohen 1978a, 69)? There is a tendency to see many causes intertwined into a 'systemic process,' a blend of factors, none of which is sufficient in itself, and which – more important – are never in the same combination, making up 'multiple roads to statehood' (Cohen 1978b, 8). The classic opposition still pits the contenders for the 'consensus' or integrative thesis against the supporters of the 'conflict' approach (Fried 1978). The former claim that there is a general acceptance by all parties of the benefits being derived from state government at its early stage (Cohen 1978b, 6–7); without denying the existence of conflicts and classes in the process, the integrative thesis stresses consent at the origin of the state. The 'conflict' school, on the other hand, emphasizes the imposition by force of an authority based upon conquest and class struggles, both of which develop from the same dynamics, one working from the outside and the other from the inside. Morton Fried is representative of the Morgan-Engels tradition which underlines the repressive character of statehood which is believed to have appeared with stratification (1967, 186, 235).

If the discussion has progressed with respect to the causes of the appearance of the state, it is still also going on over the ways of identifying statehood. What is the state? The definitions are legion. Conditions or features are usually assembled to circumscribe its distinctive character, especially when considering 'early states': specific territory, independent organization, common trade, division of labour, stratification, relationship of sovereign to subjects, and so on (Claessen 1978, 533ff.). Emphasis is usually put on the emergence of a central authority strengthened by a bureaucracy (Cohen 1978a, 69). Within this Weberian approach it is almost useless to recall the classic 'claim to the *monopoly* of the *legitimate* use of physical force' (Weber 1964, 154). It is very appealing to confer on the state a character of permanency and transcendency, as does Lawrence Krader, who sees in the state a self-perpetuating and self-serving entity providing for the 'promotion and preservation of its own existence as an end in itself' (1968, 28). But such can hardly be imputed exclusively to state governance; many other groups consider themselves in these terms – clans, lineages, tribes, associations, and the like.

The state conception of community is so widespread nowadays that it is no longer possible for anyone to escape from it. Any person is designated as falling, at any particular time and place, under the authority of a state. It is thus the compulsory feature of this social relation which is striking. The state, as a potential monopoly over all possible controls, is imposed upon the whole surface of the globe, constituting the most constraining type of authority in principle. The church may have exercised its control under the threat of excommunication, which was meaningful enough for the faithful, but at least in theory one could live – although often in dire conditions – outside it. One cannot withdraw from state authority under any circumstances. One may leave one state system, but only to be inevitably caught up by another. Stateless persons may exist in theory but never in practice, unless they let themselves be carried along indefinitely in international waters. The sovereign pretentions of the state do not authorize the analyst to conclude, however, that this authority necessarily integrates all possible collectivities. Collectivities often transcend state boundaries; the church is still a good example.

From this compulsory membership identified by Max Weber, some authors have entertained the possibility of elaborating a theory of politics. For them, politics has this obligatory social relation as its foundations, and all other social relations deriving from this initial obligatory relation qualify as political (Bergeron 1965, 29ff.). People are considered to have no choice; they are put into situations to which they are bound to submit, they have to be subjects of a unit (state, tribe, band, or any other form). Some enjoy wider choices than others because they have the advantage of mobility. Possibilities of participation – usually quite limited, under the guise of elections or otherwise – serve as official safeguards against what might be dubbed authoritarianism or arbitrary regulation.

If there is any point in discussing the reality of politics, it is probably from this feature of compulsory belonging that premises should be derived. The present-day state offers this feature in its most highly developed form, though we must not deny this character to earlier forms where it was not yet systematized to its fullest possibility of imperativeness. When regulation becomes so compelling, its effect is to intensify relations of control and conditioning. Controls become more binding, conditioning more pressing, in order to keep rules as they stand, or to operate changes.

Cultural and ideological barriers to regulation
Though the community's reactions are readily detectable in terms of thresholds of tolerance, it does not follow that no other effects upon elements of regulation are noticeable. On the contrary, the intention is first to do away with the notion of consent which purports to legitimize the institutions of regulation through the community members' presumed adhesion to these institutions. Once the notion of consent is done away with, it is imperative to pay the most careful attention to the impact of cultural and ideological values upon the different elements which make up the regulative structure. Norms accepted by all or parts of a society affect the emergence of interests and the way they are mediated – for all forms of representation are not acceptable to all communities; they identify, in general terms, who is entitled to be heard, who is entitled to represent whom. Thereafter, norms affect, to a large extent, the three layers already identified: the spirit of the rules, the rules of the game, and the types of agents acceptable. This effect should not be interpreted in terms of consent on the part of the community, but rather as the impact of cultural or ideological values and norms, shared by the community, about the components of regulation. For instance, even the most absolute monarchy still works from the values and norms of its cultural environment, and this has nothing to do with the consent of the subjects; the idea of consent probably never crossed their minds. But, deviations from these norms will trigger movements of resentment, the community reacting to the infringements of norms. Here again, the reflex springs up to forbid, not to permit.

While the community abides by cultural and ideological norms which are indirectly imposed upon the regulators, there is in contemporary societies a constant flow of new rules whose effect on the collectivity are not always easy to gauge. Empirically minded authors of the early sixties, who studied local governments, were probably more sanguine than the public policy scholars who followed a decade later. For the former it seemed relatively easy to assess rule impact in terms of people affected, kinds and amounts of resources distributed, and the overall change in the community's resource distribution (Polsby 1963, 96). For the latter rule impact seemed problematic at first but seems to have become more manageable with the passage of time (Grumm 1975; Anderson 1979; Ingram and Mann 1980; Grumm and Wasby 1981): the impact of rules with their possible 'spillover' effects rendered evaluation difficult; short-term as opposed to long-term effects and the diffusiveness, in general, of impacts require more sophisticated instruments of observation then were probably thought necessary when the public policy trend of analysis began. Responses to policies, whether the responses are positive or negative, have become the object of closer attention: compliance or non-compliance, success or failure of policies, and the unintended effects of rules that turn out to have contrary outcomes to those expected are all considerations that have contributed to putting the collectivity's response to regulative processes back on the map.[20]

With the collectivity's impact upon the components of regulation the structure is now complete, and what remains to be done is to discuss the whole.

CONCLUSION

The relationship between the collectivity and its regulating apparatus must always be considered from its structural perspective, that is, from the working of the whole rather than from linear approaches that view problems in the strict duality of one independent to one dependent variable. In some cases the dual approach may work, but in general the interaction of elements should be given priority.

It becomes analytically rewarding to juxtapose, in a global perspective, the expressions of the patterning of regulation at different levels of large collectivities. Common modes of interaction should show up in entirely different settings, whether in the family, at school, or at the office. In ideal situations absolute congruency would reproduce pure isomorphisms of behaviour. In reality, discrepancies are likely to emerge demonstrating cleavages of norms according to the level of application. Scholars who have broached this problem of congruency have had in mind the stability of a whole system or its 'democratic' content, or sometimes both (Almond and Verba 1963; Eckstein 1966; Eckstein and Gurr 1975). It is interesting, at this stage, to confront the modes of regulation adopted by units at various levels, and the degree of consistency may serve as an index of further consonance in the whole control arrangement.

Rules overseeing the congruency of the whole in terms of controls can also be submitted to the same treatment as that discussed above for the consistency of regulating patterns; cleavages are most likely to appear, showing discrepancies liable to translate into conflicts.

This same global approach should try to elucidate, or at least understand, the conditions under which issues emerge. The notion of 'mobilization of bias' partly accounts for issue emergence (Schattschneider 1960, 71). Even though this notion was originally meant to convey the impression of an undesirable twist of things, it remains serviceable to the extent that it is divested of its normative and pejorative connotations. Values, practices, and rules of the game prevent issues, so to speak, from emerging into the rule-making arena. To be of any analytical use, 'mobilization of bias' should not be conceived of as a plot, a ploy, or a

---

20 More circumscribed in its scope of investigation, the systematic evaluation of specific social programs has been in existence for more than three decades (Rossi et al. 1979).

manipulative scheme intended to divert a process of agenda setting. Bachrach and Baratz's (1963) well-known developments on non-decision which follow E.E. Schattschneider's considerations are to be used with the same reservations.

To be of any interest, 'non-decision making' has to understood, from the start, as an analytical artefact used to shed light on the functioning of the whole structure of regulation, as well as the whole conditioning mechanism adapted to it. Indeed, the rules of the game are never innocent or objective, as stated earlier; and any interests articulated by gifted strategists will exhaust all possible means to voice their points of view and prevent the expression of adverse opinions. We endow 'non-decision making' with artefact status because its full usage implies at times a reference to non-events. It covers bills that are defeated in the House as well as issues that simply never come into being. In the former instance, a bill which has been voted down can be considered an event – it can be traced back at least to the moment it was introduced; the latter instance, however, furnishes very limited grounds, and often none at all, for an evaluation in terms of concrete happenings. In such cases, non-decision can be a valuable device for showing differences between collectivities that otherwise display identical structures in their regulative functioning. The artefact is therefore contemplated as a comparative tool designed to point out variations and stimulate research to explain differences through an analysis of structural components.

Interests interact within a structure that provides channels of regulation for the exercise of controls, which are related to a collectivity's culture and diversified ideologies. The degree of consistency exhibited by controls in their relationships with interests' aspirations and the collectivity's expectations, as well as the manner in which controls are made official, should account for the degree of conflict that will unfold within the structure. Since complete or absolute consistency only exists in ideal situations, the regulative structure always works within dynamics of conflict.[21]

As already mentioned, regulation takes place in close relationship with conditioning. The two have been dissociated only for the purpose of demonstration; in fact, conditioning and regulation are meant to work together. Stephen Lukes's *Power* illustrates, for instance, a partial attempt to explain the effect of conditioning on regulation; the drawback of his analysis comes from imputing intentions to conditioners, who are somewhat reduced to the role of cynical manipulators. The integration of conditioning and regulative structures must

---

21 Expressing himself from a systemic perspective, Jean-William Lapierre (1973, 59) suggests that political decisions are resorted to when the other social systems (economic, cultural, ecological, and biosocial) are found wanting.

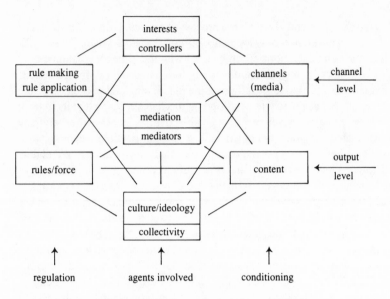

FIGURE 9 Structures of conditioning and regulation combined

ultimately lead to the identification of a single structure. When joined together (as in Figure 9), they show a single structure where the central role is mediation, which is basic to the functioning of both conditioning and regulation. Their final integration into the production structure, in the next chapter, gives a complete picture of the components and their interrelations.

6

Classes:
the coalescence of interests

Controls have been described as behaviours sustained by patterns which are in turn incorporated into roles. Furthermore, it has been established that interests, in the usage adopted, serve to denote collective values which are activated by a determined group of actors defined as controllers. This particular group may, however, be discussed in different terms. The notion of social class, among others, should be of some use, so long as it is carefully defined.

Categories, strata, and status groups
Agents may first be grouped into distinct categories according to age, sex, education, income, or other features, each category being kept independent from the others. Along this line of reasoning the possibilities of categorization are limitless. Interests of older people as opposed to other parts of the population, of men as opposed to women, of the better educated as opposed to the less well educated may be imagined, and also later examined in combinations, in order to show significant correlations.

Some combinations lead to more macroscopic views of social relations than others, by creating nominal strata which explain the allocation of resources and, in so doing, the controls within a given group of people. Such combinations cannot be summed up as mere cumulations of given factors such as education, profession, income, and so forth, for they underline the integration of these factors in making up global differentiations that cannot be accounted for when the factors are analysed separately. On this basis, many series of combinations may be imagined, the analyst articulating them himself or herself or relying upon peoples' own perception of either their own standing or that of others.

The status group, as conceived by Max Weber, works on the basis of how groups recognize each other. With the intention of reintroducing aspects of meaning and motivation that were omitted by Marx – since he considered them mere rationalizations of economic interests – Weber restricts the connotation of the notion of class to the designation of individuals' common situations in terms of their chances in life of disposing of goods or services other than those they already have. The intention is to let the concept of status group embrace a much wider and more significant reality than the notion of class. The definition of status group purports to account for the way people gauge each other, some being kept within and others outside a 'social estimation of honour' (1969, 187).[1] Not only are goods and services submitted to the rules of scarcity, but to those of prestige as well. Prestige acts as the key concept that enables one to distinguish who is who in a social hierarchy. The analytical instruments used by the founder of the comprehensive school in sociology are in evidence here. From the outset, it is not at all certain that the way a collectivity elaborates its own stratification criteria is necessarily indicative of how the analyst should proceed. Moreover, the concepts of prestige and social closure, while susceptible to systematic treatments, do not have to abide by the norms of common usage.

Prestige, after Max Weber, has become the cornerstone of the functionalists' explanation of stratification. The classic interpretation of Davis and Moore (1945) is adamant in using it as *the* explanatory factor. The needs of society as a whole translate into incentives to induce people to fulfil the most demanding and indispensable jobs, in return for rewards which have prestige as their foundation. Classes find their legitimation in their functional link to the requisites of society. Davis and Moore come to the conclusion that better remuneration, for instance, derives from stations of higher prestige. Since the selectivity of status is in conformity with relative importance to the working of society, those with higher status are entitled to better salaries. This thesis has given rise to criticisms (Tumin 1953; Wesolowski 1962), some emphasizing, quite pertinently, its untestability (Vanfossen 1979, 26ff.). The functionalists' stress on prestige still remains within the logic of parameters established along the lines of values and motivations as the factors most capable of explaining social life.

Prestige, when reintroduced into a different and wider context, may become an item, among others, whose scarcity has some significance. Although prestige should not be assigned an exclusive role, it may well serve as an indicator, or better, an asset, in the attainment of further advantages. Following Weber, it is quite admissible to retain prestige as a scarce resource, but not with the intention of constituting from it a reference group, be it called a status group or otherwise. The perspective must be much wider if prestige is to have any relevance in terms of controls.

1 F. Parkin (1971, 33) points out that 'despite the importance [Weber] assigned to status he offered little account of the factors governing its distribution.'

THE CLASS APPROACH

The class approach is more often than not couched in ambitious terms, its purpose being extensive. It attempts to explain more fully behaviour originally hemmed into categories or strata. Instead of confining the investigation to groups that are built out of an aggregation of individuals who as a sum constitute a whole, it manages the other way around, by focusing on the purported effects of the whole on individual behaviour.

Even though he was not the first to cope with the concept of class, Marx stands out as the first to develop the concept within an elaborate framework. Our understanding of Marx's disquisition on social classes puts him in direct line with Hegel. Inspired by dialectical dynamics, Marx contemplates the resolution of a fundamentally dyadic struggle – the proletariat versus the bourgeoisie – through the complete overthrow of the latter by the former, and the formation of a single whole relieved of inner contradictions. Marx saw the rise of a new universal class as a counterpart to Hegel's bureaucratic class, as the complete fulfilment of man's consciousness after the divisive cleavages that have persistently plagued humanity in its relationship with nature. It is well known that Marx's discussion on classes was cut short in the last stage of writing *Das Kapital*. Hence, his followers were reduced to relying on earlier writings. I intend to provide only a rapid look at those aspects of Marxist theory which I shall discard, and to concentrate on certain aspects which, by themselves, can hardly be labelled Marxian.

While Louis Althusser and Nicos Poulantzas take great care to avoid 'subjective' readings, as performed by adepts of the younger Marx, most followers of the great master have paid much attention to class consciousness, some, like Lukacs, putting forward interpretations with an obvious Hegelian flavour. Anyone who makes the consciousness approach his or her own is bound to call upon some criteria in his or her search to determine the degree and accurateness of political awareness achieved by the working class at a given time in its historical course. Working from a Hegelian perception, Marx considered the passage from a working class *in itself* to a working class *for itself* as the imminent progression which would result from pressure, which was becoming more and more persistent, upon the proletarian class. After him, Lenin stood for a more voluntaristic approach which banked on enlightenment from intellectual outsiders to override the strictly trade-unionist policy that workers were unmistakably about to adopt. I could set out in detail the already familiar story of internal opposition, one faction pitted against the other, the Leninist faction in favour of the so-called democratic centralism of the Communist Party and the more spontaneous schools in the Luxemburgist tradition. All in all, what counts is not, at least for the moment, the inner quarrels ripping apart the followers of the master in an unpredicted dialectical pattern, but rather the unsolvable character of their premises: up to now, Marxist theories have not furnished enough solid grounds to allow anyone to assert categorically his or her capacity to evaluate the given state of consciousness reached by any group or class. Our original renunciation of any support from the consciousness of actors is drawn largely, first, from the incapacity of the actors to express it fully and unmistakably and, second, from our very limited reliance on the faculty of third parties to discern what others, individually or collectively, wish or should wish.

For analytical as well as political reasons, Marx was induced to limit to two the number of significant classes at any one time. It suited his dialectical preoccupations and his eagerness to resolve once and for all an immemorial state of inequality and exploitation by the action of the one universal class in history, the proletariat, striking a final blow at the last of the dominant classes, the bourgeoisie, which for him concentrates in itself all the alienating factors of social life. Marx imagined this 'last shot in history' with a systematic reduction of contenders. All the remnants of former modes of production, like the peasantry and the aristocracy, as well as the byproducts of capitalism, like the petty bourgeoisie, are called upon to become part of either one or the other of the bi-polar concentrations of forces. The last engagement is a clear-cut duel under the scorching sun of equity. True, Marx's political analyses provide for more than two classes in practice. Even in the last and unfinished chapter of *Das Kapital* he recognizes the existence of three classes, and in the *Eighteenth Brumaire of Louis Napoleon*, from much earlier times, he enumerates even more, of a different nature from those described in *Das Kapital*. Personally I would be inclined to give greater credence to the *Eighteenth Brumaire* because of its attempt to bring out a more realistic picture of the actual configuration of collective actors involved. *Das Kapital* is entirely theoretical, functioning from a limited number of parameters, whereas the *Eighteenth Brumaire* applies itself to the analysis of a concrete political event.

The reduction to two parties is the result of the presumed contentious nature of both. As stated earlier, classes in the Marxist conception exist in so far as they are in conflict. While keeping at arm's length from Marx, Ralf Dahrendorf too recognizes class struggle as basic.[2]

Whatever its pretention to being scientific, Marxism has been, from its beginnings, an ethical enterprise geared not merely to the equal distribution of the fruits of labour (that is, the suppression of surplus value), which remains in Marx's

---

2 'Whoever uses the category of class without assuming the presence of class conflict abuses this category' (1968, 136). Dahrendorf insists, though, that the struggle does not have to be violent.

mind a bourgeois conception, but the ultimate Saint-Simonian achievement of 'from each according to his capacity, to each according to his need.'

In my mind controls do have moral connotations for the actors themselves. Controls are basically permeated by values that give controllers right over controllees. Furthermore, the observers themselves cannot be said to be in a constant state of indifference towards all the controls they encounter. It is more likely than not that they will feel either favourable or unfavourable to most of the controls they are called upon to analyse. They may consider some controls outrageous and others desirable; they may also find some of them outmoded, considering the stage of development of the collectivity they are studying. But whatever their state of mind, they should be in a position to recognize the existence of controls.

When Marx elaborated his partial disquisition on classes, classes were quite distinct in most people's minds, especially in Europe. Remnants of the Ancien Régime orders or estates, the aristocracy as well as the bourgeoisie, were easy to single out. The peasantry, which in most cases formed the majority, was reduced to a nondescript status. The working class was at the time a rather homogeneous group with a limited amount of specialization and differentiation compared with today's working class. Furthermore, cultures appropriate to each of these classes existed. People were readily identifiable by their clothing, their manners, their habits, and the company they kept. Having formerly enjoyed legal recognition, the upper class still stuck to its order, though in countries like Great Britain it had a propensity to keep company with the bourgeoisie while still maintaining its titles. Even today, the bourgeoisie, especially the grand bourgeoisie, make themselves known through their status as large shareholders, and can still be reckoned, even though one may easily run into trouble when it comes to accounting for the status of directors who do not necessarily own a great many shares. The proletarian class, whether in a capitalist or a communist type of economic organization, may be called the 'grande muette' – after the label that was once appended to the French army – for it seldom expresses itself except through purported representatives. If the bourgeois class may be said to be to some extent mediated by its managers, all the more reason for emphasizing the role of organizations such as trade unions and parties that vie for acceptance as spokesmen of the proletariat. While the bourgeoisie seems to have the attributes of a rather identifiable entity, such is certainly not the lot of the working class, whose confines, especially these days, are becoming more and more ambiguous. With increasing numbers of salaried people and a significant number of white-collar workers, a restrictive definition of the labouring class runs the risk of becoming almost meaningless. In any case, the Marxist tradition has constantly been troubled with the identification of the labouring class and its capacity to fend for itself. While somehow taken for granted, the class struggle has led to little clarification of the labouring class in advanced industrialized societies.[3]

This swift inquiry into the notion of class as understood by Marx should not lead us to discard the concept entirely, despite the numerous drawbacks. One might well wonder what is left after the notion has been peeled of its most common features: bipolarity, consciousness, emergent conflict, ethics, and problems of identification. Maybe the heart of the matter, the most verifiable and recognizable dimension of class, is the objective position held collectively by some agents within a given social network.

SOCIAL CLASSES: POSITIONS OF CONTROL OVER PRODUCTION

Classes account for positions of control over processes of production, positions that are not determined by biological considerations, and whose tenure (while relatively stable within an agent's lifetime) is submitted to a form of closure through social inheritance and other transmitted credentials.[4] Class is usually meant to supersede differences in status due to age and sex, and thus societies such as hunters and gatherers and the like are excluded from the discussion.[5] I am dealing here with classes exclusively as social products.

The definition calls for positions of control over the production of further resources. Classes should not be confused with static control of resources, even if, ultimately, they may well be used to achieve control over further resources. Ownership, prestige, or other features are not proposed as criteria for the identification of classes, though they are likely to serve in the acquisition of further resources.[6] One could content oneself with the actual state of resource distribution

3 Poulantzas's book on social classes (1978a), which is wholly devoted to social classes in today's capitalism, significantly puts aside the labouring class as such, preferring only to make references to it as the *other* party in the class struggle of capitalist societies.
4 The description is in contrast to Max Weber's concept of class in terms of a chance for a supply of resources (1969, 181).
5 Many authors, not to say most, with a variety of different viewpoints, rely on the idea of surplus as a condition for the emergence of classes – Davis and Moore (1945, 50) and Lenski (1966) to name a few. The economist Harry Pearson (1971) claims, on the other hand, that at best the concept has only a doubtful heuristic value, subsistence level, which is at the basis of the whole argument, being a social product to which no absolute value can be attributed. Anthropologist Marvin Harris's (1959) response recognizes that 'certain aspects of Pearson's criticism of the "surplus above subsistence" notion cannot be refuted' (185) and furnishes few convincing propositions to counter him. Jean Baudrillard (1972, 84–5) is adamant that the 'anthropological subsistence level' ('minimum vital anthropologique') does not exist: in the past, societies have always provided for a 'surplus' whatever the level of paucity being reached.
6 Some of Ralf Dahrendorf's considerations (1968) are suggestive in this respect even though he does not use the same terminology as I do and prefers to refer to authority as the general relation, leaving class independent of property and economic conditions (137).

and embark upon a statistical study of the current wealth of a nation. However, a more dynamic approach is likely to produce more significant results. The concern is not so much with who controls what is presently at hand but rather with who, in terms of status or position, controls the process of resources in the making. Production of new resources is apt to maintain, strengthen, or weaken existing controls and may even allow the emergence of new ones. Production of new resources is the fundamental process through which controls are activated.

Production
The concept of production is given a more extensive connotation here than is usually accorded to it. It covers not only the output of goods and services, as is commonly understood, but also any other production of signs and symbols, such as ceremonies of a religious or secular nature. Some productions may well be meant only to serve purposes of prestige or deference. Prestige *per se* is not, in the definition, a satisfactory condition for belonging to a class. However, the actual obtaining, through right, of a form of deference confers class status on the recipient. Sporting red high heels was, in Louis xiv's France, the privilege solely of the aristocracy; such an ensign, so to speak, certainly belongs to a set of controls, but it does not correspond, in my perspective, to a class situation. Should one obtain from this prestige resource, or simply from a title of nobility, advantages, whether material or symbolic, from somebody's else effort, then class is involved. Religious and traditional societies invest a good part of their resources (relative to their capacity) in such purposes, leading to the formation of classes entitled in many cases to receive some of these marks of respects, the bulk being devoted to strictly sacrificial or ceremonial ends. The same rationale applies to castes, orders, or estates. They may be considered relevant in so far as they account for something in the control of output endeavours.

Contemporary societies are much less inclined to devote significant parts of their production to symbolic manifestations. Industrialization has developed with great emphasis put on goods and services as they are usually understood. In accordance with this trend, the discussion that is to follow will concentrate on this type of output.

Production involves different stages, each open to controlling interventions: 1 / *production* properly speaking, which refers to intellectual or physical human effort accomplished through a division of labour which constitutes in itself a set of controls; 2 / *distribution* of income derived from the fruits of labour – also linked to division of labour; 3 / *investment* of non-distributed or unspent income, an important decision in any profitable endeavour; 4 / *consumption*, which is commonly imagined as free of controls, but which is most exposed to conditioning, while not entirely immune to controls either. How shall we situate classes given this four-tier reality? The division of labour covers at least the first three, for the investing process may also easily be considered as belonging to the division of labour. Consumption may be put aside for the time being, to be coped with after dealing with division of labour as a class-producing device.

Division of labour
Division of labour abides by two sets of rules. The first and most familiar responds to a given stage of development in the management of people and things – technology. Technology dictates, to some extent, the most efficient way to arrive at a determined output, albeit at the cost of human lives or health. It follows, as Max Weber explains, a rationality focused upon production. But technology in itself does not dictate the set of authorities which are to be adapted to technological imperatives.[7] Industrialization was formerly thought of in terms of a capitalist set of authorities at the head of the organization of industrial enterprises. Even Marx saw it this way, predicting that this mode of organization would be taken over in due course by a socialist society which would succeed the strictly industrial stage of development. Today we are readier to admit to a variety of possibilities in the authority hierarchy of enterprises; the state often intervenes by setting up rules for working conditions ranging from the age of workers, working hours, pay and collective bargaining to health conditions, retirement, and so forth. In many countries trade unions have gained the right to make certain management decisions. Nowadays, at least, we are familiar with socialist systems of all hues whose systems of controls differ significantly from one another and yet depart from the capitalist system of property. But, although the socialist societies are bent on a collectivist organization of production, they have still, in the long run, had to respect industrial imperatives of efficiency.

The division of labour entails a corresponding distribution of income accruing from the production of goods and services. It determines, first, who gets what, along the hierarchical line of production from managers to labourers. Different jobs command different rewards throughout the whole economy. Physicians are remunerated differently from plumbers. Asserting that such a distribution simply reflects the law of the market may, in some cases, be a way of avoiding further inquiries. One may at least posit the possibility of interests at work in enhancing the value of certain jobs, whether the interests are those of management or of labour. This process should be understood as an integral part of the content of conditioning, and not as an isolated event. Second, production provides, at least in principle, a surplus called salaries, profit, or rent which in turn is usually also distributed according to principles of property, either public or private property,

7 Giddens (1973, 140) underlines quite relevantly the duality within modes of production, which comes from the combination of capitalism and industrialism.

part frequently forwarded to the public treasury through taxes. The distribution of surplus will lead, at appropriate times, to an investment policy, formulated either by the enterprise's decision makers who withhold part of the profits from being distributed, or by the proprietors themselves, the shareholders, or the state. Governmental budgeting is translatable into a systematic assignment of resources legitimating and stimulating controls over specific productions: industrial, commercial, artistic, religious, and, of course, military. Government budgeting also redistributes resources by providing services or different forms of allow-ances. To dispose of funds is indeed in itself the exercise of control.

Consumption/exchange

Consumption may be considered the final stage of the process of production, although we are all aware that present consumption serves as an indication for today's and tomorrow's trends in production. Consumption thus stands at the beginning as well as at the end of the production process, which inevitably functions in a state of quasi-circularity. The system is not completely closed, however, since it is open to changes from the overall surrounding structure.

Consumption is usually entirely identified with exchange, which can be defined as follows: a patterned relationship of give and take largely based upon the presumed freedom of both parties to engage in the relationship. Exchange conveys an idea of choice between alternatives of quantity, quality, price, conditions of acquisition, and so forth. Postulating complete freedom would be a dangerous fiction, for it would obfuscate in advance the possible effects of other components of the relationship, a relationship which, at first glance, seems to imply the 'free will' of two or more parties.

In the abstract, consumption is described by the classics in terms of preferences that are givens, not to be discussed. People are imagined as indulging in exchange through personal choice, operating in a complete state of social asepsis, impervious to any outer world. John Stuart Mill's classic illustration of a purchaser's strong attraction for a musical snuff-box, for instance, is based solely upon a person's idiosyncracy (1899, 427). The whole classic argument is founded upon a person's ability to choose and discriminate. The Protestant conception of free will appears here to have had a persuasive effect upon liberal economics' outlook on trade. But, moving to the other extreme, one might take the opposite tack and posit that the whole relationship of exchange is basically determined by conditioning and controls, which leave little or no room at all for autonomous volition. The latter hypothesis has every appearance of being closer to reality than the former.

Needs and necessities are fundamentally social products. Socialization and publicity contribute in defining, by and large, the consumers' aggregate utility curves. People are conditioned to eat, dress, shelter, move, work, and recreate according to patterns that almost entirely consume their budgets. Cultures insist that their adherents furnish themselves with goods and services viewed as requisites for decent living or for life in society. Cultures prescribe rules of decency for clothing, standards on housing, religious obligations, and often moral obligations, all of which have a bearing on the personal disposal of income. Societies will, of course, differ from one another in the type of consumption they favour, as will segments of societies. From a Gallic perspective, Pierre Bourdieu (1979) has delineated the contours of social classes by examining aesthetic predilections: people are distinguished by their taste in music, for instance, the 'popular' classes' lauding of Strauss's *Blue Danube* in contrast with the upper classes' preference for Bach's *Well-tempered Clavier*.[8] One may feel free to make choices which express a discriminating taste, but more likely than not a sociologically recognizable trend will be discernible in the choices made.

Interests intervene too in inducing types of consumption. The free working of supply and demand is constantly slanted by elements that distort its idealistic pretensions. The aseptic world of utilities drawn from the blue, of perfect competition and perfect knowledge – the best abstract paragon of a control-free heaven on earth – shows its limitations whenever we are confronted with reality. Utilities, as we have seen, reveal themselves to be a reflection of external conditioning; competition turns out to be quite imperfect and knowledge limited. Monopolistic supply often dictates restrictions on the quantity, quality, price, and diversity of goods and services offered to the consumer. The consumer is thus left with a limited choice, or even Hobson's choice – the alternative of either buying or refusing to buy the only product of its kind put on the market. It goes without saying that such monopolistic conditions may be fostered by regulation which endorses an exclusive source of supply, such as the state.

Almost all forms of exchange are subject to rules and controls, whether explicit or implicit. Regulation provides producers with varying degrees of exclusive control over a market, through, for instance, protective tariffs, quotas, or patent rights, all of which contribute to restricting access to the market in the producers' favour. Regulation also advantages either the seller or the buyer whenever it defines rules for commercial exchange. No rule at all does not mean that the relationship does not ultimately come out in favour of one party. Finally, regulation may make it obligatory to furnish oneself with certain so-called necessities of life.

---

8 The book, with the *double entendre La Distinction* as its title, is in fact devoted to the topic suggested by the subtitle (with a Kantian reference): *Critique sociale du jugement.*

All these factors, conditioning, controls, and regulation contribute to making consumption a rigorously defined activity.

General conditions of employment also amount to a form of exchange of a more or less compulsory nature. Needs, necessities, or simply the desire to consume, all of which are social realities, lead one to work or to adopt less orthodox ways to arrive at the same ends. Working conditions display the requisites of a Hobbesian situation of freedom whereby one is left on one's own to decide whether, under strong social or legal pressures, one will abide by the norms and rules. Both parties involved, employers and employees, often play a game of imperfect competition and imperfect knowledge. Regulation usually strengthens or attenuates the monopolistic propensities of the parties involved. Trade unions, for instance, will be reinforced or weakened depending upon their legal status.

Ultimately, exchange amounts to a give and take of controls that are deemed acceptable, if not equitable, within the whole structure of reference. Most exchanges these days involve controls over money that are relinquished in order to get goods, services, or labour. The relationship between sellers and buyers – which includes selling or buying work – unfolds within a conditioning and regulative structure that bestows a supposed reciprocity or symmetry on the relationship. Exchange puts into relationship controls over different matters which cannot, in the absolute, be said to be either just or equal; pretending that controls can reach a state of balance or equilibrium would only add to the confusion by introducing ill-defined physical concepts into the discussion. The controls exchanged may be considered as equal or comparable in 'value' only relative to the whole structure of reference.

Working conditions at any given time indicate the degree of control the employer is in a position to exert over workers in exchange for a given salary, which in turn amounts to financial control. The employer's controls usually include a wide spectrum of activities which may extend to the workers' private lives and leisure activities. Employer's controls should never be considered isolated phenomena; they must be seen as a result of, and in relationship with, a series of factors which determine the conditions of their happening. Indeed, for some the problem is resolved by looking at society's needs, which are understood as determinate in establishing what is accepted as a fair rate of exchange (Blau 1964, 155). This functionalist mode of explanation excludes the part played by interests, at least in valorizing some types of jobs to the detriment of others. Marx too saw value as a social entity, but in a very restricted sense. For Marx, value amounted to the average labour time socially necessary for the production of a commodity. The term was meant to be applied to very standardized types of work where the amount of time spent in production is alone sufficient for the comparison of goods and services. Labour time serves as the sole measure. Skilled labour is equated with multiplied labour which can be broken down into more simple units of labour.[9] The Marxian interpretation, designed to analyse a nineteenth-century industrial reality, leaves very little room for appreciating the value margin of greatly differentiated types of work. A vexing problem for classical authors, later taken up by the Marxist school, the economic notion of value usually serves nowadays, under the guise of a materialist or even scientific discourse, to endow relations between social human beings and nature with ethical content. For Joan Robinson the notion of value 'has no operational content. It is just a word' (1974, 47). It must be added that value is at least an efficient instrument, if and when it is accepted, for promoting the complementary notion of surplus value. In sum, the notion of value is a useful criterion for establishing the foundations of any given configuration of income distribution, if we keep in mind that even in the Marxist tradition value remains a social product affected by the degree of advancement of a given social formation.

Working conditions result from the interaction of many, if not all, of the components at work within the entire social structure. They are a product of conditioning, regulation, and controls, as well as the degree of sophistication production has achieved and the demographic composition of production's network of reference.

Exchange, as a notion, leads one to discuss consumption, including labour consumption, which brings us back to the first stage of production. The exchange process corresponds to a relatively autonomous whole which includes interests that come into action to determine what resources are to be produced, distributed, invested, or consumed.

CLASSES: A CONSTRUCT

Class can help in the regrouping of seemingly unstructured, dispersed interests whose common features might otherwise go unnoticed. The notion of class, to be of any use, must bring to light sets of controls that would not be perceptible with the use of other means or instruments of observation.

To my mind, the way classes are delineated remains the analyst's concern and responsibility, for I see classes as a heuristic device and not as a description of real entities. Clearly, Marxist tradition has been inclined to bestow a sense of reality

9 Skilled labour 'counts only as simple labour intensified, or rather, as multiplied simple labour, a given quantity of skilled being considered equal to a greater quantity of simple labour' (Marx 1908, 11). Marx is even more explicit in this respect in the second chapter of his *Poverty of Philosophy*.

upon the notion of class; thus, class is frequently considered the final reference, and class struggle its basic concrete dynamics. Following Geiger and Schumpeter, Ralf Dahrendorf, who kept his distance from the Marxist school, still believes in the empirically identifiable reality of classes, even though his assertion is attenuated by other considerations (1968, 150–1). The debate, one may say, is still on. Indeed, classes are empirically verifiable in the sense that people may easily be categorized into predetermined sets, as is true of studies based on nominal strata as well. In my terms, classes do not necessarily enjoy an existence of their own. Marxists themselves have to admit the impossibility of defining concrete frontiers, even though they insist that class struggle is concrete. It is not impossible that classes do have an existence of their own, but I am far from sure that such is the case, even though some people may feel certain that they belong to a given class, or that others do.

As a construct, the notion of class can nonetheless account for actual controls wielded throughout production processes. I see class basically as an analytic instrument which allows for the establishment of correspondences between interests that interact at different levels of production. Class is a way of structuring sets of controls in relationship with other sets, and of taking into account compatibilities and incompatibilities. Classes will reveal the degree of consistency, in terms of interests, among the agents, and their positions of controls.

The Marxist approach makes the whole class system dependent to a large extent upon the notion of surplus value. Some agents are therefore identified as taking profit from working relations which enable some to extort or extract part of the value produced by others. The bourgeoisie is easily designated as the main beneficiary of the capitalist system in which productive workers feed an accumulation machine. But also drawing benefits from the capitalist system are all the ancillary functions that derive a living out of that same surplus value, either through rent or through salaries. So long as one accepts the postulates of value creation by productive workers, and of surplus value as the amount extracted from them for the working of the whole, the class system as expounded by Marxist proponents is in a good position to remain consistent within itself. But whenever these premises are put aside, the whole construction falls apart. It is no use borrowing parts and pieces from the Marxists without considering a whole new structure of explanation.

Working from the whole social structure in order to reach some conclusions about the intervention of classes in production is far removed, to start with, from a perspective that would lean towards coping with whole societies broken down into class tiers. The tendency may be strong in some cases to produce an exhaustive apparatus in which every member of society could find his or her place. This approach can be said to conform to a herbalist complex which consists of trying to classify and catalogue all species and their ramifications in a sort of social herbarium. Ordering collectivities in this manner is recognizing at the outset society's capacity to explain itself. The Durkheimian reification of society is not that far from the Hegelian intention of assigning a basic role to the state. Marx, for one, kept aloof from this particular pitfall; at least in practice he excluded the lumpenproletariat and assigned only a quasi-class status to the French peasantry, which in those days accounted for the bulk of France's population.

Since I have identified class interests in terms of positions of control over resource production, it follows that non-controllers and controllees are bound to remain out of the picture. This exclusion should apply to employees and workers inasmuch as they are kept from making policy decisions – when such is the case. Workers' opportunities for intervention are, for all practical purposes, of a negative character. Employees are, at times, in a position to impose limitations or bring production to a standstill by means of strikes. On the other hand, workers do not work for nothing; in this respect they may be said to hold control over the distribution of rewards, and often over different aspects of their working conditions. Nevertheless, their principal means of expression, when they act as a whole, within the enterprise or whenever they are grouped together, remains one of opposition. Whenever a tolerance threshold is crossed, the situation is prone to a slow-down, to 'murmuring,' protest, revolts, or, in the case of peasants, to *Jacqueries*. The argument here remains true to the reasoning used to identify the type of submissiveness collectivities usually abide by.[10] The recent Polish upheaval serves as a good example.

MEDIATION/REPRESENTATION

Marx himself at least implied, especially in the *Manifesto,* that the proletariat could not act as a class unless it proceeded to form a distinct political party administered by the most resolute and enlightened of the proletariat. In *What is to be done?* Lenin argued more explicitly that left to themselves workers would naturally veer towards trade-unionism; they therefore needed the help of intellectuals outside the proletariat. Marxist-Leninist thought posits the historical necessity of a mediator, the Communist Party, to lead the revolution to its proper end. The proletariat is not to be expected or induced to function by itself. Whether or not inspiration comes from Marxism is irrelevant; workers have been represented by trade unions and parties, exactly as any other mass movement is bound to be represented one way or another. The function of these mediators is to produce, through various symbols and signs, a representation of what the class, as

10 See pages 129–30 above.

a community this time, is or should be. The proletarian class refers, in this instance, to a creation of the mind, as any community does.

Interestingly enough, owners' controls, especially those of shareholders, have also had to follow a pattern of mediation. In the past, owners' controls were expressed by decisions emanating from proprietors, but things have changed, and mediators have interposed themselves in the process. A whole literature has grown from Berle and Means's seminal work in the thirties, which came to the conclusion that in many cases shareholders had lost their decision-making control to experts in management. Since then, some followers, like Marris (1964), Galbraith (1971), Larner (1970), Bell (1976), and others, have expounded this theory. Robert Dahl, for one, is adamant; any 'literate person' accepts the Berle and Means thesis without turning a hair.[11] However, at the risk of seeming illiterate, some authors are still discussing the pros and cons. Arguments on both sides are still being heard, and it is not certain that the cause has been won. Everybody agrees that management has a say, but opinions are at odds as to its significance. Relying heavily on motivational and microeconomic considerations, Robin Marris has suggested that, within a certain range of action, managers who enjoy a fair amount of control over decisions are likely to be more growth-oriented than shareholder-oriented. This effect has nonetheless been questioned by Robert J. Larner who, while remaining an adept of the management control thesis, comes to the conclusion that the impact on profits has been exaggerated.[12] In the same vein, research on profit maximization has been deemed inconclusive by Allen (1976, 89).

Opponents have argued that the trend in favour of managerial control has been overstated. Philip H. Burch (1972) underlines the enduring character of family control over a good number of important corporations. In a more sweeping fashion some, as reported by Maurice Zeitlin (1974), have challenged the whole argument, maintaining that whether firms are management- or owner-controlled does not make a significant difference in their profit orientation, since profits are said to remain a basic condition for any management's performance.[13] Unfortunately, such authors often rely on a very linear conception of control: some

11 'Every literate person now rightly takes for granted what Berle and Means established four decades ago in their famous study, *The Modern Corporation and Private Property* ...' (1970, 125).

12 As a matter of fact, Larner (1970, 66) concludes his book as follows: 'Although control is separated from ownership in most of America's largest corporations, the effects on the profit orientations of firms, and on stockholders' welfare have been minor. The magnitude of the effects appears to be too small to justify the considerable attention they have received in the literature for the past 38 years.'

13 'Growth, sales, technical efficiency, a strong competitive position are at once inseparable managerial goals and the determinants of high corporate profits – which, in turn, are the prerequisites of high managerial income and status' (1974, 1096).

positions are assumed to be positions of control and others, seemingly, are not. Reality is not that simple.

There is no question of submitting any answer in this area. Suffice it to register a progressive phenomenon of mediation which extends even further than management representation of shareholders' interests. Indeed, out of the dispersion of stock ownership, management has won a greater margin of autonomy in many cases, a fact that should not obfuscate the role of important minority shareholders who manage to secure a prominent position of control. Furthermore, that a thriving concentration of share ownership has fallen into the hands of financial institutions, especially commercial banks, has been noted (Chevalier 1970; Blumberg 1975),[14] and sometimes even hailed as a progression from management control to fiduciary institution control (Berle 1959).

Mediation and representation are part of any social structure, but they are probably becoming increasingly pervasive today as the defence of interests gets entrusted to professionals in the field.

The intellectuals

The concept of the intellectual serves, at least, to identify a wide range of those professionals of representation who rely upon their capacity to transmit signs and symbols in order to act as mediators of interests and who, as mediators of interests, hold interests of their own. Conceptions vary noticeably about who intellectuals happen to be. A whole tradition, along the lines of Edward Shils's suppositions, groups them into the class or category of people who share a common concern with the ultimate, thus a continuation of religious aspirations for the sacred (1972, 16, 154). This tradition is similar to Amitai Etzioni's idea of intellectuals as those who maintain a holistic evaluative stance as opposed to 'bit-oriented' experts (1968a, 184). In a somewhat narrower vein, Charles Kadushin sees intellectuals as a presumed élitist group and refers to them as élite intellectuals, that is experts who cope with 'high quality general ideas' about values and who communicate their views to a 'fairly general audience' (1974, 63). This group's medium of expression is somewhere between the specialized reviews and the common weeklies and newspapers: the *New York Review of Books*, the *New York Times Magazine* and *Book Reviews*, and others.

More recently, Régis Debray (1979) has tried his hand at circumscribing the power of intellectuals in France. He too focuses his attention on the 'haute intelligentsia' (upper intelligentsia), whom he defines as the set of persons socially authorized to publish an opinion. Debray underlines the social recognition which

14 Not all countries display the same patterns here. Niosi's thesis on the Canadian situation sustains an entirely different point of view regarding the role of financial institutions in Canada (1978).

entitles them to become involved in the political arena while still remaining unconfined by institutional or professional boundaries. This outlook comes close to Roland Barthes's viewpoint in *Degré Zéro de l'Ecriture* which situated the intellectual half-way between the 'militant' and the 'écrivain' (writer), the former term referring to the 'homme engagé' (committed man) and the latter to someone who strictly produces words.

The proponents of the limited approach frequently tend to qualify their concepts of intellectuals; they will refer to 'élite intellectuals' or 'upper intelligentsia,' leaving the impression that they are extracting a more influential part from a whole which is left out on a limb.

Being both realistic and ironic, Jean-Paul Sartre submits that an intellectual is somebody who doesn't mind his own business, one who oversteps his professional knowledge to judge situations outside his realm of proficiency (1972, 12). In this perspective the intellectual stands out as a sort of Jack of all trades who issues instructions about what others should do, especially in the governance of societies.

In contrast to this rather restrictive perception of intellectuals as the happy few who share a form of monopoly over the expression of valuable opinions, some authors have tried to give the term a more all-embracing connotation, usually with greater sociological content. S.M. Lipset's comprehensive definition illustrates this outlook well (1963, 333). For him intellectuals include all those concerned in one way or another with culture, which covers the arts, the sciences, and religion as well. It is within this type of enlarged framework that Lewis A. Coser (1965) has elaborated on certain institutional settings predominant, for instance, in eighteenth-century France and England: salons, coffee houses, scientific societies, and so forth. C.P. Snow's strictures against the widening split between two cultures, the division between scientists and intellectuals (literarily inclined scholars) within the intellectual community, remain within the boundaries of such wide range perceptions (1965).

More recently, Alvin W. Gouldner has pushed the conception much further, discerning, in Hegelian terms, the emergence of a new 'flawed universal class' which encompasses both technical and so-called intellectual producers who happen to have – in all advanced societies of the present day (including the Soviet Union and the United States) – identical interests within their own countries (1979, 6). In general, most authors shun such embracing generalizations even when they share the extensive scope of reference.

On the whole, the effort has been mostly to develop a social reality which is more or less plastic, and which lends itself to a variety of modes of identification, some more extensive, others more concentrated. What these authors have in common is a framework or an approach which is meant to be specific to intellectuals as a social entity.

Lipset and Basu (1975, 433) have made the point that studies on intellectuals have remained at a descriptive level without ever providing interpretations from a 'coherent theoretical framework.' Unfortunately, their attempt at remedying the situation remains within the confines of former approaches, since they are content with merely establishing categories of intellectual producers along the lines of innovativeness and levels of abstraction. Again, intellectuals are observed as a *sui generis* phenomenon to be analysed from within.

The Marxist approach to intellectuals
With its readiness to reintegrate any social event into the social whole, Marxism should have opened the way to rewarding developments in this field. However, very few Marxists really stand out in this respect, the tendency until recently probably having been to remain mesmerised by the 'infrastructure' of social relationships. Nevertheless, half a century ago Gramsci evolved a conception of intellectuals within an elaborate framework of society. For him, the notion of intellectuals as a class was deprived of any significance when severed from its social setting. It was meant to be integrated with the dynamics of a whole. Besides, the concept was meant to cover all the activities contributing to the processes of homogenizing value systems at different levels of society, including organizers at the enterprise level as well as politicians. Intellectuals were to be circumscribed by their functional relations with other classes. Being 'organically' related to a class, intellectuals nonetheless enjoyed a degree of relative autonomy from that class that put them in a category of their own, albeit a category which is not to be isolated from the rest of the social structure. This perspective was wrapped in the mists of historicism and dual opposition: intellectuals were arrayed as organic intellectuals, those who sustain a class on the ascendancy or in power, as opposed to traditional intellectuals who support classes on the wane or classes already passed away. Claiming, in addition, that intellectuals act as servants of the dominant group in the exercise of subsidiary functions of social 'hegemony' did not shed much light on the question as a whole. Nevertheless, some aspects of Gramsci's discussion deserve our attention: the basic idea that intellectuals do have to be interpreted from the whole they belong to and not as a separate category; that, at the same time, their mediating function confers upon them an autonomy to be reckoned with; and, finally, that a wide acceptation, which would favour a more imaginative understanding of the role, be extended to the notion.

In Gramsci's wake, Louis Althusser has centred his attention on superstructure, this time trying to lump it all together, as a vehicle of 'ideology,' into one explicative category he calls the 'ideological state apparatuses,' a reality distinct from the state's 'repressive apparatuses' (1971). His ulterior motive is probably to reveal the implicit totalitarianism of any state system. In this sense, any society is totalitarian, since it is in its name that roles are assigned. Althusser's conception has the advantage of expressing the continuous link which must be established between regulation and conditioning, but the use he makes of it is an entirely different matter.

In sum, the Marxist school is more inclined, from its holistic approach, to confront intellectuals with their function within, or effect upon, the social formation they belong to. In this respect it is more conducive to a sociological discourse on the actions of intellectuals than the rather narrow approach usually adopted by scholars exclusively concerned with intellectuals *per se*. This is not to say that the Marxist school holds any monopoly on sociological thinking. The school serves as a reminder that social objects or entities are worthless when not associated with other objects or entities in terms of social relations. The theoretical rule laid down by Easton and Dennis (1969) to the effect that no theory of political socialization can stand up without a political theory *tout court* to sustain it should be, by analogy, extended to the state of present studies on intellectuals in regard to their society of reference. No worthwhile developments can be furthered without their being connected to a more comprehensive approach, an approach which will probably not purport to exhaust explanations with a discussion of the presence of such and such intellectuals in specific situations but will rather try to explain some of the essential conditions of their ascendancy in relationship with the whole which gave rise to them.

The mediators

It is indeed much easier, and also quite tempting, to carve out a concept of the intellectual from a ready made situation, which would include all people directly concerned with the production of signs and symbols. Such a procedure would derive from an approach whose object is these producers as such. In order to avoid confusion it is advisable to propose another concept which will identify a somewhat different reality. To this effect the notion of mediator(s) is proposed as more suitable. The term refers to producers of signs and symbols of information, of values, norms, or rules, in the name of other interests. The interests thus mediated or represented do not necessarily have controls over the transmitters.

Without forming a homogeneous whole, mediators often share a good deal of mobility within their own sphere of operation and are likely, in many instances, also to have in common a comparable educational background. Mediators, in fact, use their knowledge either to organize production, to propose values, or to impose norms and rules. Their actions must be understood within the functioning of the overall structure whose three substructures – conditioning, regulation, and production – they permeate longitudinally. Moreover, the analysis has to emphasize the relational character of the mediators' presence. The mediators'

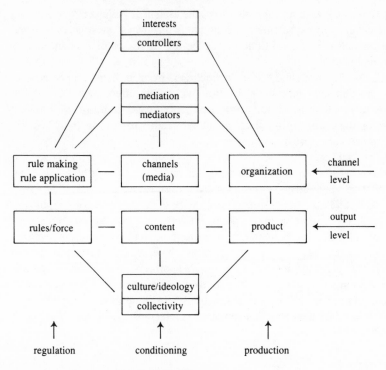

FIGURE 10 The overall social structure

actions combine with other elements of the structure: interests certainly, but also channels and culture (Figure 10). The present approach is directed against any attempt to work out a unicausal mode of explanation. From specific combinations of elements, roles are distributed to mediators, roles which determine the mediators' degree of autonomy and style and thus affect the content of their discourses as well as the type of action they engage in.

The mediators within each substructure are expected to behave according to a set of explicit or implicit norms of behaviour. Administrators in the Soviet Union, for example, are not likely to conform to the same frame of action as their North American counterparts. Conditioners will also be allocated differently, and regulators proceed from an entirely different pattern of action. Structural determinants are easy to detect when, after fundamental changes in the distribution of roles, certain features show up consistently and thus indicate the standardization of certain roles. One may hypothesize, for instance, that whenever a group has long held a form of monopoly over the cultural discourse of a society, any change, whatever its profound implications, is most likely to father a new form of monopoly. It is interesting to note that wherever clerics have enjoyed a sort of exclusivity over rostrums (be they in the church, at school, or in public), their disappearance through evolution or revolution has left a vacuum that has usually been readily filled by an intelligentsia or a totalitarian party.[15] Countries of Catholic tradition have often undergone a process of substitution whereby so called 'intellectuals' have stepped into the breach left by the clerics and taken on the aspect of priests *manqués*.

Mediators of conditioning
France's *philosophe* tradition, from the eighteenth century to the present, is one in which lay conditioners take over former clerical ascendancy in certain modes of socialization and mobilization. Tocqueville noted the movement in *The Old Régime and the French Revolution*. Referring to this collective endeavour, which can be traced back to the end of the Ancien Régime, François Bourricaud (1980) uses the label 'bricolage idéologique' (an ideological 'do it yourself').[16] The lay discourse derives from the clerical perspective of aristocratic times. For Tocqueville, the *philosophes* (who, incidentally, were more literarily than philosophically inclined) represented people ready to hold forth upon the origins of society and the fundamental rights of men, while remaining outside the political arena (book III, ch. 1). More specifically on this matter, Raymond Aron (1962, 255) stresses the propensity of 'intellectuals' to lofty abstractions in association with an indifference to the realities of life, for discussions which usually aim at the 'control,' so to speak, of things and events, by intuitive constructions that rely to a large extent upon forms rather than content. The discourse of these 'intellectuals' is also distinguished by its dissociation from established values, along the lines of an individualistic anarchism that often still claims to defend collective values.

As already noted, conditioners contribute in legitimating the creation and perpetuation of collectivities. Relations between mediators from the conditioning substructure and those working within the regulative substructure are often characterized by accommodation, or by close co-operation and reciprocal rein-forcement. Conditioners, as already mentioned, provide the legitimating elements for the origin and maintenance of states and nations. Regulators in turn often grant conditioners official recognition through an established church or other privileged

15 I use the term 'totalitarianism' only to express an order of possible extension in the right of intervention.
16 'Le bricolage idéologique' 'designates the industrious activity of those who, though they do not have mastery over the problems they refer to, modestly attend to their solution' (1980, 11; my translation).

institutions, such as the Académie française.[17] It is basically about these legitimating elements that Julien Benda complained, condemning what he considered to be their estrangement from truly universal values in favour of perverted national perspectives (1965, 32ff.). It was indeed in his time that the Ecole normale supérieure was recruiting regulators for the system, shaping up 'la République des professeurs' after it had been a seat of turmoil during the Dreyfus affair.

Mediators of regulation

Mediators operating within the regulative substructure are bound to enjoy some degree of autonomy from their counterparts in the strictly conditioning or production substructures. Even when mediators are intimately linked to particular interests, be it an aristocracy, a bourgeoisie, or other interests, they soon develop their own interests as mediators; they are also apt to defend the interests of the whole collectivity. The interests of kings have always been different from those of their barons, even though some common interests were shared in the feudal system. The instrumentalist school of C.W. Mills, Domhoff, and Miliband, on the other hand, construes the state as a device at the mercy of interests to which it is intimately linked.[18] The argument is based on physical analogies; the action of controllers is seen in terms of 'mechanically operating' forces (Offe 1974, 35). These influence theories rely on a sort of automaticity in the behaviour of mediators, and on the solidarity of controllers who do not have conflicting interests.

Like any other component, regulators should not be isolated from the rest of the social structure. The élitist school illustrates only too well a propensity to forgo this precaution in favour of an overall reductionism which concentrates on a simplified dualistic rapport between ruler and ruled. The argument usually revolves around a concerted minority subordinating a largely disorganized and impotent majority, the whole system being called upon to survive through an adapting device called the circulation of élites. Such is Mosca's view, which exemplifies quite satisfactorily the logic of the whole school which, having Machiavelli as its begetter, relies on a strictly dichotomic perspective to explain the dynamics of society. In reality, controllers may also be regulators, but they

17 'The political ambitions of successful French novelists collide with the literary ambitions of French statesmen, who dream of writing novels just as the others dream of becoming Ministers' (Aron 1962, 219). Herbert R. Lottman's *Left Bank* (1981) recounts two decades of 'intellectual' activities in France and their relations with 'politics.'

18 Inspired by the élitist tradition, John Porter's *Vertical Mosaic*, describing Canadian society, makes room for a slightly less monolithic approach.

need not be and seldom are, even in non-contemporary societies. This is no denial of multiple directorships in the governance of state institutions, advisory bodies, and other like entities which guarantee the continuous promotion of specific interests (Useem 1979). Regulation remains basically a form of mediation for a supposedly common cause. Thus, regulation necessarily calls for agents to assume the mediating functions, which may then be mediated even further by technocrats and, in some cases, by bureaucrats who are not mere executants.

At the other extreme, Nicos Poulantzas (1973) posits the existence of a relatively autonomous state whose very autonomy is indispensable to the maintenance of a capitalist class by providing for the long-run interests of the capitalist class against the segmentary claims of its individual members. The rationale is that, left to itself, the bourgeoisie is bound to fragment into fractions of irreconcilable interests. This being so, the state constitutes a necessary condition for the perpetuation of the bourgeoisie's common interests. The problem is that how the whole thing actually works remains nebulous (Gold et al. 1975, 38). We are thus left with the principle of the functional necessity of the state,[19] a sort of *deus ex machina*.

Between the two extremes – of mechanical instrumentalism and ethereal structural statism – there is room for a perspective that takes into consideration both the interests at work and the regulating devices (be they the state or other devices), as well as other elements, and that tries to comprehend an interconnected causality. Any unicausal attempt to explain the functioning of the whole is doomed in all likelihood.[20] On the other hand, the linkage assured by the mediators' horizontal action throughout the different substructures is conducive to the singling out of a reality that can only be grasped in terms of its relationships with other elements. Construing mediators as specialists in strictly one substructure, whether as professionals of broadcasting, education, business, or politics, is to miss their common status within the whole structure in favour of a more or less avowed functionalism. It is hardly necessary to reiterate that here production, conditioning, and regulating activities are the only criteria for identifying mediators as a group.

CLASS CLOSURE

Classes delineate positions of control and their mediation through social closure, to use Weber's terminology (Weber 1968, 43, 342; Parkin 1974, 3ff.). Controls

19 As time went by Poulantzas mitigated his position, recognizing that the 'popular masses' had after all made gains within the state structure (1978b, 34).
20 This interconnected causality has nothing to do with Robert Dahl's pluralism or polyarchy which purports to account for a plurality of influence in the exercise of regulation.

are maximized in the hands of some by restricting access to resources and opportunities. Classes assign attributes which act as justificatory conditions of acceptation; the prerequisites for acceptance range from physical to social characteristics: lineage, race, ethnic origin, religion, descent and so on. In reverse, the procedure amounts to a strategy of exclusion. Social scientists have examined this selective process very closely, especially in the educational system which offers a multiplicity of the facets involved in the maintenance of social barriers. Education furnishes a mode of selection, among others, for the distribution of opportunities. Rather than claim discriminatory prerequisites of access (with no pejorative connotation attributed to the term), about which little can usually be done, education, as a mode of selection, can aspire to a universality of opportunity open to all who are talented.

Randall Collins (1979) ranks among the most provocative authors in this matter: for him, the real goal of schooling is not so much technical knowledge but rather the transmission of codes – linguistic codes which include vocabulary and inflections, as well as styles of dress, aesthetic tastes, and manners – necessary to achieve status in the future. Long years of education become part of a credential system which provides a certification that raises a barrier between practioners and laymen: such are the conditions for the materialization of the medical monopoly, for instance, or for legal guilds or other professional exclusions. Such forms of exclusivity seem most obvious at the end of the educational process.

The social heritage school, on the other hand, postulates the existence of modes of cognitive expression which are already related to social classes even before attendance at school. According to the findings of this school, the working-class child, in order to understand what he or she is being told at school, must translate it into his or her own, simpler language (Bernstein 1971, 27). This phenomenon is meant to explain the lower-class child's difficulty in learning at school. Although language is integrative, it can also be divisive (119); differences in perceptions are revealed in ways of articulating the means for achieving given ends. According to this school, the 'lower class' is more likely to express itself in descriptive and concrete forms of reasoning, and the 'middle class' more likely to adopt analytic and abstract forms (Mueller 1973, 73). For the social heritage school the die is cast even before the school process begins. Education becomes an extension of pre-existing learning conditions.

While some authors in the United States – Bowles and Gintis (1976), Grannis (1970), and others – have been sensitive to the transmission of class traits through the classroom, Baudelot and Establet, two Frenchmen, have probably succeeded better in articulating a systematic thesis in this line of thought. They try to demonstrate that despite its claim to uniformity and universality, the French educational system is in reality divided, providing for two opposite networks of schooling corresponding to the social division of labour. These authors see a strong tendency to reproduce the current class configuration, the massive majority (75%) of the population being directed to vocational schools (after the elementary level), where education is based on repetition and concrete observation, and the minority being brought up in the worship of abstraction, by means of a gradual and progressive learning process. According to Baudelot and Establet's study, children drawn from the bourgeoisie have a 54% probability of success in the latter system, as against a 14% probability for children from the working class. Hence the reproduction of a class situation capable of furnishing workers for the labour market.

Bourdieu and Passeron (1970), following a different approach, work from the concept of habitus, which refers to a set of predispositions which furnish patterns of perception, appreciation, and behaviour that, by and large, are unconsciously internalized (Bourdieu 1972). Education thus proceeds not through indoctrination but by the maintenance of the current cultural, moral, and political order under the guise of neutrality and objectivity. An interesting point to add here is the importance these authors attribute to a petty bourgeoisie that acts as an intermediary in the reproduction (*La Reproduction* is the title of Bourdieu and Passeron's work) of a class, that is, a bourgeois, habitus (1970, 242ff.). One might wonder whether this petty bourgeoisie is not merely reproducing its own *Weltanschauung*. The claim that the French system of education furnishes a bourgeois conception of society has yet to be proved. The humanist content of its teachings can hardly be said to stand closer to the bourgeoisie than, for instance, the aristocracy. The hypothesis that such teachings serve a closure purpose is well founded, but that is a different matter from claiming that the concepts offered are essentially bourgeois.

On the whole, socialization sets up, through formal education and before it, a system of barriers whose effect is to invest some with privilege by securing them the resources, in terms of codes and information, to attain given sets of controls in the future.

In contrast to this too deterministic sociology, Raymond Boudon (1973), another Frenchman, attempts to demonstrate that if cultural heritage has anything to do with the educational process, it is only in the early years, and that social position (solely in terms of income) is what really explains the inequality of chances for success within the educational system in general; his argument is based upon the hypothesis that the better off people are, the better their position, in terms of risks, costs, and anticipated benefits. The education process is thus seen as a number of stages at each of which decisions have to be taken. My reservations about this argument are not so much about the approach itself, which is quite defensible despite its atomistic presuppositions, as about the limited connotation ascribed to cultural heritage: for Boudon, cultural heritage refers only to the parents' academic background. Cultural heritage, however, should also include the emphasis given to achievement, to tenacity, risk taking, boldness, and so forth, all of which is ignored by Boudon, who restricts himself to a mere statistical and more easily manageable category: income.

In the United States, Christopher Jencks and his group of scholars concluded in their early work that family environment, cognitive abilities, and educational achievements did not go very far in accounting for men's disparities in occupational positions and earnings (1972). But in a later work (1979) they tempered their opinion with respect to the impact of family background.[21] One way or another, judgments are still tentative on the question, but these studies nevertheless reveal attempts at forms of social closure.

Education furnishes the means to meet class requisites, the credentials necessary to attain coveted positions of control, the whole operation usually being carried out by mediators who do not share the status their students are on the way to achieve. Education certainly offers a propitious ground for the analysis of social closure, especially in contemporary societies where knowledge is highly valued.

Mobility, the opposite of closure, accounts for a certain adaptability achieved as the result of the circulation necessary for the maintenance of regulative channels or given sets of controls. Education, like other channels of promotion or demotion, provides stability in the assignment of roles by supplying modes of accommodation for the achievement of the status which permits the exercise of these roles and, ultimately, of controls. In other cases, mobility can permit a progressive transition to new sets of roles without requiring that the old set of roles be refurbished at a stroke.

CONCLUSION

This notion of class remains a positional interpretation of interests at work. It is used to avoid the pitfalls of morality and consciousness and yet remain aloof from the stratification school. For me, class stands at the hub of controls in the making – that is the production of resources – and of the mediations involved in the process, be they auxiliary through expertise or mediations which give rise to controls through conditioning, regulation, or both. The fact that interests must be represented whenever they are promoted for the sake of regulation and

---

21 '[The] family background as a whole [explains] about 48 percent of the variance in occupational status and 15 to 35 percent of the variance in earnings among men aged 25 to 64 in the early 1970's. These estimates imply that those who do well economically typically owe almost half of their occupational advantage and 15 to 35 percent of their earnings advantage to family background' (Jencks 1979, 81, taking into account the errata).

163 Classes: the coalescence of interests

conditioning adds a dimension to the role of the mediator: although representatives of other interests, mediators also have their own class interests.

The heuristic character of this conception of class should be put to the test by its capacity to disclose coalescences of interests before they are revealed within more readily identifiable groups like firms, associations, trade unions, and political parties. The class approach attempts to shed light on relationships that are not easily discernable from an examination of formal entities. Classes cut across such formal groupings, making use of them without being entirely subjected to them. In fact, classes permeate the whole social structure; they are an integral and inseparable part of it. As an analytic tool the notion purports to account for a level of observation that can only be verified by its effects. One should not demand more from the notion than it can accomplish.[22]

22 Anthony Giddens's disillusionment (1973, 10) with the performance of the notion of class stems from the great expectations and exaggerated demands with which analysts, including Marx, have taxed the concept. However, this is no reason to reject the notion as obsolete.

Conclusion: the overall structure and its epistemological status

The funnelling approach used to present this framework has proceeded according to a pedagogical artefact devised to progress from the simple to the complex. The thesis could have been articulated differently. The purpose was to avoid defining and developing the most basic concepts all at once. In reality, control can hardly be said to be a less complex notion than conditioning or mediation; they all work at different levels of observation, and they all belong to the same overall structure (Figure 10).

THE OVERALL STRUCTURE

From the beginning stress has been put on relations rather than on elements in so far as the relations exhibited recurring properties that lent themselves to further observation. Indeed relations alone were not expected to exhaust the meaning of any specific event. But what about the theoretical status of these relations which pull the various elements together? The different components of the structure have a limited number of aspects in common other than the fact that they are called upon to function together. Certain elements share the same level of reality – some as channels or products on a horizontal plane, others through agents on the vertical plane. Otherwise, the elements show no fundamental similarity. They have in common a link formed by an analytical device that endows them with a significance they would not have on their own, a feature inherent to any analytical construct.

The circuit described could have been called a system, but I chose structure instead in order to avoid confusion with systems analyses of functional (Parsons) or cybernetical (Deutsch and Easton) inspiration. For me, there is no one typical link between components of the structure which describes all relations; in this respect I differ with Parsons, who built his system on exchanges between components. Vincent Lemieux (1979, 122ff.) broadens the spectrum by making room for a greater number of typical links. The structure I propose does not provide for specific links which can be laid out; there is room for unexpected relationships yet to be discovered. Nobody, for instance, can determine once and for all the types of effects media are likely to have on culture, mediation, or interests. The structure is not meant to furnish a predetermined form for relationships either. In principle relationships are given a special status, but they are still not meant to be considered firmly fixed in advance. Their purpose is to stimulate the articulation of propositions about interactions among components.

The three substructures which make up the overall structure – conditioning, regulation, and production – are considered distinct solely for analytical purposes. In reality, some outputs can easily belong to two substructures at the same time; production and conditioning, for instance, often proceed together, with a common result which can be studied as an output of either. Almost all types of conditioning need a productive support which becomes, for all practical purposes, their channel. The whole has been collapsed into three major units in order to achieve a better understanding of the internal logic which sustains each of them, but in fact the three act in conjunction with each other and with other realities that at this stage of scientific knowledge have been designated as psychological, biological, and physical.

The level of observation is bound to vary depending upon the reality to be analysed. The structure is amenable to micro as well as macro situations: regulation, conditioning, and production traverse collective actions of any size, from the family to the state. Indeed, differences in size are likely to entail qualitative differences, also depending greatly on the degree of non-mobility imposed upon the actors. Modes of mobilization, patterns of conflict, rules of the game, and so on can be compared notwithstanding in some cases the population density and mobility.

The structure as a whole is not meant to reveal emergent properties other than the complexity of the interactions it puts into play. If the structure exhibits a form of holism, it is only in the interdependence of its parts. There is accordingly no magic of the whole as a whole. If the whole is not entirely identifiable from the working of its parts taken separately, the structure should, however, be comprehensible from an examination of the parts working together: the whole is more than the juxtaposition of its parts, but no more than the interplay of these same parts.

It is significant that most of the illustrations drawn from other researches in the field during the course of this work have contradicted this configuration of multiple relationships. In fact the illustrations show to what extent research has been strictly dyadic and linear, one effect following on the heels of one cause and vice versa. The structure presented here does not preclude the possibility of one feature operating as sole determinant for another feature. The trend in social sciences is still to a large extent in favour of a one-cause-one-effect mode of explanation. This satisfies the deductive requirements of science and is generally deemed the most adequate mode – so long as one is convinced of the validity of causality (Nagel 1964; Bunge 1959).[1] Proceeding from the *ceteris paribus* device so dear to economics is probably a necessity, but the device guarantees a very limited understanding of the whole reality whenever its use limits factors of variation to insignificant proportions.

Among other things, the structure provides for the postulation of a plurality of conditions indispensable to the actualization of a given effect. Determination is then to be looked at in terms of the necessity of these conditions appearing in combination. In such cases the structure does not forbid the adoption of a form of deductive reasoning. Likewise, a change in one component may well affect more than one of the other components and sometimes all of them.

Ultimately the structure is meant for the observation of interdependence within a network constructed to this effect. Calling the interdependence dialectical would open the door to numerous misunderstandings and misinterpretations. The structure is a totality which embodies a set of interrelationships between components that must maintain coherence in order to stay together. The notion of equilibrium is meaningless here, as is any reference to presumed states of homeostasis; the structure is not adapted to the cybernetic mode of functioning, no component being assigned any steering position, no single element being in charge of the management of the whole.

A HORIZONTAL REVIEW OF THE COMPONENTS OF THE STRUCTURE
AND THEIR CONTRIBUTION TO CHANGE

The entire structure is conceived in order to account for the way controls are distributed and managed within a given social network. They stand as the reference point, the social relation to be identified and explained. The whole construction is expected to shed light on the preconditions that make sets of controls possible. Such sets are not allotted at random; they are introduced and maintained by a dynamic that the structure is intended to understand.

Indeed control is a form of *découpage*; it is a construct, in the sense that it is only part of an action whose sociological dimension we retain. It is up to the analyst to

1 It is not my purpose to get entangled in the vexing debate over the status of causality that has been put in abeyance by some of the natural sciences. Nevertheless, one should not forget what causality is generally meant to refer to: 'Causality is a relation within the realm of conceptual objects. The relation of cause and effect refers to conceptual events regardless of the relation of the latter to reality ... causality must be attributed to a model which the scientist constructs out of concepts' (Lenzen 1954, 6).

recognize the patterned aspect of a specific action: in virtue of a right, an agent exercises a control. The personalized or singularized way it is performed is of no relevance here so long as it conforms to a given pattern of behaviour. In the framework the control remains the most important manifestation to be reckoned with and explained.

Interests and mediation

Although they do not constitute the basic factors of change, interests and mediation play an active part in the structure. They put into motion a series of relationships intended to produce specific effects in terms of output.

Interests identify specific relations and controls with respect to a culture or an ideology which legitimates a form of segregation, selectivity, or exclusiveness; culture and ideology are patterned to this effect. However, interests, as a concept, are not meant to take into account the aggregation of all the interests at work on all matters in a given collectivity. Everybody at one time or another finds himself or herself in the position of interest-holder. Interests are many, and many are the ways to delineate their possible configuration.

The mediatory function brings in its train the emergence of interests intimately connected with the use of most channels, channels for the production of goods and services as well as those used for the production of signs and symbols or rules. At times, mediators may even make themselves indispensable. Authoritarian regimes, especially military governments, exemplify a situation where a segment of a collectivity takes upon itself to monopolize the exercise of regulation. Such a move can only be understood in terms of the whole structure of reference. If ever the existence of a political phenomenon is posited, the description of the phenomenon should tackle mediation as next in importance to compulsory belonging. Mediation permeates all three substructures of production, conditioning, and regulation, but in a different fashion in each case. This is why the analytical articulation of the three is likely to produce rewarding results.

Social scientists have studied mediation in terms of at least two distinct realities, organizations and social classes, the former emphasizing the co-operative aspect of mediation, the latter the conflictual aspect. Whenever mediation is analysed as an organization, social classes are cast aside and, conversely, whenever mediation is viewed in terms of social classes, the organizational aspect is ignored. The specialist in organizations has a propensity to consider classes as more or less by-products of organizational apparatuses, just as his or her counterpart who specializes in classes attributes to organizations a negligible role, merely the outgrowth of class imperatives. In fact, neither organization nor social class should be ignored, even though they account for two very distinct aspects of mediation.

Channels and technology

Interests, whether mediated or not, proceed through channels. The channels imply transformation mechanisms for either production, conditioning, or regulation. The mechanism is intimately linked to technology. Techniques are standardized forms of operations whose use leads to predictable changes in objects. These forms are skills, tools, mechanical or abstract devices, rules of administration, and so forth. The objects are animate as well as inanimate – people, animals, plants, or physical entities, as well as signs and symbols. Techniques are applicable to all human types of activities, in industry, agriculture, the arts, administration, or mathematics (Freeman 1974, 5ff.; Adams 1975, 13; Perrow 1967, 195). Technology is the recognition of a set of techniques. Expressed differently, technology alters the order of energy forms or operates energy conversions (Adams 1975, 14). Techniques determine a channel's capacity. In the case of organization, for instance, some authors, like Charles Perrow (1967, 194-5), consider technology *the* defining characteristic, *the* independent variable. To go that far is to ignore context.

Technology has to be discovered, then recognized and applied. The processes of invention, acknowledgment, and conversion to use put into play all the components of the whole social structure. First of all, some collectivities are likely to be more prone to technological discoveries than others. Certainly innovation begets innovation. But some cultures or ideologies are probably more inclined to stimulate the emergence of certain types of inventions than others. Biases and prejudices can, on the other hand, impede progress in this area. Furthermore, research and development are not innocent. They are financed by private or state interests which provide institutional amenities for research and development. Information, like capital, grows in the hands of agents who already have some of it, and is liable to become monopolized. Finally, certain interests are bound to be affected, either positively or negatively, by technological advances. The utilization of techniques is not without a bearing on roles. It often enhances the control range of some and reduces the control range of others and may, in some cases, institute entirely new sets of controls. The introduction or non-introduction of techniques can easily be what is at stake in vicious conflicts. Technology metes out both rewards and penalties (Freeman 1974, 85). It often reallots roles: hence the great propensity for endangered controllers to screen out innovations that are potentially disturbing (Rogers and Shoemaker 1971, 341), whenever they are in a position to do so.

Diffusion of information must rely on conditioning channels. Acceptance of new technology stimulates the interaction of techniques and culture. R.M. MacIver (1947, 6) described the interplay a few decades ago: 'myths' affect techniques and vice versa. However, he did not take into consideration the part played by vested interests. Scholars generally agree at least on the bilaterality of the innovating process. Cultural recognition confirms a collectivity's acceptance of, or compatibility with, technical changes.[2]

Anthropologists are familiar with Leslie White's claims (1959b, 19ff.) that technology stands as *the* basic factor in culture, all other factors being dependent upon it. From this perspective, culture is understood in terms of energy transformation processes, these being the supreme cultural categories. Marvin Harris's 'cultural materialism' (1979), struggling for a science of culture, comes close to the same conclusion. From this linear causality, technology becomes the independent variable for all the other cultural components, as is the case in Perrow's conception of organization. Culture finally takes the form of a collectivity-wide organization built up to cope with the problems of 'earthly existence' (Harris 1979, ix). Cultural resistance to technology is ignored, for it would logically beg the question of technology's overriding importance.

As already mentioned, technology is basically directed at the improvement of channels, whether these are meant for conditioning, production, or regulation. By its mere existence technology is liable to have an effect, direct or indirect, upon all the other components of the social structure. Apart from affecting interests which are intimately involved in the process of new technique adoption, a change in the use of a channel is likely to have a bearing on the output itself: the type of content or product that emerges from the process and the collectivities for which it is intended.

Technical changes are not only time- and energy-saving devices, but are also likely to introduce modifications in the type of output being generated. Mass production has unmistakably opened the way to more standardized products, but it has also permitted more refined goods to come onto the market. The extensive and relatively inexpensive diffusion of sound recordings has, for instance, brought a diverse and sophisticated spectrum of listening possibilities within the reach of a wide population. These changes from the supply side are likely to bring about changes in demand, which in turn stimulate new expectations (through conditioning), and thus finally affect culture. Sophistication of taste in one area may, by osmosis, arouse more discriminating taste in others. As is more often emphasized, the reverse process of mediocrity breeding mediocrity may also occur. This process can lead to a 'McDonaldization' of culture where people become less and less discriminating in their expectations.

On a wider scale, a change occurring in one channel may affect the working

2 Katz, Levin, and Hamilton (1963, 240) sum up the whole process as follows: '*acceptance*, over *time*, of some specific *item* – an idea or practice, by individuals, groups or other *adopting units* linked to specific *channels* of communication, to a social *structure*, and to a given system of values, or *culture*' (italics in original).

of other channels. Revolution in a mode of communication (belonging to the conditioning structure) is most likely to have an effect upon channels of production through faster information devices and possibly a reduction of manpower, and may even affect the channels of regulation.

Output and environment

Outputs are the products of technology which issue from the different channels. Outputs are symbolic representations when we are dealing with regulation and conditioning, and this includes coercion when used to impress. The use of force is an exceptional output, but the potential for recourse to force is constant in most controls. When outputs come from the production substructure, they affect the environment. However, even the most symbolic event has an effect on the surroundings: writing the preceding words with a pencil marks a depletion of coal and wood resources, and the book you are holding in your hands marks a depletion of Canadian forests.

The environment refers to the physical features of the surroundings: the natural landscape and the resources underground as well as the artificial scenery, the landscape produced intentionally or unintentionally, as an effect or a consequence of human actions. With its heavy artefact import, environment becomes part of the conditioning continuum; buildings, gardens, roads, and bridges all contribute to the expression of culture and ideology. Environment understood in this fashion covers all physical resources, be they products or potential products. Environment is not merely an output; it also plays a part in input dynamics. As a result of technological changes, certain resources become important for some types of production; they set limits, so to speak, to an area of possible intervention.

Ecology as an analytical approach derives from a rather well established tradition in biology, a tradition which focuses on the interrelationship of living organisms and their environment (Vayda and Rappaport 1968, 477). Borrowed from this discipline, the term has been used in sociology and anthropology to link culture and the physical environment. The interesting debate this approach raises concerns the causal or determinant status to be extended to either culture or its environment. The common claim is that environment sets limits on culture but does not act as a determinant. Being more deterministic in his approach, Julian H. Steward prefers to talk of a 'degree of inevitability in cultural adjustments' (1957, 89). He does not put the case for environmental determinism as such but calls for greater respect to be paid to environmental factors. In his mind, these factors should not only be considered permissive or prohibitive in regard to new technologies, for local particularities may in certain cases impose social dispositions of some significance (1957, 38). In this connection Robert Murphy

(1970, 155) goes as far as to interpret Steward's view as one assigning to environment the status of a potentially creative factor.[3]

The degree of determinance to be attributed to the environment is not easy to establish – at least in theory – for, even though the environment imposes conditions upon the achievement of a social endeavour, these conditions themselves must be apprehended by culture (or ideology). Nature does not dictate courses of action in the abstract. Modes of behaviour must be acknowledged as appropriate in the first place. Any technique to cope with the environment is a cultural device intended to solve a problem of production raised and recognized as such by culture. On the other hand, the environment may be propitious and sometimes even conducive to the adoption of certain modes of behaviour that fall within given sets of values and that accord with a given level of technology. There is in this matter nothing automatic. This way of looking at the problem takes into account the possibility that, whatever their surroundings, some cultures (or ideologies) may be more prone to discoveries than others.

In the view of Marshall Sahlins, any natural selection is preceded by a cultural selection.[4] His approach assigns to culture a status of preponderance and sets no rules of conduct for the recognition of environmental influences, if any such influences even exist in his mind. Ecology for him amounts to a series of 'limit conditions'; it does not play any active part.

The rapport between culture and nature revives the moot question of the subject's autonomy towards his object of observation. The Marxist tradition has leaned in favour of the object determining the subject. Sahlins disputes this position and sides with the idealists. To propose a middle course would make little sense here. Nonetheless, any culture, like any knowledge or belief, is elaborated in reference to the surrounding objects it aims at construing. There exists a necessary connection between culture and nature. Culture is bound to select features from its environment and, by so doing, is not only limited in its choice but also most likely affected by this choice in its conception of the world.

Nevertheless, it is generally agreed that the direct conditioning effect of nature over culture is usually less perceptible as societies improve their technological capacity (Steward 1957, 40; Murphy 1970, 159).

Recognition of the declining impact of nature as technology progresses calls, in

---

3 Though interesting, Marshall Sahlins's debate over Steward's evolutionary views via Murphy is not my concern here (Sahlins 1976).

4 'It is insufficiently stressed in ecological studies that before there can be natural selection there is a cultural selection: of the relevant natural facts. Selection is not a simple natural process; it originates in a cultural structure, which by its own properties and finalities defines the environmental context specific to itself' (1976, 208).

turn, for the acknowledgment of human-made environment as a plausible factor of influence over culture. Human beings in contemporary societies are more likely to affect their own perceptions by their own works. The phenomenon of urban development may serve as an example: in this case, the environment – the city – often becomes conducive to reconsideration (through ideology) of the collectivity's own production. Some people become aware of unexpected externalities that they deem undesirable. Besides, city-dwellers are likely to develop cultural traits that contribute to reinforcing their urban values. Here is an instance of unforeseen self-conditioning features that some consider acceptable and others do not, depending upon their ideological reading of the urbanizing event.

Collectivity and demography

As environment tells us about material resources accessible at any one time and place, so demography tells us about the availability of human resources. In this way, the collectivity is dependent upon its demographic composition. And, like environment, demography is a social product affected by the social structure and yet itself a social determinant.

Demography and environment are closely related in ecological considerations. As with the environment, population configuration and density are likely to affect culture and ideology while also being affected by them. Demographic changes may be attributable to factors considered external to culture and production, but nowadays most of the changes ensue from social norms regarding marriage, birth-control, migration, and so on. In turn, these by-products of culture or regulation which take the form of population modifications in terms of age, sex, race, ethnic origin, occupation, education, or region contribute to shifts in interest strata, some strata enjoying greater weight than others. These shifts easily entail new interest expectations: ideological demands for adjustments which are believed to be in conformity with the new situation. As an example, the ever-increasing proportion of elderly people that is already noticeable in western societies is generating a new sense of 'grey power' which may in its turn evoke some form of backlash from the younger people sustaining them.

Considerations on change

Technology, demography, and environment all introduce change into the structure. Of the three, technology has long been considered *the* source of profound modifications in society. It is hardly necessary to recall Marx's insistence upon technology as the basic factor at the origin of social revolution. True, technology is often at the origin of important transformations of environment and demography. Still, the environment, in terms of its particular resources at specific times, remains determinant in fixing limits and forcing significant adaptations to the capacity for intervention. It is not inconceivable that in some cases environmental conditions may have been largely responsible for societies discovering techniques strictly as means of adapting to their surroundings. It is not always easy to draw the line between technical advance and ecological accommodation. The same rationale applies to demography, which also marks out a field of possible collective action. Like environment, demography, though interdependent with components of the structure, introduces dynamics and conditions of its own.

The degree of change is measured by the significance of the modifications brought about in the allotment of roles and controls. This process brings into the picture the part played by interests. For Sahlins, 'change begins with culture, not culture with change' and, by the same logic, culture determines utility (1976, 22, viii). True, utility is derived from culture or ideology. But before being integrated into culture, change and utility are fought out by interests. Sahlins seems impervious to the mobilizing aspect involved in the process of social mutations. Indeed, interests also derive from cultural values where they find their legitimating basis. At the same time, interests add a new dimension by introducing ideological claims which go against culture. Change is change in so far as it modifies the control organization of a given social network. In a supposedly static situation, interests only replicate claims that are in strict conformity with the culture from which they emanate; they only serve to reproduce faithfully the existing structure. Change, on the other hand, manifests itself by modifying the structure or the role network, or by making demands to this effect.[5]

Upheavals indicate a move for change by a group which has reached a level of non-tolerance owing to a discrepancy between expected controls and the controls actually or potentially ascribed to the performance of given roles. The group involved can be limited to circumscribed interests, to mediators, or to a whole collectivity. The threshold in collective expectations can be said to have been crossed whenever a state of relative deprivation (to use the terminology Ted Gurr applies to individuals) is produced owing to one of the following three circumstances: a reduction in the group's controls or, conversely, an increase in controls over the group; a change in expectations which calls for changes of controls in the group's favour; or, finally, a stabilization in the group's conditions when the group was expecting to see better days.[6] Furthermore, the justification for acting in contravention of the rules is to be found in the culture or the ideology

5 I have deliberately avoided any reference to progress, which is ultimately a normative concept. What is called progress by some may well be considered regression by others. Modernization introduces a more neutral notion by emphasizing the growing complexity of the role network. It is not my concern here to determine whether or not an element of change translates into modernity.

6 This discussion borrows and adapts from Gurr (1971) and Gurr and Duvall (1973), who rely on the psychological terminology of frustration to develop into discontent.

which sustains the group, and which provides reasons for and ways of expressing their discontent.

The regulators' potential or actual ability to withstand the move for change contributes to thwarting the move or giving it impetus. One study suggests that disloyalty on the part of the armed forces is a *sine qua non* for any successful rebellion (Russell 1974, 77ff.). The factors contributing to the making or breaking of army loyalty are therefore of some importance: one must consider not only the mix of class backgrounds among officers and conscripts, the recruitment criteria, and the contacts between the army and the civilian population (ibid. 81), but also the tradition of loyalty, the role traditionally attributed to the army in theory and practice, the culture or ideology developed through the soldiers' formative years, and so forth.

Revolutions rank as the most radical of upheavals, going to the root of things, as the etymology of 'radical' infers. Revolutions have occurred on very rare occasions, within the context of specific historical conditions of transition. For S.N. Eisenstadt, all revolutions, whether French, Russian, Turkish, or Chinese, took place only within 'imperial or imperial-feudal' types of political systems (1977, 68). These upheavals correspond to the modern revolutionary *Erlebnis*, a conscious attempt to reconstruct the social order from a lay orientation, after a severe cleavage is felt between a transcendental (religious) order and the mundane order (1978, 176). This idea of reconstruction is a direct consequence of a new capacity which has been attributed to reason, in association with promises of progress flowing from this capacity. Overall changes therefore arise under very strict structural conditions that only what is called modernity would permit, owing to the break with transcendental values, especially religion.

It is not my intention to delve into the ultimate causes of change or the nature of insurgencies and revolutions, but only to note their effects on our structure at work. The notion of change in itself opens up a new field of inquiry which I have only adumbrated, believing that it is better, for the time being, to set out the components of a structure before analysing the factors of its transformation.

My goal throughout this book has been to stake out a field of relationships to be investigated. It was not my intention to furnish answers, but rather to provide a framework for questioning. Besides, one does not test the validity of a framework; one rather tests its heuristic character from the quality of propositions that one can derive from it. Here is a structure of reference which, from a delimitation of reality, purports to provide for a specific investigation of control (as a social relation), while taking into consideration the surrounding social dynamics.

A structural view of feminism; or, What can the framework tell us about feminism?

The challenge of feminism to sociology

As a social movement feminism offers great analytic advantages in exhibiting the possibilities as well as the limits of the framework. In principle, any issue could be dealt with; we could discuss medicare or more limited cases having to do with debates developing in a restricted arena such as a city, a trade union, or a college. Feminism covers a diffuse reality which reaches everybody in one way or another. It is not, indeed, the only such issue. Religious movements, for instance, involve the adoption of patterns of behaviour that have repercussions over a whole gamut of activities, both private and public. Totalitarian ideologies, that is, ideologies with claims over all or most of people's actions, are also sustained by a type of mobilization which purports to intervene in people's private lives. Feminism is comprehensive with respect to its claim of reaching men as well as women at all levels of their social relations. From its claim to comprehensiveness – without necessarily being totalitarian – contemporary feminism is in a position to adopt modes of mobilization which aim at a wide audience.

Any movement, be it religious, ethnic, or otherwise, is usually held by its proponents as possessing a sense of its own. The movement's singularity would oblige the observer, if one followed the proponents' intentions, to develop an *ad hoc* framework of analysis, a framework that would naturally be expected to come out of the movement's own criteria of observation. The movement could thus only be understood from the inside. Any view from the outside is likely to be considered a sort of profanation, a violation of a group's own identity and sacred involvement in action. Following this rationale, only a feminist theory would be in a position to shed light on the feminist movement. This point of view is widely shared. The sense of uniqueness would disqualify in advance any attempt at analysis coming from without. The same reasoning applies to Marxism, which long ago developed a problematic of its own in order to explain the nature of the emerging labour movement and to legitimate a specific course of action. Doing likewise, the most radical forms of feminism strive for an approach that would go beyond established approaches such as Marxism, which, it is estimated, have a tendency to consider the female condition as incidental to a more significant economic or political reality. The purpose is twofold. First, the condition of women must be part and parcel of, if not central to, the chosen approach. Second, for most radicals, the new scope must be extensive enough to cover other concomitant types of discrimination such as racism. Lydia Sargent's *Women and Revolution* (1981) groups together authors who steadily underline incompatibilities emerging from the 'ménage à trois' (Joseph 1981) of Marxism, feminism, and antiracism: Marxism is judged sex-blind and race-blind while feminism is insufficiently materialist and often history-blind (Hartmann 1981). Even the notion of patriarchy which seems at times to sum up quite well the female condition is given a more descriptive than analytical status (ibid. 29). Proposing to elaborate simultaneously on how the spheres of production, reproduction, sexuality, and childrearing combine and how they vary depending upon class, race, and sex, as one author submits (Hicks 1981, 224), is quite an ambitious endeavour. The broad perspective is intended for an intervention that should take care of the recognized major forms of discrimination in the United States. The goal is basically interventionist and only secondarily analytical.

Keeping in mind that the analyst's role is one of 'disenchantment of the world,' to use Max Weber's terminology, it seems to me more appropriate to concentrate our attention on the feminist movement and, for the sake of clarity in the illustration, to consider other aspects as incidental. True, the framework deals especially with controls and the conditions necessary for their emergence, but it does not provide for a comprehensive outlook. The purpose of the present analysis is to understand not the movement as a whole but only aspects of it. Far be it from me therefore to attempt an essentialist discourse whose aim would be to grasp the total meaning of a reality, be it concrete or abstract. The objective is not to reveal, so to speak, the real meaning of feminism; this is in any case impossible. The objective is, from the outline provided by the framework, first, to situate and identify a number of elements pertaining to the structure of controls, and, second, to submit a number of relationships to investigation. Having to do with a framework and not a full-fledged theory, the goal is bound to be modest. There is nothing to prove as such; we have not reached yet this stage in the analysis. The goal is to put into interrelationship a number of factors already examined in the development of the framework.

The challenge of biology to feminism and sociology
I have established in the introduction the sociological character of the framework. Without denying the value of other approaches, I have insisted upon getting the most from the sociological perspective first. The postulate sustaining this logic is that there exists a dynamic proper to social relations. More than probably any other aspect of social life, the condition of women – that is their status and roles – is the most replete with considerations which try to explain it from points of view external to sociology, like biology.

Especially these days, biology is called upon to furnish what sometimes appear to be decisive explanations. Inspired by the behaviour of non-human primates, some authors believe in the continuity of behaviour from baboons, gorillas, and gibbons through to human beings. Numerous studies compare behaviour from one species to another, trying to underline the relevancy or irrelevancy of such an inquiry. The purpose of the biological approach is generally to show how the sexual division of labour derives from our belonging to the primate order. Lionel Tiger's often cited *Men in Groups* is representative of this tendency: to him politics derives in part from a natural process of male bonding and hierarchy found among primates and other animals. The argument was later re-enforced (Tiger and Fox, 1971, 232–40) by a more comprehensive proposition: human beings are 'programmed' into acting from a 'human social biogrammar,' a code which underlies all human behaviour. It has to do not with instincts but with 'human needs' that have to be satisfied if any society is to work well. Utopias are deemed dangerous precisely because they diverge from the basic hierarchical character of social relations. From this stream of thought Steven Goldberg (1974) extracts a reduction, which is not alien to Konrad Lorenz: the male hormonal system is said to prompt a feeling of aggression that results in the inevitable dominance of men over women. Testosterone makes *the* difference between male and female, a difference that leads to man's quasi-monopoly on high-level abstraction (204) as well as to man's preponderance in all societies without exception. Some opponents (Gough 1975) prefer to retaliate on this same ground by showing the diversity of behaviour from which no common rule can be inferred. On this matter, the biological school is often accused of selecting traits and patterns of male dominance and female subserviance when it suits what they wish to demonstrate (Leibowitz 1975). In a move to reconcile the biological and sociological schools, Janet Sayers (1982, 3) contends that sexual inequality is a product of biological as well as social and historical factors. The whole discussion is aimed at evaluating the respective influences of nature and nurture.

This vexatious problem of nature versus nurture is likely to remain insoluble for lack of conclusive data. Only an analytical artifice can strip the human being of its social character and isolate it as a biological entity. Comparisons with other animals, primates or otherwise, provide only hypothetical answers. Proponents of the biological approach take pride in imposing over and above sociological explanations the most basic laws governing social relations. True, one should always be careful about what a discipline takes for granted. For the biological analyst, sociology would generally ignore the underlying biological determinants of humanity. The point is worth keeping in mind; but the character of inevitability as put forward for instance by some authors is endowed with a sense of biological essentialism. That humankind should in the beginning have been close to the primates in its organization of social life is not surprising. Conditions were probably favourable to such a division of labour. But assigning a definitive division of roles between sexes in the name of a timeless and universal law is tantamount to Aristotle's strongly held opinion that slaves were born such by nature. Interestingly enough, proponents of biological inevitability have a tendency to match their 'scientific' pronouncements with moral ones which look more like ethical considerations in search of scientific confirmation. To them the man-woman relationship is cast forever, whatever the evolution of technology. The point about essentialism is that it can hardly be proved wrong because it posits an order of necessity in advance from an induction (which can by nature be contingent): in order to be a man, man does and must act in this or that fashion, and the same applies to woman.

The same reasoning could be applied to other social relations like the division of labour in general. From experience we know that social relations are plastic, and that controls which looked natural in the past are deemed unjustified today: slavery stands as a good example. No one is in a position to determine once and for all the allocation of controls within a given social network: the family, the school, or the government. This epistemological stand has nothing to do with a plea for freedom or humanism. It is only an appeal to analytical prudence.

Biology is by and large external to the present framework. This is no reason, however, for ignoring it. In the introduction I discarded the argument that the innate sociability of human beings was explicative of society. But the recognition of a 'double standard' distinguishing men from women in all (or almost all) societies cannot be ignored. This fact is not a matter of opinion but of reality; a reality, though, that has no sacrosanct value in itself.

When dealing with 'human nature' in chapter 3, I submitted that abilities, be they natural, ascribed, or achieved, may have an impact on collective expectations. Some exclusive abilities entitle some agents to specific roles or patterns within a role, to the exclusion of others. Biological differences, especially in terms of sex and age, generally fall into this category. The social distinctions being made between men and women may or may not have derived from our primate ancestry, but they progressively result from a cultural adjustment to an environment that changes through time and from place to place. It is most likely that in the beginning humankind was more closely linked to nature in all respects. Activities allocated respectively to each gender were probably linked to conditions that made such allocation almost imperative without being absolutely necessary. As technology progressed, the link with the environment loosened, making possible new arrangements in the cultural assignment of roles. As mentioned in the conclusion about the impact of the environment, the effect of nature on culture becomes less noticeable with the growth of technology.

I am not concerned, though, with the conformity of human actions to criteria of efficiency, whether they be of a biological, psychological, or organizational nature, or otherwise. The framework only takes into consideration controls, sets of controls, socialization, mobilization, and regulation.

THE TRADITIONAL STRUCTURE

In principle, the social structure I have proposed can be tackled from any of its components, depending upon the type of observation the analyst plans to pursue. One could start by putting the phenomenon of mediation at the centre of one's interest, or by concentrating on the impact of channels. Dealing with a social movement leads one to deal first with the patterns already existing and conveyed by culture, together with the dynamics the movement belongs to – the modes of production, socialization, and regulation – and thereafter to proceed to the analysis of new patterns as they are defended by an ideology which challenges the legitimacy or efficiency of cultural patterns. The feminist movement is no exception. Its disputation of cultural values is strong enough to validate an inquiry into the elementary forms of control as they existed in former times, should it be only to understand the breaks and continuities that might have taken place thereafter and thus make more evident the relativity of men's relationships with women.

Culture

Male dominance in terms of basic controls is generally recognized in all societies including contemporary ones, with, of course, various degrees of emphasis from one collectivity to another (Rosaldo and Lamphere 1974, 3; Dandurand 1981, 98). The existence of matriarchies, the rule of women, amounts, it seems, to sheer myth (Bamberger 1974). Bands of hunters and gatherers offer an interesting field of investigation since they display the most ancient forms of sociability that we know of today.

Until the mid-seventies, the strict sexual division of labour among hunter-gatherers was considered by most anthropologists as close to universal: man the hunter and woman the gatherer almost amounted to an established rule. The rationale behind this was, and it is still maintained today by many, that woman's functions of reproduction explained her limited role in pristine societies (Reiter 1975, 11). From the very beginning men would therefore have held a monopoly over hunting and defence, leaving women to the confines of home activities. However, more in-depth studies have called for less rigid delimitations of roles. Examples drawn from the !Kung women (Draper 1975), the Navajo Indians of New Mexico and Arizona (Lamphere 1974), and the Agta in the Philippines (Estioko-Griffin and Griffin 1981) tend to show an attenuation of this rule. Probably even more interesting is the challenge to the accepted view that hunting was the common practice right from early times. For Zihlman (1981) it most likely developed late in human evolution, extending from the technological and social bases of the gathering stages: bows and arrows, widely used nowadays by bands, are relatively recent artefacts.

All this concern for the ancient past is obviously intended to dispute the widespread consensus among social scientists as to the minor role assigned to women in comparison with the major controls held in men's hands. There is already, at this stage of analysis, an ideological purpose in opposing the western cultural reading of pristine society as it has been elaborated by male anthropologists. Establishing the egalitarian character of ancient bands would demonstrate the cultural nature of subsequent controls as they were introduced by successive civilizations. It seems to be widely admitted, for instance, that women were submitted to a regime of greater confinement as urbanization progressed in Ancient Egypt and Greece (Boulding 1977); women were, so to speak, withdrawn from the productive network they had been part of.

Culture is not only made up of patterns of behaviour; it is also made up of forms regarding aesthetics of all sorts, and ultimately of forms concerning the code of communication: language. Now the code itself happens to be biased in favour of males. Such is the case in English, especially in its syntax and semantics (Spender 1980; Kramarae 1981). It is even more obvious in French, which has genders, and in which the masculine is set as the universal gender: in any situation the masculine embraces the feminine. Should there be one man in an audience of ten thousand women, the adjectives used in the plural form to qualify this collectivity necessarily have to be masculine. The word 'naïve' borrowed by English and derived from the feminine form in French sounds awkward to a Gallic ear whenever the adjective is applied to a man (notwithstanding the cultural bias in favour of the realism of males). Being a cultural form, language is not neutral: it is 'man made' (Spender 1980, 139), a product of control exercised by men over it. Having enjoyed a position of high and nearly exclusive public visibility (in the arts and literature, as well as in government), they have been in a position to influence the setting and the linguistic rules and norms in their favour. Any linguistic code is likely to carry within itself traits of the setting it emerged from.

The traditional culture marks the differentiation of sexes in terms of distinct spheres of activities, the domestic and the public (Rosaldo 1974, 23ff.). Most women spend a large part of their adult life in giving birth to children and rearing them, and because of this pattern of mothering, women are confined to the domestic sphere. The consequences are important because they entail a whole series of patterns in attitudes and behaviour that underline the differences between the sexes and their respective spheres of action. Males are born as boys who must show some skills in order to secure themselves the status of men. It is assumed to be an achieved status (even though almost all boys happen to become men). Women, on the contrary, are ascribed a status: they are sisters, wives, or mothers. Females are seen as deriving their status from nature (Ortner 1974, 73), whereas males come to be looked at as products of culture.[1] Men's role is largely considered as an accomplishment through stages and rites of passage, and women's as cycles of nature recorded, so to speak, by culture. (This does not exclude rites for women too, but they are probably performed in accordance with nature's imperatives.)

To this twofold model, then, correspond intellectual and personality traits which are supposed to characterize each sex. Numerous inquiries and cross-cultural surveys agree in confirming general perceptions of sex roles which are explained and corroborated by sex traits (Williams and Best 1982). Gender-typing does not only entail differences in clothing and activities; it seems also to affect the means of expression. There seems to be a female language style (Delamont 1980, 21). Women's intonation, pronunciation, and even syntax and vocabulary are said to produce a more hesitant and less positive discourse than man's, putting women in a position of subordination.

In conformity with this cultural vision of sex roles, authors like Parsons and Bales differentiated between functions in the family, attributing to the father activities high in 'instrumentality' and to the mother activities high in 'expressive-ness.' The authors confirm in academic parlance the traditional dichotomy of men as made for the outside and women for the inside (1955, 45, 47). The interest-ing aspect of this contribution is its conformity to cultural values. In a bolder fashion, Freud wrote about women's penis envy, which is meant to translate into

---

1 This view is challenged by Peggy R. Sanday (1981, 4–5), who argues that men are also bound to nature, being subject to death, destruction, and animality, as are women. The point in dispute is not a question of fact – whether males are as linked to nature as females or not – but simply a question of appreciation as expressed by culture. Ortner's wording is clear: women are 'seen' as closer to nature.

psychological language an already accepted situation of dependence. Culture easily pervades the theoretical field because it has all the trappings of naturalness and common sense. The lower status of women did not have to be proved by psychology or sociology, but simply explained.

This very sketchy attempt at circumscribing the role of women is only intended to demonstrate briefly the sort of components that can shape a discussion on culture in relation to feminism. The elements will vary according to the types of controls the analyst wants to investigate. It is essential to keep in mind that culture remains throughout the discussion a construct of factors chosen for their pertinence. These may sometimes appear far removed from observable reality; again it is up to the analyst to demonstrate the relevancy of his or her outline in accordance with the set of controls he or she wants to put in evidence. There is therefore no reality existing in advance, a given which we would call culture. Its extensiveness depends largely upon the use being made of it. Culture is utilized as a heuristic device, no more. Now, the farther the limits are pushed, the more extensive the explanation is likely to be, since its explanatory capacity applies to a wider range of events.

The setting up of values, norms, and patterns as levels of culture has some meaning in so far as it is put in relationship within one of three dynamics already proposed: conditioning, production, and regulation. Some controls may be situated outside these dynamics, but the most significant controls have something to do with one if not all three substructures.

Conditioning
Control of conditioning has long been exercised exclusively by males. The major outlets for expression, whether on the hustings, in the academy, or in the arts or sciences, were male monopolies. More specifically, men held exclusive rights over public channels of diffusion, attributing a position of high visibility to themselves whereas women were left in the 'intimacy' of their homes. In this division of labour, male interests were well served. The routine, repetitious, and tedious functions of primary socialization have always been entrusted to women's care. Risks of deviation in the socializing process were limited, for women's interventions were confined to their own individual families and were thus limited and compartmentalized. The sole relationships possible among females were by and large social or parasocial ones. Women did not, on the whole, form communities, as men did in the army, the government, or the club.

Primary schools in western societies often remained women's responsibility. In this case, the programs they taught were not defined by them, and even pedagogical activities were strictly circumscribed. Further socialization conceived for boys would usually fall within a direct male sphere of influence (Ortner 1974, 80).

The socialization of girls has long been oriented towards low expectations based on values of dependency, submissiveness, and conformity (Iglitzin 1974, 25–6). A whole literature, at least from Simone de Beauvoir through Betty Friedan and onward, has emphasized the making of the passive woman. It is interesting to note, though, that the model proposed has not always been that persistent, even if in practice women have remained outside the public sphere. In traditional rural settings women were accustomed to work in the fields and share other tasks with their husbands. The advent of a stratum of prosperous merchants and industrialists combined with a growing number of people whose incomes permitted them to employ domestic help gave rise to the exaltation of idle wives remaining close to their homes. Emulating the aristocratic way of life, successful bourgeois tried to replicate it in another fashion. In contrast with the nobility, the bourgeoisie enhanced family values and imposed a new way of life. Whereas aristocrats kept themselves to themselves as a class, the bourgeois extended their range of relationships while at the same time establishing a firmer distinction between public and private life. The family became the centre of great attention: severed from the public sphere, it was henceforth perceived as an autonomous and self-sufficient cell of society (Laurin-Frenette 1981, 162). Family life was expected to secure prosperity and social order. At this stage, liberal individualism was prescribed for the heads of families, that is for men. (It is, indeed, because of this same principle of liberal individualism that women soon demanded the same treatment.) With the progressive disappearance of servants, good housekeeping became the entire responsibility of wives. Ruth Schwartz Cowan (1976) exposes very convincingly what the transition meant and how an ideology of duty was built up on the need for housewives to satisfy new imperatives: child care became more demanding, as did standards of housekeeping. Even though the number of children per family declined on the average and household technology improved, the time spent on housework by non-employed housewives remained relatively the same between 1920 and 1970 (Cowan 1976, 15; Thrall 1982, 182). According to Cowan, an ideology of 'guilt' developed in the twenties. Magazines and their advertisements created a world of obligations for women towards their families. Betty Friedan's 'feminine mystique' describes this mission of women at its apex, when it was losing its ideological character and becoming integrated into cultural heritage. The era of magazines, which was at that time moulding a way of life, is interesting to analyse. As part of the structure of conditioning, before the advent of television, magazines were providing visual and reading vistas of national dimension. Whereas newspapers and even radio stations had local standing, magazines furnished a sense of belonging to a new and much wider community.

They were not meant, for the most part, to air conflicting opinions but rather to convey an exquisite feeling of well-being in North America. Norman Rockwell's covers for the *Saturday Evening Post* illustrate this ethos better than anything, and the suburban lifestyle became a fuller embodiment of it.

The dynamics of conditioning created by the era of magazines and later modified by the introduction of television was made possible by a structure of components: a new mode of expression (a new channel) by itself, the magazine format and periodicity, interests ready to invest, advertisers ready to bank on a new form of influence, a new type of content, and finally a type of culture oriented towards consumption. The ultimate effect is the creation of a new world of communications spreading standards of behaviour on a nationwide scale. Television reinforced this same dynamics when it superseded the function of some magazines which had to fold through lack of advertising revenue. Diffusion through magazines and television was the result of technological changes introduced into the conditioning structure. Especially in the case of women's magazines, advertising has been used to publicize advances in the technology of household appliances and house-cleaning. The overall content conveys a lifestyle: stories, pictures, advice, advertising, and the magazine format itself contribute to making a domestic whole together with the implicit values it holds.

It is a common practice to analyse the content of mass media. There are studies (Tuchman, Daniels, and Benet 1978; Butler and Paisley 1980) that suggest that the roles assigned to women in commercials, magazine advertisements and stories, films, and television programs are usually secondary to those of men. Up to the seventies, women were defined by their relationship or absence of relationship with men, working women being set aside as untypical. Analysts of the female condition often adopt a feminist stance and condemn media content for being sexist or for alienating women. It is obviously not my purpose to proceed with this approach. My intent is not to label roles but only to distinguish them from others without making a judgment about their appropriateness. In this respect, it is worth noting that from the end of the second world war to the sixties mass media content in the United States was largely oriented towards what was called the middle-class lifestyle. Here were depicted the true Americans. Workers and blacks were seldom featured. Indeed, content analysis reveals patterns sustained through a whole discourse. The most subtle ones are the most interesting to expose. For instance, the 'voice-over' in commercials, in which a male voice delivers the substantive message – 'Yes ladies, "Removall" soap is made for you' – in the course of time sanctions men's ascendency over the opposite sex. In the same category can be placed afternoon radio programs, whose plays, phone-ins, and medical advice are intended to fill the time of women at home (Karpf 1980). Content analysis would also be appropriate, for instance, in the study of comic strips on a comparative basis through time: one could compare Dagwood with Blondie and ask who is the more stupid? Two generations of French-speaking children have been socialized by the *Tintin* series and many studies in France have been written on different aspects of this work. Interestingly enough, the only female character of any importance is 'la Castafiore,' an aquiline-nosed diva whose behaviour is ludicrous. The objective, in this case, would not be to point out the author's misogyny but to investigate the type of roles held by women in stories intended for children.

Most of these instances seem to illustrate a cultural appreciation, not in that they accurately reflect the factual situation but because they express the ideal life of women as it has been accepted for some time. For this reason the patterns being shown or implied look so natural to the audience in general that they do not have to be legitimated, defended, or explained. They are part of the culture, and their means of transmission are part of a socialization process which develops, as explained in chapter 2, in a climate of spontaneous acceptability. This is not to deny the existence of interests. Far from it. The functionalist approach would have us believe that consensus becomes a sign of normal integration which would erase the existence of interests. Culture is the product of interests which in turn derive their reference values from culture. Male interests are, so to speak, recognized by culture, but they also perpetuate the values that legitimate them through conditioning and regulation.

Male interests are sustained through the actual exercise of controls and through the pattern-maintenance assumed by a socialization process that is mainly under male control. If socialization has any significant impact, it is on the division of labour that it is expected to work most efficiently.

Male interests have managed to keep a constant hold on the major networks of output or what are culturally held to be so. This does not mean, however, that men have always been more useful or more indispensable to their collectivities. Far from it; it is agreed by some, for example, that gathering was often essential for the physical well-being of the band whereas the products of hunting were of secondary importance. But the value (prestige) attributed to the activities of males (Rosaldo and Lamphere 1974, 19) has always been more culturally appreciated, possibly because men were in a better position to impose the evaluation of their own works and to socialize women to it.

Production
The traditional setting invests males with control over what are considered the major fields of decision making. The distinction between the public and the domestic world already sets spheres of activities which respond to dynamics that are worth discussing separately.

So far as the sexes are concerned, the public market operates from what appears to be a dual division of labour. Women are mainly allocated positions that imply low control in the organization, a high level of uncertainty, little upward mobility, and a low salary (Barron and Norris 1976; Kanter 1977). Following what Kanter calls the feminization of clerical work, decision-making positions remain men's prerogative even in sectors where women make up the overwhelming majority. And whenever women are part of an administration, chances are great that they will be attributed staff roles rather than management ones. This tradition dates back to the time when office work was introduced. In its early stages, office work was 'asexual,' indifferent to the occupant's sex. In the second half of the nineteenth century, clerical work was assumed predominantly by men (Wilson 1982, 83), but the whole process became progressively feminized (Davies 1982). After some controversy as to whether or not it was proper for women to indulge in such activities, office work became recognized as a function that devolved upon them. Made routine through 'scientific' management, it provided a low-paying job designed for a transient work force (before marriage). Teaching, which was originally a male job, also evolved into a category of female, inexpensive labour. By contrast, professions were originally closed to women, leaving to men exclusive control over the ability to regulate the conditions of access and exercise of such disciplines. Even though barriers have been lifted since then, the credential system (Collins 1979) is still in effect, establishing thresholds or rites of passage which serve to limit the flow of admissible candidates. Sally Hacker (1983) argues that the 'culture of engineering' prescribes a strong concentration on mathematics in the formative years in order to separate those who will later enjoy jobs requiring managerial skills from those in the lower stratum who will have to content themselves with routine jobs susceptible to automation. Within this context, one may contend that owing to their former socialization women are more likely to exclude themselves, feeling less inclined to study mathematics. This point of view, whether we adhere to it or not, underlines the effects of socialization on expectations and the will to persist. The gender division of labour derives from a double cultural exclusion: resistance on the part of male employers and the socialization of women to lower expectations (Descarries-Bélanger 1980). Not only have women been excluded from major controls in the organization of production and relegated to subservient functions or menial work, but their earnings have remained much lower than those of males; comparative analyses show gaps that can be quite variable, the female labour force faring much better, for instance, in France than in Great Britain (Oakley 1981, 161). To this must be added the factor of part-time employment, where women proportionately far outnumber men.

The distinction between public and domestic markets has varied over time. In some periods, like Antiquity, the distinction was quite marked, whereas in others, like the Middle Ages, private and public spheres were more fused together. Mercantile activities, from the beginnings in the Late Middle Ages to the industrial revolution in the first half of the nineteenth century, have brought about the compartmentalization of roles which resulted in a sharp distinction between the public and the domestic spheres.

At the beginning of the industrial era men were more in demand as employees than women, even though the latter were the mainstay of the sweated textile industry. This led to a corresponding division of labour in the family: men were involved in life outside the family whereas women were restricted to that sphere. Men were, so to speak, removed from their households whereas very few women, in fact, were involved in factory life (Tilly and Scott 1978, 77). Women were more or less left with the domestic responsibility. This new organization of family life and labour translated into a clearer demarcation line between male and female occupations and roles. The long-term result, thanks to appropriate mobilization to that effect, was to confirm women's role as professional homemakers (Laurin-Frenette 1981, 164). As conditions made it possible for labourers' families to live on only one salary, wives preferred to adopt the Victorian pattern and stay at home (Wilson 1982, 53). This confirmed the tendency to divide labour according to gender much as the public sphere was divided from the private.

France offers an interesting field for observation because of the unadulterated character of its experience. It can almost be taken as an extreme case, and using it as a yardstick, one can gauge less extreme situations in the western hemisphere. Historians note the revival in France of Roman law between the thirteenth century and the eighteenth, a revival that is concomitant with the consolidation of private property (Flandrin 1979, 125). Paternal and marital authority are therefore reinforced. The father assumes the double role of head of the household (*chef de famille*) and head of family property (*chef de la communauté*); in a word, he is the master of the house (Bodard Silver 1977). The practice of patronymic surnames appears to date from the fourteenth century. The Napoleonic Code of 1804 (which inspired the Quebec Civil Code of 1866) integrated the principles drawn from Roman law (*pater familias*) with traditional law (Coutume de Paris and others) in vesting the father with the role of supreme authority in the family, enjoying 'control over the use and disposal of property on one hand, and control over family members in the household on the other' (ibid. 263). Married women were reduced to the status of minors, losing their rights over their own persons, property, and children. The French civil code served as an instrument of consolidation for a rising bourgeoisie – a class built from the accumulation of capital and direct control over capital investment. Nevertheless, many questions remain unanswered; France was not particularly developed at the time, its system of production relied more on the petty bourgeoisie – small shopkeepers – than on a true bourgeoisie.

In many respects the Napoleonic Code serves to consolidate the patrimony of the *rentiers*, but this is another question.

In view of the fact that husband and wife no longer work together but separately, one for the other, both for the matrimonial community, but under the husband's tutelage, it is admissible to talk about an implicit contract. Kenneth Boulding (1978) sees this relationship as one of exchange and reciprocity that differs from a commercial contract, among other things owing to the psychological value at stake. The aim here is not to fathom the emotional content of the matrimonial relationship but more sociologically to extract the social aspect involved in it. Symmetry in reciprocity or exchange is culturally or ideologically determined, so much so that it is impossible to determine in advance an ideal or objective state of equilibrium. For more than a century and up until quite recently, the engagement binding husband and wife compelled the former to guarantee a living and the latter to provide household labour. Rights and duties were established thus and culturally accepted, with the control they implied. There was an exchange of implicit controls: one on the fruits of the husband's labour and the other on the wife's disposal of time.

Recently more attention has been paid to housework as a productive activity, though in the United States housewives are considered, for statistical purposes, to be 'economically inactive' and so outside the productive process (Wolpe 1978, 294). Some accusingly refer to this as the 'legal pickpocketing of each woman's paycheck' (Ahern and Bliss 1976, ix) which cynically denies the woman's contribution to the couple. It is interesting to note, as Christine Delphy points out,[2] that since all domestic services furnished by wives are actually available on the market, they do have a value that is translatable into a given salary. When performed outside one's home these services are accountable in the gross national product. Indeed, the discussion has been extended to cover men's work in the house as well. But whenever both husband and wife work outside the home, household tasks are, on the whole, assumed by the wife, following a pattern illustrated by the 'superwoman syndrome' (Scanzoni and Szinovacz 1980, 20), which is also observed in the Soviet Union (Deckard 1975, 230).

It is not my concern to determine whether any arrangement or division of labour is justified or not, at any one time. The forms vary but must be considered by the analyst as given while keeping in mind that, up to the present time, men have been in control of the major channels through which all three substructures – conditioning, production, and regulation – work.

Regulation
Men's roles as public interveners and decision makers led to their recognition in all

2 Quoted in Andrée Michel (1978, 193–4) from *Partisans* 1970, no. 54–5

major sectors of regulation. With very few exceptions like Cleopatra, Elizabeth I, and Catherine the Great, women have generally been excluded from the world of governance, which was held to be the preserve of men. The traditional structure of exclusive male preponderance works from a consistency of the three substructures, while regulation confirms man's capacity to lay down the rules which are bound to work in his favour. The structure as a whole works from the interplay of its parts; the more consistent interests are with culture in their dynamics within production, conditioning, and regulation, the fewer conflicts there are in any of these substructures. The tight coherence of the whole structure in favour of men was broken down from outside. Ironically, it took place when male labour was made distinct from the household; in other words when technology introduced a new way of organizing work. With this conversion to industrialization, which also directly affected some women, although to a lesser degree, one begins to see the first signs of overall change.

STRUCTURES IN MUTATION

The impact of culture on ideology: the first feminist wave
The analytical interest of mobilization is that it offers an opportunity to uncover factors which would be harder to detect in a static situation. Conflict strengthens ideological choices, and change in one component, in this case the technology of production, modified the activities of men and, in so doing, affected the traditional arrangement of roles.

Working conditions for women in the nineteenth century and well into the twentieth were established in terms of a man's world. Jobs were segregated by sex, from the start, with most adult white men being allotted a 'family wage.' The others – young people, women, blacks, and so on – were reduced to depressed wages, incidentally with the support of the trade unions (Hartmann 1981, 21–2; Wilson 1982, 84). But however hard and painful the conditions may have been for these women, it is not from this group that discontent emerged. There may have been disgruntlement at times, but there was no real movement of mobilization. It is well established that the first feminist wave was sustained by what is often referred to as a middle-class liberalism (Evans 1977). There may have been predecessors in France, Germany, and Great Britain, like the 'citoyennes républicaines révolutionnaires,' but they were still marginal.

The first expression of feminism was articulated by people from middle-class backgrounds. This raises two questions: why this stratum of society, and why the feminist solution?

Liberalism derives in great part from the principles of individuality laid out by Protestantism. These provide for the personal responsibility of each human being for his or her own salvation. It becomes a right and a duty to decide in one's own conscience what is right and what is wrong. It is not surprising, therefore, that liberalism laid its foundation on the Protestant bedrock of individuality, responsibility, and freedom of conscience. And gender was not expected to make any significant modification of these principles. Some sects in fact extended forms of religious authority to women, and the Quakers became carriers of feminist ideas and leadership.

Indeed, liberalism may be expressed as a fusion of Protestantism and eighteenth-century rationalism and enlightenment. But the impulse given by Protestantism to values of involvement in this world, to work as a continuation of God's creation, clearly contributed to endowing liberalism with values of action as a moral imperative. The work ethic has certainly affected a segment of women who were inactive, not to say idle, maybe arousing a feeling of guilt which was alien to their Catholic counterparts. Aristocratic societies with Catholic loyalties such as France felt little compassion for those suffering from inequalities derived from the system. The world was thus created and willed by God. The idle lifestyle of a whole leisure class aroused little resentment. It was felt that some were born to work and others were not, a situation that Voltaire recognized in the eighteenth century as natural and desirable. Until the nineteenth century, the bourgeois ideal in France was to earn as much money as possible in order to enjoy later the fruits of other people's labour through a *rente*, as the aristocrats did. That bourgeois women in that country should feel the same aspirations as their husbands and revel in social life should come as no surprise. As a matter of fact, there is no inherent impulse either to spend one's life in fashionable society or conversely to devote it to work or sacrifice. Culture provides for these values, and religion (which is often part of culture) provides an even stronger impetus.

The bourgeois ideal that arose from Protestantism was one of incessant work in order to reinvest and accumulate the fruits of labour. There were certainly provisions for leisure, but probably much more for the conspicuous expression of wealth which amounted to a necessary condition in order to be in a position to acquire even more wealth. There was also the search for social recognition, a desire to be considered equal to the best. Assigning 'middle-class' women to a passive role of pleasure or partial idleness was not totally consistent with the liberal ethic. The feminist ideology emerged as a solution to an ideological-cultural predicament. In Catholic societies, bourgeois women tried to emulate their aristocratic counterparts who were living on unearned income; being bourgeois did not involve any break with the lifestyle or the expectations of the nobility. In France, the grande bourgeoisie tried to adapt to the standards of the nobility, whereas in Britain, from a process of intermixing, the nobility became involved in commercial ventures and capitalists obtained a certain degree of recognition, albeit only because of the importance of the City.

All ideologies emerge from cultural roots and stand as an adaptation to a changing situation. There is no such thing as total ideological antithesis to cultural values. Marxism is not the antithesis of liberalism but an attempt to surpass capitalism. Feminism is consistent with liberalism and forces liberal principles to their logical conclusions. Feminism appeared when liberalism was in the ascendant; it simply stated that the individualism which is exercised by men should be exercised by women in some specific fields of activity.

The feminist movement happened to be strong in societies where Protestant and liberal principles were widely accepted: the United States, Great Britain, English Canada, Australia, New Zealand, and the Scandinavian countries. In various forms and with different emphases, the movement upheld values of interest to people who stood to gain some control if the same rules were applied to all.

Many demands pertained to legal and property controls: rights to hold property, to sign contracts, to sue or be sued, to earn a living (Giele and Smock 1977, 308), and to gain access to the professions (Evans 1976, 2). In Great Britain, the emphasis was put on the right to respectable jobs. There was an increase in the number of single women as a result of male emigration (Vicinus 1977, xvi; Klein 1967, 464). Simultaneously there were campaigns for temperance in order to improve the lot of some married women who, having no control over the family's property, were particularly vulnerable to abuse caused by alcohol (Wilson 1982, 116). The right to vote was claimed with a view to adding more weight to these demands. Significantly, it was largely in Anglo-Saxon countries with Protestant and liberal traditions that women were first granted the right to vote, with the first world war accelerating the process in some cases.

Countries with strong Catholic traditions were more hesitant. In France, many legislative actions in favour of women were adopted by the Chamber of Deputies between the two world wars but were turned down by the Senate, and until 1938 French women owed complete obedience to their husbands. The right to vote was ultimately recognized by the De Gaulle regime in 1944. In Latin America, most countries waited until after the second world war to grant women the right to vote in national elections (although Brazil, Uruguay, and Cuba introduced it in the thirties; Chaney 1979, 67). In Quebec, around the turn of the nineteenth century, the legislature had inadvertently given women the right to vote, although this was revoked in 1834. For decades the clerical media, with Henri Bourassa as their leader, claimed that politics was not women's business and that a move in this direction would go against natural law. However, in 1940, despite a campaign on the part of the clergy and its allies in the media, the Liberal government of the day passed the woman suffrage bill (Stoddart 1973). Although Germany is largely Protestant, a coalition of the church, the army, and an authoritarian government, all hostile to woman suffrage, made conditions rather difficult for women there too (Evans 1976, 6).

I have touched here on the most obvious aspects of the mobilizing process, its outputs: rules, as they have been legislated and have later been applied and interpreted. But this is only the tip of the iceberg. Mobilization puts in motion a whole structure of components that more recent expressions of feminism have placed under a new light.

Organized mobilization

The second wave of feminism came in response to changes and inconsistencies of some components in the structure, especially in regard to the cultural setting. This new form of feminism, articulated through more numerous and diversified demands, has proceeded through three stages, organized mobilization, succeeded by a period of spontaneous and face-to-face activism, superseded in turn by a reorganized mode of action.

In its first stage in the early sixties, new feminism was, on the whole, a reaction by women who had been educated, that is socialized, for professions or administrative work to which they were later denied access in one way or another. The right of access to college education was recognized by society, however unenthusiastically, but actual professional practice was not yet really accepted. More and more women, many of them married, were attracted into low-paying clerical work; the sixties were years of manpower shortage, a situation that seemed likely to benefit women, but this need for woman power did not noticeably affect the upper strata of professional work despite the increase in higher education among women (Banks 1981, 211; Wilson 1982, 126).

Betty Friedan's classic 'problem that has no name,' which is explained by her as a 'problem of identity' (1963, 77), is better understood by Jo Freeman (1975, 31), who sees it in terms of 'relative deprivation,' which is close to Gurr's language. True, Gurr's approach is permeated with psychology, but the notion can be given a collective connotation. In my mind, feelings of frustration of strictly psychological origin certainly exist, but whenever a feeling of dissatisfaction is generalized to a whole stratum of agents occupying essentially the same role, it is more likely to be a feeling of social origin. When Friedan writes that women feel the 'need to grow and fulfill their potentialities as human beings,' (77) she is expressing a Protestant liberal point of view about the nature of man and woman. The 'problem that has no name' is more satisfactorily explained as a cultural disjunction between a form of education oriented towards action and the subsequent state of agents who are brought back to a former cultural state of living: the household. The ideology triggered off is simply one in search of consistency between socialization and practical action. Better-educated women, as a group, reacted to a situation they could compare with the lot of their husbands and former male classmates (Freeman 1975, 31; Chafe 1977, 3). The feminist ideology takes over as a response to a cultural contradiction between the values transmitted by education and the absence of corresponding patterns in the division of labour.

The foundation of NOW (the National Organization of Women) in the United States in 1966 marked the resumption of a former mode of mobilization: the claim to identical rights to those of males through an organized body. Usually made up of middle-aged women, the women's rights groups were directly oriented towards regulative solutions to issues such as job discrimination, equal pay, and property laws (Teather 1976, 217). The Canadian Royal Commission on the Status of Women appointed in 1967 is characteristic of the goals being pursued at the time. The mobilization was directed by official representatives towards the regulative bodies. The message conveyed was liberal, as were the means of conveying it. In this case, there was coherence between the conditioning and the regulative structures.

Diffused mobilization
The second stage corresponds to an entirely different dynamics mainly brought about by a change in the conditioning structure itself. The mobilization was this time directed at the cultural base, the female collectivity at large, and not immediately through regulative channels. This change of tack entailed a modification in the use of conditioning channels. Instead of the traditional patterns of communication – meetings, leaflets, official gatherings – feminist groups turned to face-to-face encounters as a new channel of mobilization. And such a medium of mobilization in turn implied a new mode of mediation, a new set of mediators – communicators or leaders – and a new type of content. All the components of this new conditioning structure are considered as working consistently with the others.

Let us look at the aspect which is the most obvious without being necessarily the most significant. (No element of the structure is deemed more important as such than the others.) The women's liberation movements had in common a reading of social relations as phenomena of oppression or exploitation. Having evolved from similar analyses of the condition of blacks, labourers, and students, the approach only had to apply the same reasoning to women. The problem it raised was to determine whether the oppression of women is part and parcel of a more comprehensive reality, such as the capitalist system, or if it is in itself a recurring phenomenon in all types of societies. This distinction led to a split, with one group analyzing class and trying to reconcile feminism with Marxism and the other pointing towards an autonomous framework peculiar to the condition of women. In countries like France, Great Britain, and Germany, where social militancy has by tradition been stronger, socialist or Marxist feminism is more common than in the United States, where, it seems, men have more often constituted the major enemy (Bouchier 1978, 105).

The notion of patriarchy around which radical feminism often evolved permitted an extension of scrutiny to all levels of social activity, and especially aspects of socialization that were formerly taken for granted. The universality of the battle of sexes, it was contended, showed to what extent it was possible to bring to light a variety of controls exercised upon women in all spheres of life. In some cases, lesbianism was considered the best way out of the male stranglehold.

It is not my purpose to analyse in detail the different variants that arose during the late sixties and early seventies. With leaders coming from different backgrounds (civil rights movements, NOW, and leftist militant organizations), the ideology was bound to make up a diversified whole. It was flexible, open to additions and discoveries of all sorts so long as these conformed to a common denominator about male dominance and the improvement of women's situation. The ideology did not prescribe strict canons of orthodoxy integrated into a hierarchy of modes of mobilization.

The format of mobilization was consistent with the ideology as well as with a strategy designed for a cultural gender revolution. Workers' movements, trade unions, and political parties have often been the creations of intellectual mediators who acted as the bona fide representatives of the interests of labour. Such movements usually have from the outset both a hierarchy of functions and a co-optive method of replacing officers. The women's liberation movement, on the other hand, intended to start from the grass roots and to remain at that level.

Mobilization was based upon the principle of 'consciousness raising' and took place in small groups, a format that facilitates confidential meetings. Through a process of face-to-face relationships, participants were led to discover among themselves shared grievances originating in sex differences. The format did not preclude cathartic forms of expression whereby people freed themselves of psychological burdens. The emphasis was deliberately put on spontaneity and self-expression. Discussions might apply to general situations shared by all the participants or to more specific experiences peculiar to divorced or widowed women or to lesbians, for instance. The idea of consciousness raising sessions may well have been borrowed from New Left discussion groups (Carden 1974, 33). They had the definite advantage of being adapted to a form of ideology that relied on personal commitment prior to any collective action. The internalization of new values was thus likely to be better guaranteed.

No mode of mobilization is entirely neutral, objective, or innocent. Consciousness raising sessions were conceived to bring participants from what were considered moderate positions to more progressive ones (ibid. 40); the sessions acted as a mode of resocialization. Little is known of the people in charge of these gatherings. Any grass-roots meeting, however informal, is inspired and to some extent oriented by people who feel, as a group, a responsibility to hold the meeting. They amount to mediators of a cause, even though they may well deny any intervention on their part. There emerges a form of social leadership that goes beyond the strictly psychological ascendency of some individuals over others. But there is no question of implying that this was a subtle form of manipulation. This notion lies outside my framework, for it suggests the derogatory use of symbols with the intention of deceiving others. There is no indication to this effect here; and should there be any, it would make no difference. The framework is resistant to any considerations of that nature. Nonetheless, it is still interesting to know what sort of people acted as mobilizers; the sociologist or the political scientist is not expected to be a strong believer in spontaneous generation.

The informal meetings were well-adapted to college-educated participants who were relatively at ease expressing their emotions and opinions compared with ordinary working people, who were less suited for unstructured and sometimes endless discussions. As a matter of fact, this mode of mobilization attracted young, middle-class people 'schooled in the campus politics of the New Left groups' and often from relatively affluent milieux (Teather 1976, 321; Chafe 1977, 124; Banks 1981, 251). As William Chafe (1977, 128) points out, the 'absence of structure helped to narrow the movement's class base.'[3]

True, this form of conditioning avoided the 'star' or 'élite' system, and the movement often reacted to what was considered to be a sort of usurpation of representation (Freeman 1975, 120; Bouchier 1978, 104). Any attempt at institutionalization was likely to appear to be a remnant of male culture; leaders were deemed unnecessary (Chafe 1977, 127). The movement was loath to become an organization, which led Jo Freeman to suggest the possibility of a 'tyranny of structurelessness' (1973, 202–14). This and the relative homogeneity of the participants did not, however, preclude the presence of some leaders. We may hypothesize that some female mediators, having left male progressive groups because they were kept on the fringes of them, adapted to a new mode of mobilization. There were very likely enough groups to keep a good number of mobilizers busy.

Interestingly enough, the strategy of feminism was to penetrate and transform society before intervening at the regulative level. Some have referred to it as a 'guerilla movement.' The metaphor is suggestive: the movement spread surreptitiously into the very homes and families of its future members, subverting values and norms before obtaining their confirmation through regulation.

This underground mobilization led the mass media to designate leaders since they lacked obvious cues from the movement's members. With about fifteen

---

3 'The emphasis of movement supporters on intragroup compatibility unintentionally reinforced a tendency toward middle-class homogeneity' (Chafe 1977, 128).

thousand groups (Carden 1974) at one time in the United States and no central organization, any person put in the limelight ran the risk of being labelled unrepresentative. This situation underlines the degree of incompatibility between two methods of conditioning: on the one hand an instrument of mobilization working at the level of primary groups and, on the other, the mass media whose basic aim was to transmit cultural values (socialization) to large audiences. It seems that protests reported by newspapers at times had a positive effect on recruitment by the movement (Carden 1974, 33). In general, though, there has been much criticism of the way in which feminist demonstrations were covered. The same applies to the way in which liberated women have been portrayed on television – looking pretentious, being carried away by their proselytising fervour, and losing sight of the world's 'real' problems (Baehr 1980, 37–8).

Antifeminist positions usually rely on cultural values; clearly antifeminists have culture on their side, they do not have to legitimate a whole platform in favour of the traditional woman. They are likely to content themselves with a patchwork ideology of pattern-preservation; they only have to remain on the defensive because the burden of proof is on the assailants. The feminist ideology, on the other hand, has to explain and defend its positions down to basic principles, as any ideology of some magnitude has to do. As yet, to my knowledge, no fullfledged antifeminist or 'masculinist' ideology has developed. Some, like John Gordon in *The Myth of the Monstrous Male* published by the Playboy Press (1982), may try to send the ball back into the feminists' court, but the reaction is usually limited to specific issues, such as abortion.

Although the feminist movement may have had a limited following and failed to attract mass support for its public demonstrations (Banks 1981, 248), of all the movements of the late sixties it is the only one to have had an uninterrupted, lasting effect. Changes that are periodically submitted to the regulative structure bespeak changes that have taken place in people's thinking, whatever the original following of the movement may have been in the past. There are now few feminists but a better audience for specific issues that derive from the feminist movement.

Institutionalization and professionalization
The trend towards the institutionalization of feminism in the seventies is widely admitted (Banks 1981; Bouchier 1979). Institutionalization here means a situation in which representatives claim the right to speak officially in the name of a movement and are recognized to do so by others, be they individuals, groups, or governments. Usually this representation is enshrined in a full-fledged organization.

For many authors, the feminist movement has transformed itself into traditional modes of pressure because it failed to obtain mass support and thus deradicalized its program (Banks 1981, 236, 248) after being absorbed by the middle-class environment (Bouchier 1979, 394).

We may wonder whether the movement became deradicalized because it evolved progressively towards institutionalization, or whether, on the contrary, it became institutionalized because it resigned itself to deradicalization. In other words, did the channel determine the content or vice versa? Or was it, in North America, the culture of incremental change which finally imposed itself upon the more globalistic approach of radical feminism (Gelb and Palley 1982, 7)? There is nothing in my framework that excludes a hypothesis of unicausality, that is a hypothesis which establishes the relation of one cause, one effect, or one component towards another. But it seems more rewarding first to assume a dynamics of the structure as a whole, and later investigate factors of change. In other words, I emphasize the logic of the whole and later examine the breaks in its functioning by comparing the new mode of functioning with the previous one.

What is most striking is that the movement adopted a new mode of mobilization, this time within the structure of regulation. This mode appears to fall back on the traditional one of earlier feminism. Such is not the case, however, since the mediation factor works very differently. There is no recourse to large organizations, but rather the mediating groups are fragmented. Representation specializes in specific issues (abortion, child day-care, equal pay, and so on) at the same time as the function of representation is professionalized. Mediators are dispersed, although not to the same degree as they were in the sixties; now they are highly concentrated either in terms of issues or in terms of their fields of intervention, such as a political party, a trade union, a university, or a state committee.

The content which was couched by the women's liberation movement in terms of oppression and alienation is then broken down into issues which in turn can be grouped together in terms of roles corresponding to patterns of control to be introduced or removed.

In their role as human beings, feminists claim equality of treatment with men: equal job and equal pay opportunities, that is, equal control over the production and distribution of goods and resources. These demands relate to 'role equity' as opposed to 'role change'; the former would extend to women rights already existing for men whereas the latter introduces new patterns tailored to the situation of women, which are usually harder to satisfy (Gelb and Palley 1982, 7).

In their role as women, feminists claim personal control over their own reproductive capacities (birth control assistance, abortion on demand), the removal of society's control over their bodies (the sexism of modern medicine, anti-abortion laws), and, on the other hand, better control by society of crimes such as sexual harassment, rape, and violence. Control over means of socialization would extend to advertising (showing women as sex objects) and text books (showing women in traditional roles of housewives, secretaries, and nurses). For wives, feminists seek paid domestic labour and economic security as well as publicly funded day-care facilities, and rights over the revenue generated by the couple.

Almost all these issues (which serve only as examples, since there are many more) are articulated by more or less specialized groups which operate in a variety of spheres that sometimes impinge on unexpected aspects of life.

One interesting inroad made by feminists is the one in social research. Being personally implicated both as researchers and feminists, some women find themselves in a strategic position of mobilization in favour of their sex group. In the United States there would appear to be some three hundred women's studies program, implying that there are some thirty thousand courses in colleges and universities (Boxer 1982). For some, in the field, academic is political; scholarship is considered integrated into politics (ibid. 661, 676). From this perspective, feminist studies are clearly identified as a 'partisan enterprise' against the androcentric nature of present theories which are in turn the reflection of a sexist society (Gould 1980, 461). Other authors feel a danger of exclusion; the sociology of women has become, for instance, a recognized concentration but, at the same time, may turn out to become a ghetto (Laurin-Frenette 1981, 8).

History is usually among the first disciplines affected by an ideology in formation. As is the case with any collectivity in the making, feminists have applied themselves to the rehabilitation of women in history. Books are written to redress biased accounts in which men presumably celebrate their own deeds – visible activities (or activities that have been made visible) like wars, feats of arms, 'momentous' events in industry or politics, which in Canada translated into free trade, ministerial responsibility, the construction of the Grand Trunk, and so on (Gordon, Buhle, and Dye 1976; Dumont et al. 1982). Apart from vindicating the part played by female personalities in the past, such as in the history of technology (Stanley 1983), feminist history aims at bringing out the basic contributions of female peasants, workers, and mothers, not to mention, of course, those who fought for the liberation of women.

The social sciences have undergone similar modifications of content and, even more, of approach. Feminist anthropology and sociology, from which some aspects have been borrowed for the present illustration, have tried to readjust the focus of their respective disciplines and make sure that women are considered significant social actors.

True, scholarship serves here as an instrument of mobilization in so far as it has as its objectives the promotion of women and, ultimately, changes in patterns of control. This, indeed, poses the problem of objectivity and neutrality for which, in my mind, there exist, for the time being, no satisfactory solution.

Whether in universities, trade unions, political parties, state bureaucracies, or local governments, the participation of women has been on the increase as a result of the strategy of specialization. Committees on the status of women in different countries have contributed to maintaining a constant instrument of representation for feminists, even if not all have agreed with the mediators chosen for the job. Women's interests are more and more represented on an official basis, providing channels for demands of many kinds.

Women's participation at the top levels of national legislatures and governments is still very limited. The Scandinavian countries are about the only ones with more than the token representation seen in other countries (Randall 1982, 69–75; Sanzone 1981). Though impressive as a personal feat, Margaret Thatcher's accession to the prime ministership of Great Britain has not been translated into a more open cabinet for women. Of course the situation is likely to vary according to parties. Taking the case of Britain, where socialist feminism is entrenched in socialist and labour movements (Banks 1981, 259), opportunities are likely to be better for women in leftist groups than in the United States, for instance, where such a tradition does not exist.

Resistance to women's taking part in the different steps of regulation (rule making and rule application) is embedded in culture but enhanced by rules of the game that facilitate or thwart attempts to introduce change. For example, the American presidential system and the French method of designating ministers (who do not have to be members of the National Assembly) both offer the possibility of recruiting people from outside the traditional reservoir of politicians. On the other hand, the parliamentary system allows a party more easily to impose minimum quotas of female candidates for general elections (with all the problems of getting nominated in favourable constituencies and subsequently getting elected); this is even more the case in systems using proportional representation (Simard 1984, 33). The electoral system also can work for or against potential female candidates. It seems that, as long as they are kept out of administrative jobs, women will have a harder time than their male counterparts in finding campaign funds, because of a lack of business contacts (Epstein and Coser 1981, 139). Here, then, is a vicious circle of resource gathering in favour of men. Indeed, the costs of getting elected vary according to the restrictions the rules of the game impose in terms of sources of funds and in terms of spending.

If women's representation is thin in the regulative structure, it is probably stronger in the achievement of some outputs. Active mediating groups form a sort of invisible network; they may disagree at times but are likely to take united stands in favour of some basic demands. Through official recognition in the regulatory sphere, like advisory councils on the status of women or, in some cases, a ministry which has a role of standing watch over female interests, representation is assured in many sectors of society and especially at the top. But, as a counterpoint, offices of some importance occupied by women in government bureaucracies remain, on the whole, outside the circle of senior executives and of significant productive sectors (Randall 1982, 79–80; Simard 1984, 40).

Although outputs have not always been very impressive in comparison with the intensity of demand, they have nonetheless produced increased sensitivity to new rights, translated into, for instance, greater control by married women of the financial assets of the household: in Quebec the family house can no longer be disposed of without the wife's consent and in Ontario housewives have been recognized as having a right to share in the family assets if a marriage breaks up. Similar changes have come about in many countries, especially on women's rights in marriage, but major breakthroughs like the Equal Rights Amendment in the United States have often been denied.

In sum, this mode of mobilization, which hinges on some concentration of expertise, is directed towards actions to be undertaken by regulative bodies. The specialization and institutionalization of the feminist movement have called for persons who are articulate enough to present and defend issues in a diversity of channels, public as well as private. From this process the format (channels) has changed, together with the content and the audience for which it is intended. The people acting as representatives are likely to be somewhat older than their predecessors. The militants of the sixties were usually students who were of age, who could speak for themselves. In the seventies and eighties the new mode of mobilization required added capacities: a thorough knowledge of the matter, experience with the people concerned, and the capacity to communicate through the channels of administration and government. Between the former militants and the present representatives there is no basic incompatibility, and the generation gap has been closed with time. The present-day activists are not necessarily the same ones (though they may well be), but they probably come from the same background so far as age, education, and social milieu are concerned. The demographic factor is likely to have had an effect of some sort. It would account for the professionalization of some in a large age-group in search of permanent status.

CONCLUSION

It is noticeable that from the start in the nineteenth century down to the present, feminism has usually attracted a public that comes roughly from the middle class. The concept of middle-classness is imprecise, very approximate, perhaps meaningless; at best, it may serve as a vague indication. In the case of the feminist movement we are concerned with a group of people who are determined to act as mediators in one sense or another – in administrations, legislatures, governments, political parties, pressure groups, and the mass-media – or, in other words, in the mediating sector of all three substructures: production, regulation, and conditioning. This change of tack probably responds to demographic pressure due to an impressively large cohort coming into the prime of life, but such changes do not have automatic effects; the consequences vary depending upon the way the changes are, so to speak, managed by the structure. The second world war left the western world with a demographic disproportion between men and women which had no significant repercussions on the allocation of gender roles. Great numbers of women, having received a college education with a view to a career, nowadays see every reason for mobilizing against discriminating forms of barriers (just as Quebec's Parti québécois kept its popularity high among the mediating group so long as the party was perceived as the purveyor of possible jobs for mediators; it lost a lot of support when the government sent the message – by eliminating positions in the civil service, in teaching, and in hospitals – that the good times were over). This trend has not prevented less-favoured female groups in society (workers, immigrants, and the poor) from becoming organized (Fitzgerald, Guberman, and Wolfe 1982; Banks 1981, 251). Still, it would be interesting to know how the mobilizers of these groups operate and who they are.

Like demographic changes which have effects depending upon the way culture or ideology react to these changes, technology, being 'used as a means to nontechnological ends' (Thrall 1982, 194), operates in the same fashion. As a factor of change, technology rests on two cultural determinants: first, it usually emerges in collectivities that promote this type of novelty, and second, it is subordinate to the use being made of new techniques. Women's situation has been greatly affected, as we have seen, by the introduction of technology at the different stages of industrialization. Today women face again the advantages and disadvantages of such changes: the increasing use of computers is clearly reducing the demand for office workers, but on the other hand new machinery used in industry improves women's chance of obtaining jobs exclusively held by men in the past. The division of labour, which used to be dependent to a large extent upon biological capacities and the value placed on them by culture, has restricted the field of work for women. With the advantage of technology, biological differences are less and less likely to be considered major criteria of selection. As noted earlier, the impact of environment on human behaviour tends to decrease as more and more artefacts are introduced, so that the increasing use of machinery in industry is likely to reduce the amount of sexual discrimination on the basis of physical abilities. This trend does not, however, preclude social or psychological considerations from being used to maintain or create conditions that exclude women.

Demography and technology, as we have seen, are factors of change but under strict social conditions. They both affect and are affected by the overall social structure. And the changes they introduce usually have repercussions on the components of whole substructures: conditioning, production, regulation, or all three acting in unison. Conflicts show to what extent modes of mobilization can be at odds, their incompatibility revealing how some groups work from dynamics that are alien to those of others; in the sixties, for instance, the traditional culture was quite vulnerable to the surreptitious and underground action developed by spontaneous and face-to-face female groups.

The present framework only aims at circumscribing a dynamics of selected social relations that are expected to interact along some detectable patterns: control, conditioning, conflict, and regulation. The framework does not purport to cope with matters of happiness, alienation, self-fulfilment, dignity, self-respect, or lucidity. These are among the high values that may or may not be retained by cultures or ideologies. Normative aspects too, like domination and oppression, lie outside the framework which applies itself only to recording what actually happened or happens but has nothing to do with what should or should not happen within a given range of events.

This consideration of feminism referred to an initial outline which delineates the field of observation in advance to the exclusion of other aspects. I could have decided to enlarge the outline in order to cover closely related aspects like the condition of blacks and other visible minorities, labourers, immigrants, and so forth, for some women may find themselves in all these categories. Each of these questions is amenable to the same analysis as the one applied to feminism. It is, indeed, a sociological approach; it does not intend to elaborate on the inner sense of these events or to find solutions. I selected feminism not necessarily through personal inclination but for its analytical richness. Of course the choice of any topic is already a *parti pris*; that, nobody can escape.

Bibliography

Aberdach, Joel D., R.D. Putnam, B.A. Rockman, et al., 1981. *Bureaucrats and Politicians in Western Democracies*. Cambridge, Mass.: Harvard University Press

Abrahamson, M., E.H. Mizruchi, and C.A. Hornung, 1976. *Stratification and Mobility*. New York: Macmillan

Adams, Richard N., 1975. *Energy and Structure*. Austin, Texas: University of Texas Press

Adams, Robert McC., 1966. *The Evolution of Urban Society*. Chicago, Ill.: Aldine

Adams, William C., 1978. 'Network News Research in Perspective: A Bibliographic Essay' In Adams and Schreibman, 11–46

Adams, William C., and Fay Schreibman, 1978. *Television Network News*. Washington, DC: George Washington University

Adler, Norman, and Charles Harrington, 1970. *The Learning of Political Behavior*. Glennview, Ill.: Scott, Foresman

Ahern, Dee Dee, and Betsy Bliss, 1976. *The Economics of Being a Woman*. New York: McGraw Hill

Akin, William E., 1977. *Technocracy and the American Dream*. Berkeley, Calif.: University of California Press

Albrow, Martin, 1970. *Bureaucracy*. New York: Praeger

Aldrich, Howard E., 1979. *Organizations and Environments*. Englewood-Cliffs, NJ: Prentice-Hall

Allen, Elizabeth, et al., 1978. 'Against Sociobiology' in Caplan, 259–94

Allen, Michael P., 1976. 'Management Control in the Large Corporation: Comment on Zeitlin' in 'Commentary and Debate,' *American Journal of Sociology*, vol. 81, no. 4, Jan. 1885–94

Allison, Graham T., 1971. *Essence of Decision*. Boston: Little, Brown

Almond, Gabriel A., and G.B. Powell, 1966. *Comparative Politics*. Boston: Little, Brown

204 Bibliography

Almond, Gabriel A., and Sidney Verba, 1963. *The Civic Culture*. Princeton, NJ: Princeton University Press
- 1980. *Civic Culture Revisited*. Boston: Little, Brown
Altheide, David L., 1976. *Creating Reality, How TV News Distorts Events*. Beverly Hills, Calif.: Sage Publications
Altheide, David L., and Robert P. Snow, 1979. *Media Logic*. Beverly Hills, Calif.: Sage Publications
Althusser, Louis, 1970 (1965). *For Marx*. New York: Vintage Press
- 1971 (1970). 'Ideology and Ideological State Apparatuses' in *Lenin and Philosophy*. London: New Left Books
- 1976 (1974). *Essays in Self-Criticism*. London: New Left Books
Alzon, Claude, 1978. *Femme mythifiée, femme mystifiée*. Paris: Presses universitaires de France
Ambler, John, 1975. 'Trust in Political and Nonpolitical Authorities,' *Comparative Politics*, vol. 8, no. 1, Oct., 31– 58
Amundsen, Kirsten, 1971. *The Silenced Majority*. Englewood Cliffs, NJ: Prentice-Hall
Anderson, James E., 1979. *Public Policy-Making*. New York: Holt, Rinehart & Winston
Anderson, Perry, 1976. *Lineages of the Absolute State*. London: New Left Books
Armer, Michael, and Allen D. Grimshaw, 1973. *Comparative Social Research*. New York: John Wiley & Sons
Armstrong, John A., 1982. *Nations Before Nationalism*. Chapel Hill, NC: University of North Carolina Press
Aron, Raymond, 1962. *The Opium of the Intellectuals*. New York: W.W. Norton
Bachrach, Peter, 1967. *The Theory of Democratic Elitism*. Boston: Little, Brown
Bachrach, P., and M. Baratz, 1963. 'Decision and Nondecisions: An Analytical Framework,' *American Political Science Review*, vol. 57, no. 3, Sept., 632–42
- 1970. *Power and Poverty*. New York: Oxford University Press
Badie, Bertrand, and Pierre Birnbaum, 1982 (1979). *Sociologie de l'Etat*. Paris: Grasset
Baehr, Helen (ed.). 1980. *Women in the Media*. Oxford: Pergamon Press
Baier, K., and N. Rescher, 1969. *Values and the Future*. New York: Free Press
Bailey, F.G., 1969. *Stratagems and Spoils*. Oxford: Basil Blackwell
Baker, R.K., and S.J. Ball (eds), 1969. *Mass Media and Violence, Report to the National Commission on the Causes and Prevention of Violence*. Washington, DC: US Government Printing Office
Balandier, Georges, 1969. *Anthropologie politique*. Paris: Presses universitaires de France
Balbus, Isaac D., 1971. 'The Concept of Interest in Pluralist and Marxian Analysis,' *Politics and Society*, vol. 1, no. 2, Feb., 151–77
Bamberger, Joan, 1974. 'The Myth of Matriarchy: Why Men Rule in Primitive Society' in Rosaldo and Lamphere, 263–80

Banks, Olive, 1981. *Faces of Feminism*. New York: Saint Martin's Press

Barlow, George W., and James Silverberg (eds), 1980. *Sociobiology: Beyond Nature/Nurture*. Boulder, Colo.: Westview Press

Barnard, Chester I., 1938. *The Functions of the Executive*. Cambridge, Mass.: Harvard University Press

Barnet, R.J., and R.E. Muller, 1974. *Global Reach*. New York: Simon & Schuster

Barnouw, Erik, 1978. *The Sponsor*. New York: Oxford University Press

Barron, R.D., and G.M. Norris, 1976. 'Sexual Divisions and the Dual Labour Market' in *Dependence and Exploitation in Work and Marriage*, ed. Diana L. Barker and Sheila Allen, 47–69. London: Longman

Barry, Brian, 1965. *Political Argument*. London: Routledge & Kegan Paul

– (ed.), 1976. *Power and Political Theory*. London: John Wiley

Batscha, Robert M., 1975. *Foreign Affairs News and the Broadcast Journalist*. New York: Praeger

Baudelot, C., and R. Establet, 1971. *L'Ecole capitaliste en France*. Paris: François Maspero

Baudrillard, Jean, 1972. *Pour une critique de l'économie politique du signe*. Paris: Gallimard

Bauer, Raymond A., 1973. 'The Audience' in de Sola Pool and Schramm, 141–52

Bauman, Zygmunt, 1973. *Culture as Praxis*. London: Routledge & Kegan Paul

Beardsley, Philip L., 1980. *Redefining Rigor*. Beverly Hills, Calif.: Sage Publications

Becker, L.B., M.E. McCombs, and J.M. McLeod, 1975. 'The Development of Political Cognitions' in Chaffee, 21–63

Bélanger, André-J., 1974. *L'Apolitisme des idéologies québécoises*. Québec: Presses de l'Université Laval

– 1977. *Ruptures et constantes, quatre idéologies du Québec en éclatement*. Montréal: Hurtubise HMH

– 1984. 'Le politique, concept mystificateur?' *Canadian Journal of Political Science*, vol. 17, no. 1, Mar., 49–64

Bell, Daniel, 1960. *The End of Ideology*. Glencoe, Ill.: Free Press

– 1976. *The Coming of Post-Industrial Society*. New York: Basic Books

Bell, David, 1975. *Power, Influence, and Authority*. New York: Oxford University Press

Bell, David, and Lorne Tepperman, 1979. *The Roots of Disunity*. Toronto: McClelland & Stewart

Benda, Julien, 1965 (1927). *La Trahison des clercs*. Utrecht: J.-J. Pauvert

Bendix, R., and S.M. Lipset (eds), 1953. *Class, Status and Power*. Glencoe, Ill.: Free Press

– (eds), 1966. *Class, Status and Power* (2nd ed.). New York: Free Press

Bensman, Joseph, 1979. 'Max Weber's Concept of Legitimacy: An Evaluation' in Vidich and Glassman, 17–73

Benson, J. Kenneth, 1977. 'Innovation and Crisis in Organizational Analysis,' *Sociological Quarterly*, vol. 18, Winter, 3–16

Bentley, Arthur F., 1967 (1908). *The Process of Government*. Cambridge, Mass.: Harvard University Press

Berelson, Bernard, 1948. 'Communications and Public Opinion' in Schramm (1960), 527–43

Berelson, Bernard, and Patricia J. Salter, 1946. 'Majority and Minority Americans: An Analysis of Magazine Fiction,' *The Public Opinion Quarterly*, vol. 10, no. 2, Summer, 168–90

Berger, Peter L., 1979. 'The Worldview of the New Class: Secularity and its Discontents' in Bruce-Briggs, 49–66

Berger, Peter L., and Thomas Luckmann, 1967. *The Social Construction of Reality*. New York: Anchor Books

Berger, Suzanne, 1981. *Organizing Interests in Western Europe*. Cambridge: Cambridge University Press

Bergeron, Gérard, 1965. *Le Fonctionnement de l'Etat*. Paris: Armand Colin

Berle, Adolf A., 1959. *Power Without Property*. New York: Harcourt, Brace

Berle, Adolf A., and Gardiner C. Means, 1968 (1932). *The Modern Corporation and Private Property*. New York: Harcourt, Brace & World

Bernard, Jessie, 1981. *The Female World*. New York: Free Press

Bernardi, Bernardo (ed.), 1977. *The Concept and Dynamics of Culture*. The Hague: Mouton

Bernstein, Basil, 1971. *Class, Codes and Control*. London: Routledge & Kegan Paul

Bertaux, Daniel, 1977. *Destins personnels et structure de classe*. Paris: Presses universitaires de France

Bettelheim, Bruno, 1970. *The Children of the Dream*. New York: Avon

Bierstedt, Robert, 1950. 'An Analysis of Social Power,' *American Sociological Review*, vol. 15, no. 6, Dec., 730–8

Binder, Leonard, et al. (eds), 1971. *Crises and Sequences in Political Development*. Princeton, NJ: Princeton University Press

Blake, J., and K. Davis, 1964. 'Norms, Values and Sanctions' in *Handbook of Modern Sociology*, ed. R.E.L. Faris, 456–84. Chicago, Ill.: Rand McNally

Blalock, Hubert M., 1964. *Causal Inferences in Nonexperimental Research*. Chapel Hill, NC: University of North Carolina Press

Blau, Peter M., 1963. 'Critical Remarks on Weber's Theory of Authority,' *American Political Science Review*, vol. 57, no. 2, June, 305–16

– 1964. *Exchange and Power in Social Life*. New York: John Wiley & Sons

Blau, Peter M., and O.D. Duncan, 1967. *The American Occupational Structure*. New York: John Wiley & Sons

Blau, Peter M., and Charles H. Page, 1956. *Bureaucracy in Modern Society*. New York: Random House

Blau, Peter M., and W.R. Scott, 1963. *Formal Organizations*. London: Routledge & Kegan Paul

Blondel, Jean, 1978. *Political Parties*. London: Wildwood House

Blumberg, Phillip I., 1975. *The Megacorporation in American Society*. Englewood Cliffs, NJ: Prentice-Hall

Blumler, Jay G., 1979. 'The Role of Theory in Uses and Gratifications Studies,' *Communication Research*, vol. 6, no. 1, Jan., 9–36

Blumler, Jay G., and E. Katz, 1974. *The Uses of Mass Communication*. Beverly Hills, Calif.: Sage Publications

Bodard Silver, Catherine, 1977. 'France: Contrasts in Familial and Societal Roles' in Giele and Smock, 257–99

Bodin, Louis, 1962. *Les Intellectuels*. Paris: Presses universitaires de France

Bon, F., and M.-A. Burnier, 1971. *Les Nouveaux intellectuels*. Paris: Editions du Seuil

Bostian, Lloyd R., 1970. 'The Two-Step Flow Theory: Cross-Cultural Implications,' *Journalism Quarterly*, vol. 47, no. 1, Spring, 109–17

Bottomore, T.B., 1966a. *Classes in Modern Society*. New York: Pantheon Books

– 1966b. *Elites and Society*. Harmondsworth: Penguin Books

Bottomore, T.B., and Robert Nisbet (eds), 1978. *A History of Sociological Analysis*. London: Heinemann

Bouchier, David, 1978. *Idealism and Revolution*. New York: Saint Martin's Press

– 1979. 'The Deradicalization of Feminism: Ideology and Utopia in Action,' *Sociology*, vol. 13, no. 3, Sept., 387–402

Boudon, Raymond, 1968. *A quoi sert la notion de 'structure'?* Paris: Gallimard

– 1973. *L'Inégalité des chances*. Paris: Armand Colin

Boulding, Elise, 1976. *The Underside of History*. Boulder, Colo.: Westview Press

– 1977. 'Nomadisme, mobilité et statut des femmes' in Michel, 85–100

Boulding, Kenneth E., 1959 (1952). *The Image*. Ann Arbor, Mich.: University of Michigan Press

– 1978. 'Réciprocité et échange: l'individu et la famille dans la société' in Michel, 21–37

Bourdieu, Pierre, 1972. *Esquisse d'une théorie de la pratique*. Paris: Droz

– 1979. *La Distinction*. Paris: Editions de Minuit

Bourdieu, Pierre, and J.-C. Passeron, 1970. *La Reproduction*. Paris: Editions de Minuit. English translation *Reproduction in Education*. London: Sage Publications, 1977

Bourque, Gilles, 1977. *L'Etat capitaliste et la question nationale*. Montréal: Presses de l'Université de Montréal

Bourricaud, François, 1980. *Le Bricolage idéologique*. Paris: Presses universitaires de France

Bowles, Samuel, 1977. 'Unequal Education and the Reproduction of the Social Division of Labor' in Karabel and Halsey, 137–53

Bowles, Samuel, and Herbert Gintis, 1976. *Schooling in Capitalist America*. New York: Basic Books

Boxer, Marilyn J., 1982. 'For and about Women: The Theory and Practice of Women's Studies in the United States,' *Signs*, vol. 7, no. 3, Spring, 661–95

Breuer, Georg, 1982. *Sociobiology and the Human Dimension*. Cambridge: Cambridge University Press

Bruce-Briggs, B. (ed.), 1979. *The New Class?* New Brunswick, NJ: Transaction Books

Bryce, James, 1901. *Studies in History and Jurisprudence*, vol. 2. Oxford: Clarendon Press

Buckley, Walter, 1958. 'Social Stratification and the Functional Theory of Social Differentiation' in Lipset and Smelser, 478–84

Bunge, Mario, 1959. *Causality*. Cambridge, Mass.: Harvard University Press

Burch, Philip H., 1972. *The Managerial Revolution Reassessed*. Lexington, Mass.: Lexington Books

Butler, Matilda, and W. Paisley, 1980. *Women and the Mass Media*. New York: Human Science Press

Caplan, Arthur L. (ed.), 1978. *The Sociobiology Debate*. New York: Harper & Row

Caplow, Theodore, 1968. *Two Against One*. Englewood Cliffs, NJ: Prentice-Hall

Carden, Maren Lockwood, 1974. *The New Feminist Movement*. New York: Russell Sage Foundation

Carroll, Berenice A. (ed.), 1976. *Liberating Women's History*. Urbana, Ill.: University of Illinois Press

Cater, Douglas, and R. Adler (eds), 1975. *Television as a Social Force*. New York: Praeger

Catlin, George E.G., 1930. *A Study of the Principles of Politics*. London: George Allen & Unwin

Catton, William R., 1969. 'Value Modification by Mass Media' in Baker and Ball, 285–97

Chafe, William H., 1977. *Women and Equality*. New York: Oxford University Press

Chaffee, Steven H. (ed.), 1975. *Political Communication: Issues and Strategies for Research*. Beverly Hills, Calif.: Sage Publications

Chaney, Elsa W., 1979. *Supermadre*. Austin, Texas: University of Texas Press

Chevalier, Jean-Marie, 1970. *La Structure financière de l'industrie américaine*. Paris: Edition Cujas

Chomsky, Noam, 1969. *American Power and the New Mandarins*. New York: Pantheon Books

Claessen, H.J.M., 1978. 'The Early State: A Structural Approach' in Claessen and Skalnik, 533–96

Claessen, H.J.M., and P. Skalnik (eds), 1978. *The Early State*. The Hague: Mouton Publishers

– (eds), 1981. *The Study of the State*. The Hague: Mouton Publishers

Clastres, Pierre, 1974. *La Société contre l'Etat*. Paris: Editions de Minuit

Clausen, John A., et al., 1968. *Socialization and Society*. Boston: Little, Brown
Cobb, R.W., and C.D. Elder, 1972. *Participation in American Politics*. Boston, Mass.: Allyn & Bacon
Cohen, Bernard C., 1963. *The Press and Foreign Policy*. Princeton, NJ: Princeton University Press
Cohen, Ronald, 1978a. 'State Origins: A Reappraisal' in Claessen and Skalnik, 31–75
– 1978b. 'Introduction' in Cohen and Service
Cohen, Ronald, and E.R. Service (eds), 1978. *Origins of the State*. Philadelphia, Penn.: Institute for the Study of Human Issues
Cohen, Yolande (ed.), 1981. *Femmes et politique*. Montréal: Le Jour
Cole, B., and M. Oettinger, 1978. *Reluctant Regulators*. Reading, Mass.: Addison-Wesley
Collins, Randall, 1979. *The Credential Society*. New York: Academic Press
Connolly, W.E., 1972. 'On "Interests" in Politics,' *Politics and Society*, vol. 2, no. 4, Summer, 459–75
Corning, Peter A., 1976. 'Toward a Survival Oriented Policy Science' in Somit, 127–54
Coser, Lewis A., 1965. *Men of Ideas*. New York: Free Press
– 1975. *The Idea of Social Structure*. New York: Harcourt Brace Jovanovich
Courtney, Alice E., and T.W. Whipple, 1974. 'Women in TV Commercials,' *Journal of Communication*, vol. 24, no. 2, Spring, 110–18
Cowan, Ruth Schwartz, 1976. 'The "Industrial Revolution" in the Home: Household Technology and Social Change in the 20th Century,' *Technology & Culture*, vol. 17, no. 1, Jan., 1–23
Crenson, M.A., 1971. *The Un-politics of Air Pollution*. Baltimore, Md.: Johns Hopkins Press
Crozier, Michel,1964. *The Bureaucratic Phenomenon*. Chicago, Ill.: University of Chicago Press
Crozier, Michel, and E. Friedberg, 1980 (1977). *Actors and Systems*. Chicago, Ill.: University of Chicago Press
Curran, J., M. Gurevitch, and J. Woollacott (eds), 1977. *Mass Communications and Society*. London: Edward Arnold
Currie, E., and J.H. Skolnick, 1970. 'A Critical Note on Conceptions of Collective Behavior,' *The Annals*, vol. 391, Sept., 34–45
Cutler, Neal E., 1975. 'Toward a Generational Conception of Political Socialization' in Schwartz and Schwartz, 254–88
– 1977. 'Political Socialization Research as Generational Analysis' in Renshon, 294–326
Czudnowski, Mosche M., 1976. *Comparing Political Behavior*. Beverly Hills, Calif.: Sage Publications
Dahl, Robert A., 1961. *Who Governs?* New Haven, Conn.: Yale University Press
– 1967. *Pluralist Democracy in the United States*. Chicago, Ill.: Rand McNally

- 1970. *After the Revolution?* New Haven, Conn.: Yale University Press
- 1976. *Modern Political Analysis.* Englewood Cliffs, NJ: Prentice-Hall
Dahlberg, Frances (ed.), 1981. *Woman the Gatherer.* New Haven, Conn.: Yale University Press
Dahrendorf, Ralf, 1968 (1959). *Class and Class Conflict in Industrial Society.* Stanford, Calif.: Stanford University Press
Dandurand, Renée B., 1981. 'Famille du capitalisme et production des êtres humains,' *Sociologie et Sociétés*, vol. 13, no. 2, 95–111
Davies, James C., 1963. *Human Nature in Politics.* New York: John Wiley & Sons
- 1977a. 'The Development of Individuals and the Development of Politics' in Fitzgerald, 74–95
- 1977b. 'The Priority of Human Needs and the Stages of Political Development' in Pennock and Chapman, 157–96
Davies, Margery W., 1982. *Woman's Place Is at the Typewriter.* Philadelphia: Temple University Press
Davis, Kingsley, and W.E. Moore, 1945. 'Some Principles of Stratification' in Bendix and Lipset (1966), 47–53
Davis, Morton D., 1970. *Game Theory.* New York: Basic Books
Dawson, R.E., and K. Prewitt, 1969. *Political Socialization.* Boston, Mass.: Little Brown
Debray, Régis, 1979. *Le Pouvoir intellectuel en France.* Paris: Editions Ramsay
- 1980. *Le Scribe, genèse du politique.* Paris: Bernard Grasset
Deckhard, Barbara Sinclair, 1975. *The Women's Movement.* New York: Harper & Row
de Fleur, Melvin, 1966. *Theories of Mass Communication.* New York: David McKay
de Huszar, G.B. (ed.), 1960. *The Intellectuals, A Controversial Portrait.* Glencoe, Ill.: Free Press
Delamont, Sara, 1980. *The Sociology of Women.* London: George Allen & Unwin
Descarries-Bélanger, Francine, 1980. *L'Ecole rose ... et les cols roses.* Montréal: Editions coopératives Alfred Saint-Martin
de Sola Pool, I., and W. Schramm (eds), 1973. *Handbook of Communication.* Chicago, Ill.: Rand McNally
Deutsch, Karl W., 1966a. *Nationalism and Social Communication.* Boston, Mass.: MIT Press
- 1966b. *The Nerves of Government.* New York: Free Press
Deutsch, Karl W., and W.J. Foltz (eds), 1966. *Nation-Building.* New York: Atherton Press
Devereux, Edward C., Jr, 1961. 'Parsons' Sociological Theory' in *The Social Theories of Talcott Parsons*, ed. Max Black, 1–64. Englewood Cliffs, NJ: Prentice-Hall
Dion, Léon, 1971. *Sociéte et Politique.* Québec: Presses de l'Université Laval

Dolbeare, Kenneth M. (ed.), 1975. *Public Policy Evaluation*. Beverly Hills, Calif.: Sage Publications

Domhoff, G. William, 1967. *Who Rules America?* Englewood Cliffs, NJ: Prentice-Hall

Donohue, G.A., P.J. Tichenor, and C.N. Olien, 1972. 'Gatekeeping: Mass Media System and Information Control' in Kline and Tichenor, 41–69

Downs, Anthony, 1957. *An Economic Theory of Democracy*. New York: Harper & Row

– 1967. *Inside Bureaucracy*. Boston: Little Brown

Draper, Patricia, 1975. '!Kung Women: Contrasts in Sexual Egalitarianism' in Reiter, 77–109

Dubin, Robert, 1978. *Theory Building*. New York: Free Press

Duesenberry, J.S., 1960. 'Comment' in Universities National Bureau Committee for Economic Research, *Demographic and Economic Change in Developed Countries*. Princeton, NJ: Princeton University Press

Dumont, Micheline, et al., 1982. *L'Histoire des femmes au Québec*. Montréal: Quinze

Durkheim, Emile, 1897. Review of A. Labriola's *Essais sur la conception matérialiste de l'histoire* in *Revue philosophique de la France et de l'étranger*, vol. 44, Dec., 645–51

– 1966 (1938). *The Rules of Sociological Method*. New York: Free Press

Easton, David, 1953. *The Political System*. New York: Alfred A. Knopf

– 1965. *A Systems Analysis of Political Life*. New York: John Wiley & Sons

Easton, David, and Jack Dennis, 1969. *Children in the Political System*. New York: McGraw Hill

Easton, David, and Robert D. Hess, 1961. 'Youth and the Political System' in Lipset and Lowenthal, 226–51

Eckstein, Harry, 1966. *Division and Cohesion in Democracy*. Princeton, NJ: Princeton University Press

– 1973. 'Authority Patterns: A Structural Basis for Political Inquiry,' *American Political Science Review*, vol. 67, no. 4, Dec., 1142–61

Eckstein, Harry, and Ted R. Gurr, 1975. *Patterns of Authority*. New York: John Wiley & Sons

Edelman, M., 1964. *Symbolic Uses of Politics*. Urbana, Ill.: University of Illinois Press

– 1971. *Politics as Symbolic Action*. Chicago, Ill.: Markham

Eichler, Margrit, 1980. *The Double Standard*. New York: Saint Martin's Press

Eisenstadt, S.N., 1977. 'Sociological Theory and an Analysis of the Dynamics of Civilizations and of Revolutions,' *Daedalus*, vol. 106, no. 4, Fall, 59–78

– 1978. *Revolution and Transformation of Societies*. New York: Free Press

Eisenstadt, S.N., and S.R. Graubard, 1973. *Intellectuals and Tradition*. New York: Humanities Press

Ekeh, Peter P., 1974. *Social Exchange Theory*. Cambridge, Mass.: Harvard University Press

Eldersveld, Samuel J., 1964. *Political Parties*. Chicago, Ill.: Rand McNally

Elsner, Henry, 1967. *The Technocrats*. Syracuse, NY: Syracuse University Press

Emerson, Rupert, 1962. *From Empire to Nation*. Cambridge, Mass.: Harvard University Press

Epstein, Cynthia F., 1970. *Woman's Place*. Berkeley, Calif.: University of California Press

Epstein, Cynthia F., and Rose L. Coser (eds), 1981. *Access to Power*. London: George Allen & Unwin

Epstein, E.J., 1974. *News from Nowhere*. New York: Vintage Books

Erbring, L., E.N. Goldenberg, and A.H. Miller, 1980. 'Front Page News and Real-World Cues: A New Look at Agenda-Setting by the Media,' *American Journal of Political Science*, vol. 24, no. 1, Feb., 16–49

Estioko-Griffin, Agnes, and P.B. Griffin, 1981. 'Woman the Hunter: The Agta' in Dahlberg 121–51

Etzioni, Amitai, 1964. *Modern Organizations*. Englewood Cliffs, NJ: Prentice-Hall

– 1968a. *The Active Society*. New York: Free Press

– 1968b. 'Basic Human Needs,' *American Sociological Review*, vol. 33, no. 6, Dec., 870–85

Eulau, Heinz, John C. Wahlke, et al., 1978. *The Politics of Representation*. Beverly Hills: Sage Publications

Evans, Richard J., 1976. *The Feminist Movement in Germany*. London: Sage Publications

– 1977. *The Feminists*. New York: Harper & Row

Evans-Pritchard, E.E., 1947 (1940). *The Nuer*. Oxford: Clarendon Press

Ferber, Marianne A., 1982. 'Women and Work: Issues of the 1980's,' *Signs*, vol. 8, no. 2, Winter, 273–95

Finer, S.E., 1966 (1958). *Anonymous Empire*. London: Pall Mall Press

Fink, Clinton F., 1968. 'Some Conceptual Difficulties in the Theory of Social Conflict,' *Journal of Conflict Resolution*, vol. 12, no. 4, Dec., 412–60

Fishman, Mark, 1980. *Manufacturing the News*. Austin, Texas: University of Texas Press

Fitzgerald, M., C. Guberman, and M. Wolfe (eds), 1982. *Still Ain't Satisfied*. Toronto: Women's Press

Fitzgerald, Ross (ed.), 1977. *Human Needs and Politics*. Australia: Pergamon Press

Flandrin, Jean-Louis, 1979 (1976). *Families in Former Times*. Cambridge: Cambridge University Press

Frank, Robert S., 1973. *Message Dimensions of Television News*. Lexington, Mass.: D.C. Heath & Co

Freeman, David M., 1974. *Technology and Society*. Chicago, Ill.: Rand McNally

Freeman, Jo, 1973. 'The Tyranny of Structurelessness' in Jaquette, 202–14

- 1975. *The Politics of Women's Liberation*. New York: David McKay

Fried, Morton H., 1967. *The Evolution of Political Society*. New York: Random House

- 1978. 'The State, the Chicken, and the Egg; or, What came First?' in Cohen and Service, 35-47

Friedan, Betty, 1963. *The Feminine Mystique*. New York: W.W. Norton

Friedrich, Carl J. (ed.), 1959. *Community*. New York: Liberal Arts Press

Froman, Lewis A., 1962. 'Learning Political Attitudes,' *Western Political Quarterly*, vol. 15, no. 2, June, 304-13

Galbraith, John K., 1971. *The New Industrial State*. Boston: Houghton Mifflin

Galtung, J., and M.H. Ruge, 1970. 'The Structure of Foreign News' in Tunstall, 259-98

Gamson, W.A., 1975. *The Strategy of Social Protest*. Homewood, Ill.: Dorsey Press

Gans, Herbert J., 1979. *Deciding What's News*. New York: Pantheon Books

Geertz, Clifford, 1973. *The Interpretation of Cultures*. New York: Basic Books

Gelb, Joyce, and Marian Lief Palley, 1982. *Women and Public Policies*. Princeton, NJ: Princeton University Press

Gella, Aleksander, 1976. *The Intelligentsia and the Intellectuals*. Beverly Hills, Calif.: Sage Publications

Gerth, H.H., and C. Wright Mills, 1969. *From Max Weber*. New York: Oxford University Press

Giddens, Anthony, 1973. *The Class Structure of the Advanced Societies*. London: Hutchison University Library

Giele, J. Zollinger, and A. Chapman Smock (eds), 1977. *Women: Roles and Status in Eight Countries*. New York: John Wiley & Sons

Gitlin, Todd, 1980. *The Whole World is Watching*. Berkeley, Calif.: University of California Press

Glasgow University Media Group, 1976. *Bad News*. London: Routledge & Kegan Paul

- 1980. *More Bad News*. London: Routledge & Kegan Paul

Gluckman, Max, 1965. *Politics, Law and Ritual in Tribal Society*. Oxford: Basil Blackwell

Goffman, Erving, 1974. *Frame Analysis*. Cambridge, Mass.: Harvard University Press

Gold, D.A., C.Y.H. Lo, and E.O. Wright, 1975. 'Recent Developments in Marxist Theories of the Capitalist State,' *Monthly Review*, vol. 27, no. 5, Oct., 29-43, and no. 6, Nov., 36-51

Goldberg, Steven, 1974. *The Inevitability of Patriarchy*. New York: William Morrow

Goldmann, Lucien, 1955. *Le Dieu caché*. Paris: Gallimard

Goldstone, Jack A., 1980. 'Theories of Revolution: The Third Generation,' *World Politics*, vol. 32, 425-53

Goode, William J., 1972. 'The Place of Force in Human Society,' *American Sociological Review*, vol. 37, no. 5, Oct. 1972, 507-19

Goodenough, Ward H., 1964. 'Cultural Anthropology and Linguistics' in *Language in Culture and Society*, ed. Dell Hymes. New York: Harper & Row: 36–9
– 1971. *Culture, Language and Society*. Philippines: Addison-Wesley
Goodin, Robert E., 1980. *Manipulatory Politics*. New Haven, Conn.: Yale University Press
Goodman, Nelson, 1969. *Languages of Art*. London: Oxford University Press
Gordon, A.D., M.J. Buhle, and N.S. Dye, 1976. 'The Problem of Women's History' in Carroll, 75–92
Gordon, John, 1982. *The Myth of the Monstrous Male*. New York: Playboy Press
Goslin, D.A., 1969. *Handbook of Socialization*. Chicago, Ill.: Rand McNally
Gough, Kathleen, 1975. 'The Origin of the Family' in Reiter, 51– 76
Gould, Meredith, 1980. 'The New Sociology,' *Signs*, vol. 5, no. 3, Spring, 459–67
Gouldner, Alvin W., 1979. *The Future of Intellectuals and the Rise of the New Class*. New York: Continuum
Grannis, Joseph C., 1970. 'The School as a Model of Society' in Adler and Harrington, 137–48
Greenstein, Fred I., 1969. *Children and Politics*. New Haven, Conn.: Yale University Press
Greenstein, Fred I., et al., 1974. 'The Child's Conception of the Queen and Prime Minister,' *British Journal of Political Science*, vol. 4, part 3, July, 257–87
Greenstein, Fred I., and Nelson W. Polsby (eds), 1975a. *Governmental Institutions and Processes, Handbook of Political Science*, vol. 5. Reading, Mass.: Addison-Wesley
– (eds), 1975b. *Policies and Policymaking*. Philippines: Addison-Wesley
Gregory, M.S., A. Silver, and D. Sutch (eds), 1978. *Sociobiology and Human Nature*. San Francisco, Calif.: Jossey-Bass
Grumm, John G., 1975. 'The Analysis of Policy Impact' in Greenstein and Polsby (1975b), 439–73
Grumm, John G., and S.L. Wasby, 1981. *The Analysis of Policy Impact*. Lexington, Mass.: D.C. Heath
Gurr, Ted Robert, 1971. *Why Men Rebel*. Princeton, NJ: Princeton University Press
– (ed.), 1980. *Handbook of Political Conflict*. New York: Free Press
Gurr, Ted Robert, and Raymond Duvall, 1973. 'Civic Conflict in the 1960s, A Reciprocal Theoretical System with Parameter Estimates,' *Comparative Political Studies*, vol. 6, no. 2, July, 135–69
Hacker, Sally L., 1983. 'Mathematization of Engineering: Limits on Women and the Field' in Rothschild, 38–58
Hall, Richard H., 1977. *Organizations: Structure and Process*. Englewood Cliffs, NJ: Prentice-Hall
Harris, Marvin, 1959. 'The Economy Has No Surplus?' *American Anthropologist*, vol. 61, no. 2, April, 185–99

– 1979. *Cultural Materialism*. New York: Random House

Hart, H.L.A., 1967. *The Concept of Law*. Oxford: Clarendon Press

Hartmann, Heidi, 1981. 'The Unhappy Marriage of Marxism and Feminism: Towards a more Progressive Union' in Sargent, 1–41

Hartz, Louis, 1964. *The Founding of New Societies*. New York: Harcourt, Brace & World

Hayes, Carlton J.H., 1966 (1926). *Essays on Nationalism*. New York: Russell and Russell

Hechter, Michael, 1977. *Internal Colonialism*. Berkeley, Calif.: University of California Press

Heclo, Hugh, 1973. 'Presidential and Prime Ministerial Selection' in *Perspectives on Presidential Selection*, ed. Donald R. Matthews. Washington, DC: Brookings Institution

Hess, R.D., and J.V. Torney, 1967. *The Development of Political Attitudes in Children*. Chicago, Ill.: Aldine Publishing

Hicks, Emily, 1981. 'Cultural Marxism: Nonsynchrony and Feminist Practice' in Sargent, 219–37

Hinings, C.R., et al., 1967. 'An Approach to the Study of Bureaucracy,' *Sociology*, vol. 1, no. 1, Jan., 61–72

Hirsch, Paul M., 1977. 'Occupational, Organizational, and Motivational Models in Mass Media Research' in Hirsch, Miller, and Kline, 13–42

Hirsch, Paul M., P.V. Miller, and F.G. Kline, 1977. *Strategies for Communication Research*. Beverly Hills, Calif.: Sage Publications

Hirschman, Albert O., 1970. *Exit, Voice and Loyalty*. Cambridge, Mass.: Harvard University Press

– 1977. *The Passions and the Interests*. Princeton NJ: Princeton University Press

Hoebel, E. Adamson, 1964. *The Law of Primitive Man*. Cambridge, Mass.: Harvard University Press

Hoffmann, Stanley, et al, 1963. *In Search of France*. Cambridge, Mass.: Harvard University Press

Hofstetter, C.R., 1976. *Bias in the News*. Columbus, Ohio: Ohio State University Press

Holt, Robert T., and John E. Turner, 1970. *The Methodology of Comparative Research*. New York: Free Press

Homans, George C., 1961. *Social Behavior*. New York: Harcourt, Brace & World

– 1962. *Sentiments and Activities*. New York: Free Press of Glencoe

Homans, George C., and David M. Schneider, 1955. *Marriage, Authority and Final Causes*. Glencoe, Ill.: Free Press

Hoyt, Elizabeth E., 1961. 'Integration of Culture: A Review of Concepts,' *Current Anthropology*, vol. 2, no. 5, Dec., 407–26

Hume, David, 1854. 'Of the First Principles of Government' in *The Philosophical Works*, vol. 3. Boston: Little, Brown

Huntington, Samuel P., 1968. *Political Order in Changing Societies*. New Haven, Conn.: Yale University Press

Iglitzin, Lynne B., 1974. 'The Making of the Apolitical Woman' in Jaquette, 25–36

Ingram, H.M., and D.E. Mann (eds), 1980. *Why Policies Succeed or Fail*. Beverly Hills Calif.: Sage Publications

Innis, Harold A., 1951. *The Bias of Communication*. Toronto: University of Toronto Press

Jackson, J.A. (ed.), 1968. *Social Stratification*. London: Cambridge University Press

Jacob, P.E., and H. Teune, 1964. 'The Integrative Process' in Jacob and Toscano, 1–45

Jacob, P.E., and J.V. Toscano (eds), 1964. *The Integration of Political Communities*. Philadelphia: J.B. Lippincott

Jaquette, Jane J. (ed.), 1974. *Women in Politics*. New York: John Wiley & Sons

Jencks, Christopher, 1972. *Inequality*. New York: Basic Books

Jencks, Christopher, and D. Riesman, 1968. *The Academic Revolution*. Garden City, NY Doubleday

Jencks, Christopher, et al., 1979. *Who Gets Ahead?* New York: Basic Books

Johnson, Dale L. (ed.), 1982. *Class and Social Development: A New Theory of the Middle Class*. Beverly Hills, Calif.: Sage Publications

Joseph, Gloria, 1981. 'The Incompatible Ménage à Trois: Marxism, Feminism and Racism' in Sargent, 91–107

Kadushin, Charles, 1974. *The American Intellectual Elite*. Boston, Mass.: Little, Brown

Kanter, Rosabeth M., 1977. *Men and Women in the Corporation*. New York: Basic Books

Kaplan, Abraham, 1964. *The Conduct of Inquiry*. San Francisco, Calif.: Chandler Publishing

Karabel, J., and A.H. Halsey, 1977. *Power and Ideology in Education*. New York: Oxford University Press

Karpf, Anne, 1980. 'Women and Radio' in Baehr, 41–54

Katz, Elihu, 1960. 'The Two-Step Flow of Communication' (1957) in Schramm, 346–6

Katz, Elihu, G. Blumler, and M. Gurevitch, 1974. 'Utilization of Mass Communication by the Individual' in Blumler and Katz, 19–32

Katz, Elihu, M. Gurevitch, and H. Haas, 1973. 'On the Use of the Mass Media for Important Things,' *American Sociological Review*, vol. 38, no. 2, April, 164–81

Katz, Elihu, and P.F. Lazarsfeld, 1966 (1955). *Personal Influence*. New York: Free Press

Katz, Elihu, M.L. Levin, and H. Hamilton, 1963. 'Traditions of Research on the Diffusion of Innovation,' *American Sociological Review*, vol. 28, no. 2, April, 237–52

Katz, Richard S., 1980. *A Theory of Parties and Electoral Systems*. Baltimore, Md.: Johns Hopkins University Press

Keat, R., and J. Urry, 1975. *Social Theory as Science*. London: Routledge & Kegan Paul

Keeler, John T.S., 1981. 'Corporatism and Official Union Hegemony: The Case of French Agricultural Syndicalism' in Suzanne Berger, 185–208

Kelsen, Hans, 1961 (1945). *General Theory of Law and State*. New York: Russell & Russell

King, Anthony, 1975. 'Executives' in Greenstein and Polsby (1975a), 173–256

Klapp, Orrin E., 1969. *Collective Search for Identity*. New York: Holt, Rinehart, Winston

Klapper, Joseph T., 1967 (1960). *The Effects of Mass Communication*. New York: Free Press

Klein, Viola, 1967. 'Great Britain' in *Women in the Modern World*, ed. Raphael Patai, 463–88. New York: Free Press

Kline, F.G., and P.J. Tichenor (eds), 1972. *Current Perspectives in Mass Communication Research*. Beverly Hills, Calif.: Sage Publications

Kluckhohn, Clyde, 1962 (1951). 'Values and Value Orientation in the Theory of Action' in Parsons and Shils, 388–433

Kohn, Hans, 1945. *The Idea of Nationalism*. New York: Macmillan

Konrad, G., and I. Szeliny, 1979. *The Road of the Intellectuals to Class Power*. New York: Harcourt Brace Jovanovich

Kornhauser, William, 1959. *The Politics of Mass Society*. New York: Free Press

Korpi, Walter, 1974. 'Conflict, Power and Relative Deprivation,' *American Political Science Review*, vol. 68, no. 4, Dec., 1569–78

Krader, Lawrence, 1968. *Formation of the State*. Englewood Cliffs, NJ: Prentice-Hall

Kramarae, Chevis, 1981. *Women and Men Speaking*. Rowley, Mass.: Newbury House

Kranow, E.G., and L.D. Longley, 1978. *The Politics of Broadcast Regulation*. New York: Saint Martin's Press

Krasner, Stephen D., 1978. *Defending the National Interest*. Princeton NJ: Princeton University Press

Kraus, Sidney, and Dennis Davis, 1976. *The Effects of Mass Communication on Political Behavior*. University Park, Penn.: Pennsylvania State University Press

Kroeber, A.L., and C. Kluckhohn, 1952. *Culture, A Critical Review of Concepts and Definitions*. New York: Vintage Books

Kroeber, A.L., and T. Parsons, 1958. 'The Concepts of Culture and of Social System,' American Sociological Review, vol. 23, no. 5, Oct., 582–3

Kuhn, Thomas S., 1970. *The Structure of Scientific Revolutions*. Chicago: University of Chicago Press

Ladd, E.C., and S.M. Lipset, 1975. *The Divided Academy*. New York: McGraw-Hill

Ladd, John, 1959. 'The Concept of Community: A Logical Analysis' in Friedrich, 269–93

Lafont, Robert, 1968. *Sur la France*. Paris: Gallimard

Lamphere, Louise, 1974. 'Strategies, Cooperation and Conflict among Women in Domestic Groups' in Rosaldo and Lamphere, 97–112

218 Bibliography

La Palombara, Joseph, 1964. *Interest Groups in Italian Politics*. Princeton, NJ: Princeton University Press
Lapierre, Jean-William, 1973. *L'Analyse des systèmes politiques*. Paris: Presses universitaires de France
Larner, Robert J., 1970. *Management Control and the Large Corporation*. New York: Dunellen Publishing
Larrain, Jorge, 1979. *The Concept of Ideology*. Athens, Ga.: University of Georgia Press
Laski, Harold J., 1957. *A Grammar of Politics*. London: George Allen & Unwin
Lasswell, Harold D., 1948. 'The Structure and Function of Communication in Society' in *The Communication of Ideas*, ed. Lyman Bryson, 37–51. New York: Harper & Brothers
– 1968. 'The Future of the Comparative Method,' *Comparative Politics*, vol. 1, no. 1, Oct., 3–18
– 1979. *The Signature of Power*. New Brunswick, NJ: Transaction Books
Lasswell, Harold D., and Abraham Kaplan, 1965. *Power and Society*. New Haven, Conn.: Yale University Press
Laurin-Frenette, Nicole, 1981. 'Féminisme et anarchisme: quelques éléments théoriques et historiques pour une analyse de la relation entre le mouvement des femmes et l'Etat' in Yolande Cohen, 147–91
Lawson, Kay, 1976. *The Comparative Study of Political Parties*. New York: Saint Martin's Press
– (ed.), 1980. *Political Parties and Linkage*. New Haven, Conn.: Yale University Press
Lazarsfeld, Paul F., B. Berelson, and H. Gaudet, 1968 (1944). *The People's Choice*. New York: Columbia University Press
Lazarsfeld, Paul F., and Robert K. Merton, 1948. 'Mass Communication, Popular Taste and Organized Social Action' in Schramm, 492–512
Leach, Edmund R., 1964 (1954). *Political Systems of Highland Burma*. London: G. Bell & Sons
Leach, Edmund R., 1976. *Culture and Communication*. Cambridge: Cambridge University Press
Leclercq, Jean-Michel, 1979. *La Nation et son idéologie*. Paris: Anthropos
Le Goff, Jacques, 1976. *Les Intellectuels au Moyen Age*. Paris: Editions du Seuil
Leibowitz, Lila, 1975. 'Perspectives on the Evolution of Sex Differences' in Reiter, 20–35
Lemieux, Vincent, 1979. *Les Cheminements de l'influence*. Québec: Presses de l'Université Laval
Lenski, G.E., 1966. *Power and Privilege*. New York: McGraw-Hill
Lenzen, Victor F., 1954. *Causality in Natural Science*. Springfield, Ill.: Charles C. Thomas
Lerner, Gerda, 1979. *The Majority Finds Its Past: Placing Women in History*. New York: Oxford University Press

Levine, D.M., and M.J. Bane, 1975. *The 'Inequality' Controversy*. New Press: Basic
  Books
Lévi-Strauss, Claude, 1958. *Anthropologie structurale*. Paris: Plon
– 1974. *Tristes Tropiques*. New York: Atheneum
Lijphart, Arend, 1968. *The Politics of Accommodation*. Berkeley, Calif.: California
  University Press
– 1971. 'Comparative Politics and the Comparative Method,' *American Political Science
  Review*, vol. 65, no. 3, Sept., 682–93
– 1975. 'The Comparable-Cases Strategy in Comparative Research,' *Comparative
  Political Studies*, vol. 8, no. 2, July, 158–77
Linton, Ralph, 1945. *The Cultural Background of Personality*. New York: D. Appleton-
  Century
Lippmann, Walter, 1960 (1922). *Public Opinion*. New York: MacMillan
Lipset, S.M., 1963. *Political Man*. Garden City, NY: Doubleday
– 1964. *The First New Nation*. London: Heinemann
– 1970. *Revolution and Counterrevolution*. Garden City, NY: Anchor Books
Lipset, S.M., and A. Basu, 1975. 'Intellectual Types and Political Roles' in Coser,
  433–70
Lipset, S.M., and Leo Lowenthal (eds), 1961. *Culture and Social Character*. Glencoe,
  Ill.: Free Press
Lipset, S.M., and N.J. Smelser, 1961. *Sociology, The Progress of a Decade*. Englewood
  Cliffs, NJ: Prentice-Hall
Litman, Barry Russell, 1979. *The Vertical Structure of the Television Broadcasting
  Industry*. East Lansing, Mich.: MSU Business Studies
Lively, Jack, 1976. 'The Limits of Exchange Theory' in Barry, 1–13
Lottman, Herbert R., 1981. *The Left Bank*. New York: Wallace & Sheil
Lukes, Stephen, 1974. *Power, A Radical View*. London: Macmillan
Lumsden, Charles J., and Edward O. Wilson, 1981. *Genes, Mind and Culture: The
  Coevolutionary Process*. Cambridge, Mass.: Harvard University Press
Luxton, Mag, 1982. 'The Home, a Contested Terrain' in Fitzgerald, Guberman, and
  Wolfe, 112–21
MacCormack, Carol P., et M. Strathern, 1980. *Nature, Culture and Gender*. Cambridge:
  Cambridge University Press
Machlup, Fritz, 1962. *The Production of Knowledge in the United States*. Princeton, NJ:
  Princeton University Press
– 1980. *Knowledge and Knowledge Production*. Princeton, NJ: Princeton University Press
MacIver, R.M., 1947. *The Web of Government*. New York: MacMillan
Mack, R.W., and R.C. Snyder, 1957. 'The Analysis of Social Conflict – Towards an
  Overview and Synthesis,' *Journal of Conflict Resolution*, vol. 1, no. 2, June,
  212–48

Mackenzie, W.J.M., 1967. *Political and Social Science*. Harmondsworth: Penguin Books

– 1978. *Political Identity*. Harmondsworth: Penguin Books

MacKuen, M.B., and S.L. Coombs, 1981. *More than News*. Beverly Hills, Calif.: Sage Publications

McLuhan, Marshall, 1962. *The Gutenberg Galaxy*. Toronto, University of Toronto Press

Macpherson, C.B., 1977. 'Needs and Wants: An Ontological or Historical Problem?' in Fitzgerald, 26–35

– 1979. 'Second and Third Thoughts on Needs and Wants,' *Canadian Journal of Political and Social Theory*, vol. 3, no. 1, Winter, 46–9

McQuail, Denis (ed.), 1972. *Sociology of Mass Communication*. London: Penguin Books

– 1976. *Review of Sociological Writing on the Press*. London: Royal Commission on the Press, Her Majesty's Stationery Office

– 1977. 'The Influence and Effects of Mass Media' in Curran, Gurevitch, and Woollacott, 70–91

McQuail, D., and M. Gurevitch, 1974. 'Explaining Audience Behaviour: Three Approaches Considered' in Blumler and Katz, 287–301

Macridis, Roy C., 1967. *Political Parties, Contemporary Trends and Ideas*. New York: Harper & Row

Mair, Lucy, 1962. *Primitive Government*. Baltimore, Md.: Penguin Books

Manes, Audrey L., and Paula Melnyk, 1974. 'Televised Models of Female Achievement,' *Journal of Applied Social Psychology*, vol. 4, no. 4, Oct.–Dec., 365–74

Mannheim, Karl, 1936. *Ideology and Utopia*. New York: Harcourt, Brace & World

– 1952. *Essays on the Sociology of Knowledge*. New York: Oxford University Press

March, James G. (ed.), 1965. *Handbook of Organizations*. Chicago, Ill.: Rand McNally

Marris, Robin, 1964. *The Economic Theory of 'Managerial' Capitalism*. London: Macmillan

Martin, Roderick, 1977. *The Sociology of Power*. London: Routledge & Kegan Paul

Marx, Karl, 1908. *Capital*. London: Swan Sonnenschein

Maslow, Abraham H., 1954. *Motivation and Personality*. New York: Harper & Row

Matheson, Gwen (ed.), 1976. *Women in the Canadian Mosaic*. Toronto: Peter Martin

Meadow, Robert G., 1980. *Politics as Communication*. Norwood, NJ: Ablex

Mennell, Stephen, 1979. 'Theoretical Considerations on the Study of Cultural "Needs,"' *Sociology*, vol. 13, no. 2, May, 235–57

Merriam, Charles E., 1950. *Political Power*. Glencoe, Ill.: Free Press

Merton, Robert K., 1951 (1949). *Social Theory and Social Structure*. Glencoe, Ill.: Free Press

Meynaud, Jean, 1968. *Technocracy*. New York: Free Press

Michel, Andrée (ed.), 1977. *Femmes, sexisme et sociétés*. Paris: Presses universitaires de France

- 1978. *Les Femmes dans la société marchande*. Paris: Presses universitaires de France
Michels, Roberto, 1966. *Political Parties*. New York: Free Press
Miliband, Ralph, 1969. *The State in Capitalist Society*. London: Weidenfeld & Nicolson
Mill, J.S., 1899. *Principles of Political Economy*, vol. 1. New York: Colonial Press
Miller, J.D.B., 1969. *The Nature of Politics*. Harmondsworth: Penguin Books
Millett, Kate, 1970. *Sexual Politics*. Garden City, NY: Doubleday
Mills, C. Wright, 1967. *The Sociological Imagination*. London: Oxford University Press
Mitchell, Juliet, 1971. *Woman's Estate*. New York: Pantheon Books
Moe, Terry M., 1980. *The Organization of Interests*. Chicago, Ill.: University of Chicago Press
Monaco, James (ed.), 1978. *Media Culture*. New York: Delta Books
Moore, Gwen, 1979. 'The Structure of a National Elite Network,' *American Sociological Review*, vol. 44, October, 673–92
Moore, Sally F., 1978. *Law as a Process*. London: Routledge & Kegan Paul
Morgan, Edward P., 1977. *Inequality in Classroom Learning*. New York: Praeger
Mosco, Vincent, 1979. *Broadcasting in the United States*. Norwood, NJ: Ablex
Mouzelis, Nicos P., 1975. *Organisation and Bureaucracy*. London: Routledge & Kegan Paul
Mueller, Claus, 1973. *The Politics of Communication*. New York: Oxford University Press
Murphy, Robert F., 1970. 'Basin Ethnology and Ecological Theory' in *Languages and Cultures of Western North America*, ed. Earl H. Swanson, 152–71. Pocatello, Idaho: Idaho State University Press
Nadel, S.F., 1961 (1942). *A Black Byzantium*. London: Oxford University Press
Nagel, Ernest, 1964. *The Structure of Science*. New York: Harcourt, Brace & World
Nagel, Jack H., 1975. *The Descriptive Analysis of Power*. New Haven: Yale University Press
Nettl, J.P., 1967. *Political Mobilization*. London: Faber & Faber
Nimmo, Dan, 1978. *Public Communication and Public Opinion in America*. Santa Monica, Calif.: Goodyear Publishing
Niosi, Jorge, 1978. *The Economy of Canada*. Montreal: Black Rose Books
Nordlinger, Eric A., 1981. *On the Autonomy of the Democratic State*. Cambridge, Mass.: Harvard University Press
Oakley, Ann, 1981. *Subject Women*. Oxford: Martin Robertson
Oberschall, Anthony, 1973. *Social Conflict and Social Movements*. Englewood Cliffs, NJ: Prentice-Hall
Offe, Claus, 1974. 'Structural Problems of the Capitalist State' in *German Political Studies*, ed. Klaus von Beyme, 31–57. Beverly Hills, Calif.: Sage Publications
- 1981. 'The Attribution of Public Status to Interest Groups: Observations on the West German Case' in Suzanne Berger, 123–58

Olson, Mancur, 1965. *The Logic of Collective Action*. Cambridge, Mass.: Harvard
University Press
Ortner, Sherry B., 1974. 'Is Female to Male as Nature is to Culture?' in Rosaldo and
Lamphere, 67–87
Ossowski, Stanislaw, 1963. *Class Structure in the Social Consciousness*. London:
Routledge & Kegan Paul
Oyengar, Shanto, 1979. 'Television News and Issue Salience,' *American Politics
Quarterly*, vol. 7, no. 4, Oct., 395–416
Paletz, David L., and Roberta E. Pearson, 1978. 'The Way You Look Tonight:
A Critique of Television News Criticism' in Adams and Schreibman, 65–71
Panitch, Leo, 1980. 'Recent Theorizations of Corporatism: Reflections on a Growth
Industry,' *British Journal of Sociology*, vol. 31, no. 2, June, 159–87
Parkin, Frank, 1971. *Class Inequality and Political Order*. New York: Praeger
– (ed.), 1974. *The Social Analysis of Class Structure*. London: Tavistock Publications
Parsons, Talcott, 1960. *Structure and Process in Modern Societies*. Glencoe, Ill.: Free
Press
– 1961. 'An Outline of the Social System' in *Theories of Society*, ed. T. Parsons et al.,
30–79. New York: Free Press of Glencoe
– 1966. *Societies*. Englewood Cliffs, NJ: Prentice-Hall
– 1967. *Sociological Theory and Modern Society*. New York: Free Press
– 1969. *Politics and Social Structure*. New York: Free Press
– 1972. 'Culture and Social System Revisited,' *Social Science Quarterly*, vol. 53, no. 2,
Sept., 253–66
Parsons, Talcott, and R.F. Bales, 1955. *Family*. Glencoe, Ill.: Free Press
Parsons, Talcott, and Edward A. Shils (eds), 1962. *Toward a General Theory of Action*.
New York: Harper & Row
Partridge, P.H., 1971. *Consent and Consensus*. London: Pall Mall
Pearson, H.W., 1971 (1957). 'The Economy has no Surplus: Critique of a Theory of
Development' in Polanyi, Arensberg, and Pearson, 320–41
Pennock, J.R., and J.W. Chapman (eds), 1977. *Human Nature in Politics*. New York:
New York University Press
Perrow, Charles, 1967. 'A Framework for the Comparative Analysis of Organizations,'
American Sociological Review, vol. 32, no. 2, April, 194–208
– 1972. *Complex Organizations*. Glenview, Ill.: Scott, Foresman
Peyrefitte, Alain, 1981. *The Trouble with France*. New York: Alfred A. Knopf
Piaget, Jean, 1968. *Le Structuralisme*. Paris: Presses universitaires de France
Piotte, Jean-Marc, 1970. *La Pensée politique de Gramsci*. Montréal: Editions Parti
pris
Pitts, J.R., 1963. 'Continuity and Change in Bourgeois France' in Hoffmann et al.,
235–304

Polanyi, K., C. Arensberg, and H. Pearson (eds), 1971 (1957). *Trade and Market in the Early Empires*. Chicago, Ill.: Gateway Edition

Polsby, Nelson W., 1963. *Community Power and Political Theory*. New Haven, Conn.: Yale University Press

Popper, Karl, 1961. *The Poverty of Historicism*. London: Routledge & Kegan Paul

– 1965. 'Three Views Concerning Human Knowledge' in *Conjectures and Refutations*, 97–119. New York: Harper & Row

Portelli, Hugues, 1972. *Gramsci et le bloc historique*. Paris: Presses universitaires de France

Porter, John, 1965. *The Vertical Mosaic*. Toronto: University of Toronto Press

Poulantzas, Nicos, 1973. *Political Power and Social Classes*. London: New Left Books

– 1978a. *Classes in Contemporary Capitalism*. London: New Left Books

– 1978b. *State, Power, Socialism*. London: New Left Books

Przeworski, Adam, and Henry Teune, 1970. *The Logic of Comparative Social Inquiry*. New York: John Wiley & Sons

Putnam, Robert D., 1976. *The Comparative Study of Political Elites*. Englewood Cliffs, NJ: Prentice-Hall

Pye, Lucian W., 1962. *Politics, Personality and Nation Building*. New Haven, Conn.: Yale University Press

– 1966. *Aspects of Political Development*. Boston: Little, Brown

– 1971. 'Identity and the Political Culture' in Binder et al., 101–34

Pye, Lucian W., and S. Verba, 1965. *Political Culture and Political Development*. Princeton, NJ: Princeton University Press

Randall, Vicky, 1982. *Women and Politics*. London: Macmillan

Raphael, D.D., 1967. *Political Theory and the Rights of Man*. Bloomington, Ind.: Indiana University Press

Ratner, Ronnie S. (ed.), 1980. *Equal Employment Policy for Women*. Philadelphia: Temple University Press

Ravetz, Jerome R., 1971. *Scientific Knowledge and Its Social Problems*. Oxford: Clarendon Press

Reiter, Rayna R. (ed.), 1975. *Toward an Anthropology of Woman*. New York: Monthly Review Press

Renan, Ernest, 1887. 'Qu'est-ce qu'une nation?' (1882) in *Discours et conférences*. Paris: Calmann-Lévy

Renshon, Stanley A., 1975. 'The Role of Personality Development in Political Socialization' in Schwartz and Schwartz, 29–68

Renshon, Stanley A., 1977. *Handbook of Political Socialization*. New York: Free Press

Rieff, Philip, 1970. *On Intellectuals*. Garden City, NY: Anchor Books

Riker, William H., 1962. *The Theory of Political Coalitions*. New Haven, Conn.: Yale University Press

- 1964. *Federalism*. Boston, Mass.: Little Brown
- 1975. 'Federalism' in Greenstein and Polsby (1975a), 93–172
Riker, William H., and P.C. Ordershook, 1973. *Introduction to Positive Political Theory*. Englewood Cliffs, NJ: Prentice-Hall.
Robbins, Lionel, 1952. *An Essay on the Nature and Significance of Economic Science*. London: Macmillan
Robinson, Joan, 1974. *Economic Philosophy*. Harmondsworth: Penguin Books
Robinson, John P., 1976. 'Interpersonal Influence in Election Campaigns: Two Step-Flow Hypotheses,' *Public Opinion Quarterly*, vol. 40, no. 3, Fall, 304–19
Rocher, Guy, 1972. *Talcott Parsons et la sociologie américaine*. Paris: Presses universitaires de France
Rogers, Everett M., 1962. *Diffusion of Innovations*. New York: Free Press
- 1973. 'Mass Media and Interpersonal Communication' in de Sola Pool and Schramm, 290–310
Rogers, Everett M., and F.F. Shoemaker, 1971. *Communication of Innovations*. New York: Free Press
Rosaldo, Michelle Z., 1974. 'Woman, Culture and Society: A Theoretical Overview' in Rosaldo and Lamphere, 17–42
Rosaldo, Michelle Z., and Louise Lamphere (eds), 1974. *Woman, Culture and Society*. Stanford, Calif.: Stanford University Press
Roscho, Bernard, 1975. *Newsmaking*. Chicago, Ill.: University of Chicago Press
Rose, Arnold M., 1967. *The Power Structure*. New York: Oxford University Press
Rosengren, Karl Erik, 1974. 'Uses and Gratifications: A Paradigm Outlined' in Blumler and Katz, 269–86
Rossi, Alice S., 1982. *Feminists in Politics*. New York: Academic Press
Rossi, P.H., H.E. Freeman, and S.R. Wright, 1979. *Evaluation: A Systematic Approach*. Beverly Hills, Calif.: Sage Publications
Rothschild, Joan (ed.), 1983. *Machina ex Dea*. New York: Pergamon Press
Russell, D.E.H., 1974. *Rebellion, Revolution and Armed Force*. New York: Academic Press
Russett, Cynthia E., 1966. *The Concept of Equilibrium in American Social Thought*. New Haven: Yale University Press
Sahlins, Marshall, 1976. *Culture and Practical Reason*. Chicago: University of Chicago Press
- 1977. *The Use and Abuse of Biology*. London: Tavistock Publications
Salaman, Graeme, 1979. *Work Organizations*. London: Longman
Sanday, Peggy R., 1981. *Female Power and Male Dominance*. Cambridge: Cambridge University Press
Sanzone, Donna S., 1981. 'Women in Politics' in Epstein and Coser, 37–51
Sargent, Lydia (ed.), *Women and Revolution: The Unhappy Marriage of Marxism and Feminism*. London: Pluto Press

Sartori, Giovanni, 1976. *Parties and Party Systems*. Cambridge: Cambridge University Press

Sartre, Jean-Paul, 1972. *Plaidoyer pour les intellectuels*. Paris: NRF Gallimard

Sayers, Janet, 1982. *Biological Politics*. London: Tavistock

Scanzoni, John, and M. Szinovacz, 1980. *Family Decision-Making*. Beverly Hills, Calif.: Sage Publications

Schapera, I., 1956. *Government and Politics in Tribal Societies*. London: Watts

Schattschneider, E.E., 1960. *The Semisovereign People*. New York: Holt, Rinehart & Winston

Schlozman, K.L., and S. Verba, 1979. *Injury to Insult*. Cambridge, Mass.: Harvard University Press

Schmitter, Philippe C., 1974. 'Still the Century of Corporatism?' *The Review of Politics*, vol. 36, no. 1, Jan., 85–131

– 1982. 'Reflections on Where the Theory of Neo-Corporatism Has Gone and Where the Praxis of Neo-Corporatism May Be Going,' in *Patterns of Corporatist Policy-Making*, ed. Gerhard Lehmbruch and P.C. Schmitter, 259–79. Beverly Hills, Calif.: Sage Publications

Schneider, Louis, and Charles M. Bonjean (eds), 1973. *The Idea of Culture in the Social Sciences*. London: Cambridge University Press

Schramm, Wilbur (ed.), 1960. *Mass Communications*. Urbana, Ill.: University of Illinois Press

Schramm, Wilbur, and D.F. Roberts, 1974. *The Process and Effects of Mass Communication*. Urbana, Ill.: University of Illinois Press

Schubert, Glendon, 1960. *The Public Interest*. Glencoe, Ill.: Free Press

Schumpeter, Joseph A., 1976 (1947). *Capitalism, Socialism and Democracy*. New York: Harper & Row

Schwartz, David C., and Sandra K. Schwartz (eds), 1975. *New Directions in Political Socialization*. New York: Free Press

Seaton, S.L., and H.J.M. Claessen, 1979. *Political Anthropology, the State of the Art*. The Hague: Mouton

Shafer, Boyd C., 1955. *Nationalism, Myth and Reality*. New York: Harcourt, Brace

Shaw, Donald L., and C.L. Clemmer, 1977. 'News and the Public Response' in Shaw and McCombs, 33–51

Shaw, Donald L., and Maxwell E. McCombs (eds), 1977. *The Emergence of American Political Issues*. St Paul, Minn.: West Publishing Co.

Shibutani, T., and K.M. Kwan, 1965. *Ethnic Stratification*. New York: Macmillan

Shils, Edward, 1956. *The Torment of Secrecy*. Glencoe, Ill.: Free Press

– 1972. *The Intellectuals and the Powers*. Chicago, Ill.: University of Chicago Press

Siegel, Arthur, 1983. *Politics and the Media in Canada*. Toronto: McGraw Hill Ryerson

Sigal, Leon V., 1973. *Reporters and Officials*. Lexington, Mass.: D.C. Heath

Sigel, Roberta, and M.B. Hoskin, 1977. 'Perspectives on Adult Socialization' in Renshon, 259–93

Silverman, David, 1970. *The Theory of Organisation*. London: Heinemann

Simard, Carolle, 1984. 'Changement et insertion des femmes dans le système politique,' *Politique*, no. 5, 27–49

Simmel, Georg, 1930. *The Sociology of Georg Simmel*, transl. K.H. Wolff. Glencoe, Ill.: Free Press

Smelser, Neil J., 1963. *Theory of Collective Behavior*. New York: Free Press of Glencoe

– 1973 'The Methodology of Comparative Analysis' in Warwick and Osherson, 42–86

Smith, Anthony D., 1971. *Theories of Nationalism*. London: Duckworth

Smith, David N., 1974. *Who Rules the Universities?* New York: Monthly Review Press

Smith, M.G., 1960. *Government in Zazzau*. London: Oxford University Press

Snow, C.P., 1965. *The Two Cultures and a Second Look*. Cambridge: Cambridge University Press

Snyder, Louis L., 1972 (1954). *The Meaning of Nationalism*. Westport, Conn.: Greenwood Press

Somit, Albert (ed.), 1976. *Biology and Politics*. The Hague: Mouton

Spender, Dale, 1980. *Man Made Language*. London: Routledge & Kegan Paul

Stanley, Autumn, 1983. 'Women Hold Up Two-Thirds of the Sky: Notes for a Revised History of Technology' in Rothschild, 5–22

Stein, Arthur A., 1976. 'Conflict and Cohesion,' *Journal of Conflict Resolution*, vol. 20, no. 1, March, 143–72

Steward, Julian H., 1957. *Theory of Culture Change*. Urbana, Ill.: University of Illinois Press

Stewart, J.D., 1958. *British Pressure Groups*. Oxford: Clarendon Press

Stoddart, Jennifer, 1973. 'The Woman Suffrage Bill in Quebec' in *Women in Canada*, ed. Marylee Stephenson, 129–47. Toronto: New Press

Stoll, C.S., 1974. *Female and Male*. Dubuque, Iowa: Wm. C. Brown

Stretton, H., 1969. *The Political Sciences*. London: Routledge & Kegan Paul

Suleiman, Ezra N., 1978. *Elites in French Society*. Princeton, NJ: Princeton University Press

Suppe, Frederick, 1974. *The Structure of Scientific Theories*. Urbana, Ill.: University of Illinois Press

Sutton, F.X., et al., 1956. *The American Business Creed*. Boston: Harvard University Press

Swanson, David L., 1977. 'The Uses and Misuses of Uses and Gratifications,' *Human Communication Research*, vol. 3, no. 3, Spring, 214–21

– 1979. 'Political Communication Research and the Uses and Gratifications Model,' *Communication Research*, vol. 6, no. 1, Jan., 37–53

Swartz, M.J., V.W. Turner, and A. Tuden (eds), 1966. *Political Anthropology*. Chicago, Ill.: Aldine Publishing

Teather, Lynne, 1976. 'The Feminist Mosaic' in Matheson, 301–46
Thrall, Charles A., 1982. 'The Conservative Use of Modern Household Technology,'
 Technology & Culture, vol. 23, no. 2, Apr., 175–94
Tiger, Lionel, 1969. *Men in Groups*. London: Thomas Nelson
Tiger, Lionel, and Robin Fox, 1971. *The Imperial Animal*. Toronto: McClelland &
 Stewart
Tilly, Charles, 1978. *From Mobilization to Revolution*. Reading, Mass.: Addison-Wesley
– (ed), 1975. *The Formation of National States in Western Europe*. Princeton, NJ:
 Princeton University Press
Tilly, Louise A, and Joan W. Scott, 1978. *Women, Work and Family*. New York: Holt,
 Rinehart & Winston
Tocqueville, Alexis de, 1953 (1835). *Democracy in America*, vol. 1. New York: Alfred
 A. Knopf
– 1955 (1856). *The Old Regime and the French Revolution*. Garden City, NY:
 Doubleday-Anchor Books
Toulmin, Stephen, 1972. *Human Understanding*, vol. 1. Princeton, NJ: Princeton
 University Press
Touraine, Alain, 1971 (1969). *The Post-Industrial Society*. New York: Random House
Tuchman, Gaye, 1973. 'Making News by Doing Work: Routinizing the Unexpected,'
 American Journal of Sociology, vol. 79, no. 1, July, 110–31
– 1978, *Making News*. New York: Free Press
Tuchman, Gaye, A.K. Daniels, and J. Benet, 1978. *Hearth and Home*. New York:
 Oxford University Press
Tumin, Melvin M., 1953. 'Some Principles of Stratification, a Critical Analysis' in
 Bendix and Lipset (1966), 53–8
Tunstall, J. (ed.), 1970. *Media Sociology*. Urbana, Ill.: University of Illinois Press
Useem, Michael, 1979. 'The Social Organization of the American Business Elite and
 Participation of Corporation Directors in the Governance of American Institutions,'
 American Sociological Review, vol. 44, August, 553–72
Van den Berghe, Pierre L., 1978. 'Bridging the Paradigms: Biology and the Social
 Sciences' in Gregory, Silver, and Sutch, 33–52
Vanfossen, Beth E., 1979. *The Structure of Social Inequality*. Boston: Little, Brown
Vayda, Andrew P., and Roy A. Rappaport, 1968. 'Ecology, Cultural and Non-Cultural'
 in *Introduction to Cultural Anthropology*, ed. James A. Clifton, 477–97. Boston,
 Mass.: Houghton Mifflin
Veblen, Thorstein, 1957. *The Higher Learning in America*. New York: Sagamore Press
Verba, Sydney, 1965. 'Comparative Political Culture' in Pye and Verba, 512–60
Vermeersch, Etienne, 1977. 'An Analysis of the Concept of Culture' in Bernardi, 9–73
Vicinus, Martha, 1977. *A Widening Sphere*. Bloomington, Ind.: Indiana University
 Press

Vidich, A.-J., and R.M. Glassman (eds), 1979. *Conflict and Control*. Beverly Hills, Calif.: Sage Publications

Waldman, Sidney R., 1972. *Foundations of Political Action*. Boston, Mass.: Little, Brown

Wallace, William A., 1974. *Causality and Scientific Explanation*. Ann Arbor, Mich.: University of Michigan Press

Walter, E.V., 1969. *Terror and Resistance*. London: Oxford University Press

Warriner, Charles K., 1956. 'Groups are Real, a Reaffirmation,' *American Sociological Review*, vol. 21, no. 5, Oct., 549–54

Warwick, Donald P., and Samuel Osherson (eds), 1973. *Comparative Research Methods*. Englewood Cliffs, NJ: Prentice-Hall

Weber, Eugen, 1976. *Peasants into Frenchmen*. Stanford, Calif.: Stanford University Press

Weber, Max, 1949. *The Methodology of the Social Sciences*. Glencoe, Ill.: Free Press

– 1964 (1947). *The Theory of Social and Economic Organization*, ed. Talcott Parsons. New York: Free Press

– 1968. *Economy and Society*. New York: Bedminster Press

– 1969 (1946). *Essays in Sociology*, ed. H.H. Gerth and C.W. Mills. New York: Oxford University Press

Wesolowski, Wlodzimiers, 1962. 'Some Notes on the Functional Theory of Stratification' in Bendix and Lipset (1966), 64–9

Westergaard, J., and H. Resler, 1976. *Class in a Capitalist Society*. Harmondsworth: Penguin Books

White, D.M., 1950. 'The "Gatekeeper": A Case Study in the Selection of News,' *Journalism Quarterly*, vol. 27, Fall, 383–90

White, Leslie A., 1959a. 'Concept of Culture,' *American Anthropologist*, vol. 61, no. 2, April, 227–51

– 1959b. *The Evolution of Culture*. New York: McGraw-Hill

Wiegele, Thomas C., 1979. *Biopolitics: Search for a More Human Political Science*. Boulder, Colorado: Westview Press

Wilkinson, Paul, 1971. *Social Movement*. New York: Praeger

Williams, John E, and D.L. Best, 1982. *Measuring Sex Stereotypes*. Beverly Hills, Calif.: Sage Publications

Williams, Robin M., Jr, 1968. 'Value,' *International Encyclopedia of Social Sciences*, vol. 16, 283–4. New York: Macmillan Free Press

Wilson, Edward O., 1975. *Sociobiology: The New Synthesis*. Cambridge, Mass.: Harvard University Press

– 1978a. *On Human Nature*. Cambridge, Mass.: Harvard University Press

– 1978b. 'Foreword' in Caplan

Wilson, James Q., 1973. *Political Organizations*. New York: Basic Books

Wilson, S.J., 1982. *Women, the Family and the Economy*. Toronto: McGraw-Hill Ryerson

Wolpe, Ann Marie, 1978. 'Education and the Sexual Division of Labour' in *Feminism and Materialism*, ed. Annette Kuhn and Ann Marie Wolpe, 290–328. London: Routledge & Kegan Paul

Wright, Erik O., 1978. *Class, Crisis and the State*. London: New Left Books

– 1979. *Class Structure and Income Determination*. New York: Academic Press

Wrong, Dennis H., 1961. 'The Oversocialized Conception of Man in Modern Sociology,' *American Sociological Review*, vol. 26, no. 2, April, 183–93

– 1976. *Skeptical Sociology*. New York: Columbia University Press

– 1979. *Power*. Oxford: Basil Blackwell

Wylie, L., 1963. 'Social change at the Grass Roots' in Hoffmann et al., 159–234

Zeitlin, Maurice, 1974. 'Corporate Ownership and Control: The Large Corporation and the Capitalist Class,' *American Journal of Sociology*, vol. 79, no. 5, March, 1073–119

Zetterberg, Hans L., 1965. *On Theory and Verification in Sociology*. New York: Bedminster Press

Zihlman, Adrienne L., 1981. 'Women as Shapers of the Human Adaptation' in Dahlberg, 75–120

Zucker, Harold G., 1978. 'The Variable Nature of News Media Influence' in *Communication Yearbook, No. 1*, ed. B.D. Ruben, 225–40. New Brunswick, NJ: Transaction Books

Index

DATE DUE

MAR 2 8 1996			
REC'D MAR 2 6 1996			